The Pastors Wives Cookbook

By Sybil DuBose

Published by
WIMMER COOKBOOKS

International Standard Book Number – 0-918544-13-0

WIMMER
C O O K B O O K S
ConsolidatedGraphics

1-800-548-2537
Printed in China

Table of Contents

Menus

And be ye kind one to another, tenderhearted, forgiving one another, even as God for Christ sake has forgiven you. Eph. 4:32

 # Breakfast

---

BREAKFAST

**Orange-Grapefruit Sections
with Bing Cherries On The Stem
Eggs Benedict
Sour Cream Coffee Cake
Coffee**

EGGS BENEDICT

4 English muffins, split   4 eggs, poached
4 large thin slices ham, cooked   Hollandaise Sauce

Cook ham and have ready. Cook eggs in egg poacher until of desired doneness. Toast and butter split English muffins. Top each muffin with cooked ham slice, then poached egg. Generously spoon hollandaise sauce on top. Garnish with parsley sprigs. Serves 4.

HOLLANDAISE SAUCE
3 egg yolks   1½ tablespoons lemon juice
½ cup butter or margarine, melted   Dash cayenne
3 tablespoons hot water

In top of double boiler with wire whisk, beat egg yolks until smooth. (Boiler should not touch water in pan below) Slowly stir in butter. Gradually add hot water, beating constantly. Stir in seasonings and lemon juice. Cook until thick. Cover and keep hot over water until serving time. Reheat over hot water if necessary.

SOUR CREAM COFFEE CAKE

1 cup butter or margarine	1 teaspoon baking powder
2 cups sugar	¼ teaspoon salt
2 eggs	1 cup pecans, chopped
1 cup sour cream	4 tablespoons brown sugar
1 teaspoon vanilla	1 teaspoon cinnamon
2 cups all purpose flour, sifted	

Cream butter and sugar well. Add eggs, one at a time, beating well after each addition. Fold in sour cream and vanilla. Add dry ingredients which have been sifted together. Pour ½ of this batter into greased and floured bundt pan or angel food cake pan. Mix together pecans, brown sugar and cinnamon. Sprinkle ¾ of mixture over batter (Don't let touch side of pan). Top with rest of batter and sprinkle rest of nut mixture on top. Bake at 350 degrees for 45 to 60 minutes. Cool cake for 10 minutes before turning out of pan.

Mrs. Fred V. Brown (Norma)
Spartanburg, South Carolina

Mrs. John B. Cunningham (Isobel)
Alberta, Canada

Mrs. Earl L. Pounds (Esther)
St. Louis, Missouri

BREAKFAST

Honeydew Melon Wedges
Oven Fried Bacon   Cheese Omelet
Angel Biscuits
Raspberry Jam   Butter
Coffee

OVEN FRIED BACON

Place bacon strips in 13 x 9-inch baking pan. Place in 400 degree oven and bake 10 minutes. Watch carefully. Do not overcook.

CHEESE OMELET

6 eggs	2 tablespoons butter or margarine
5 tablespoons light cream	⅛ teaspoon pepper
½ teaspoon salt	⅓ cup Cheddar cheese, grated

Beat eggs until well blended. Add salt, pepper and light cream. Heat skillet until moderately hot. Add butter or margarine. When butter begins to sizzle, add egg mixture. Reduce heat. Cook eggs slowly; when they begin to set, lift mixture very gently with spatula as to allow liquid to flow to bottom. Tip skillet now and then to aid uncooked mixture to reach bottom. When top of omelet becomes firm, spread ⅓ cup grated Cheddar cheese over half of omelet. Fold opposite half over cheese. Serve at once.

ANGEL BISCUITS

5 cups all-purpose flour	½ cup warm water
1 teaspoon salt	1 package dry yeast
1 teaspoon soda	¾ cup cooking oil
3 teaspoons baking powder	1 teaspoon sugar
2 cups buttermilk	

Sift together dry ingredients. Dissolve yeast in warm water. Add with oil and buttermilk to dry ingredients. Mix well and knead several times, adding flour as needed as dough will be sticky. Roll out and make into biscuits. (You do not have to let these rise first). Place on greased cookie sheet. Bake in 400 degree oven until nicely browned. Serves approximately 36. DELICIOUS!

Mrs. Bill Bailey (Faye)
Elizabethtown, Kentucky

Mrs. Albert Moore (Lorraine)
Whiting, Indiana

Mrs. L. H. Fowler (Mildred)
Langley, South Carolina

Mrs. E. Harmon Moore
Indianapolis, Indiana

Mrs. John A. Moore (Julia)
Greenville, North Carolina

Mrs. Elbert L. Smithen (Jo)
Midland, Texas

Mrs. Ronald D. Rhodus (Virginia)
Mt. Zion, Illinois

BREAKFAST

Morning Fruit Bowl
Blueberry Pancakes   Favorite Maple Syrup
Smoked Sausage Links
Coffee or Tea

MORNING FRUIT BOWL

Wash, peel and slice fresh peaches (or use frozen peaches). Mix with fresh whole strawberries. Add sugar to taste. Spoon into fruit bowls and serve.

SMOKED SAUSAGE LINKS

Cook sausage slowly in small amount of water about 15 minutes or until done. Let pan become dry or pour off excess water. Continue cooking until sausages are nicely browned on all sides. NOTE: Sausages may be placed in baking pan and cooked in oven, uncovered. Add small amount of water and bake at 350 degrees for 15-20 minutes or until done.

BLUEBERRY PANCAKES

2¼ cups flour, sifted	2 cups milk
3 teaspoons baking powder	2 eggs, separated
1 teaspoon salt	4 tablespoons shortening, melted
2 teaspoons sugar	½ cup blueberries

Beat egg yolks until light and fluffy. Add 2 cups milk, beat until well blended. Sift together flour and dry ingredients. Slowly beat in egg and milk mixture. Add melted shortening. Beat egg whites until stiff. Fold into pancake batter. Gently stir in blueberries. Drop from tablespoon onto hot griddle. Let cook until pancakes are puffy, full of bubbles and edges are cooked. Turn and cook other side until done.

BUTTERED BISCUITS

2 cups self-rising flour
1 stick butter or margarine

⅔ cup milk

Cut butter into flour. Add milk and stir. Roll out and cut with biscuit cutter. Bake at 450 degrees for 10 minutes.

Mrs. Ted Callahan
Jackson, South Carolina

Mrs. Kay Ellis
Louisville, Mississippi

FAVORITE MAPLE SYRUP

1 teaspoon Maple flavoring
2 cups sugar

1 cup water
¼ cup light corn syrup

Combine sugar, water and corn syrup in saucepan. Heat, stirring occasionally, until mixture boils. Cover, and boil gently 10 minutes. Remove from heat. When syrup is cool, add maple flavoring and blend thoroughly. Serve over pancakes, waffles or French toast. Yield: 1¼ cups syrup.

Mrs. Bobby W. Barnett (Mary)
Bradford, Rhode Island

BREAKFAST

Orange Juice
Country Ham   **Scrambled Eggs**
With Red Eye Gravy   **Cheese Grits**
Buttered Biscuits   **Blackberry Jam**
Coffee

COUNTRY HAM

Slice country ham into serving pieces. Soak in water overnight in refrigerator. Rinse well. Put cooking oil in skillet, about 2 tablespoons. Heat to sizzling. Place ham slices in skillet and cook until meat becomes brown on each side.

RED-EYE GRAVY

Add 1 cup water to ham drippings. Bring to a boil and heat until all particles are released from bottom of skillet, stirring constantly. Serve over ham or grits.

CHEESE GRITS

4 cups water
1 cup quick grits
1 teaspoon salt
1 stick margarine

½ pound sharp Cheddar cheese
2 eggs
¼ cup Parmesan cheese
Corn flakes

Put grits into boiling water and cook until thick. Add margarine and grated Cheddar cheese. Cool. Add slightly beaten eggs. Place in 9 x 9-inch greased casserole dish. Top with crushed corn flakes mixed with Parmesan cheese. Bake 45 minutes in a 350 degree oven. Serve with baked ham or pork chops instead of potatoes.
Mrs. Roger Harrington
Ft. Pierce, Florida

SCRAMBLED EGGS

6 eggs
⅓ cup light cream
2 tablespoons butter or margarine

½ teaspoon salt
Pepper to taste

Break eggs into cup, one by one. If good quality, transfer to mixing bowl. Add salt and pepper to taste. Stir in light cream. Mix thoroughly. Place skillet on medium heat. Put margarine in skillet and let get hot to sizzling. Add egg mixture. Reduce heat and cook, lifting from bottom and sides of skillet until eggs are uniformly done throughout. Do not overcook.

 # Luncheon

---

LUNCHEON

Crabmeat Pie

Chicken Tetrazzini   **Green Bean Bundles**
Nell's Apricot Salad   **Freezer Yeast Rolls**
Butter
Luscious Cheese Cake
Coffee or Tea

CRABMEAT PIE

1 large unbaked pie shell	2 eggs, beaten
2 tablespoons flour	½ cup mayonnaise
½ cup milk	2 cans crabmeat (one claw meat and
⅓ cup green onions, sliced	one white meat)
1 package Swiss cheese, cubed	1 can shrimp

Beat eggs and add slowly flour, mayonnaise and milk. Stir in the shrimp, crabmeat, cheese and onions. Bake at 350 degrees for 40 minutes. Serve in small portions. Use as appetizer.
Mrs. Bobby Perry (Sue)
Moss Point, Mississippi

NELL'S APRICOT SALAD

2 3-ounce packages apricot gelatin	1 8-ounce package cream cheese
⅔ cup sugar	2 jars apricot baby food
⅔ cup water	1 small can crushed pineapple, drained
1 tall can milk, chilled	Chopped nuts

Bring to boil the gelatin, sugar and water. Remove from fire and add cream cheese, apricot baby food and crushed pineapple. Beat the milk, which has been chilled, and fold into mixture. Top with chopped nuts. Chill until firm.
Mrs. J. R. White (Nell)
Montgomery, Alabama

CHICKEN TETRAZZINI

1 large fryer or hen
1 onion, chopped
1 cup celery, chopped
2 carrots, sliced
1 clove garlic
Salt and pepper to taste
1½ cans tomato soup

½ can pimento, chopped
½ to ¾ pound American cheese, grated
1 small jar stuffed olives
½ can ripe pitted olives, chopped
15-ounces thin noodles
Mushrooms

Boil chicken with carrots, onion, celery, salt, pepper and garlic. Cook until done. Strain stock. Cut chicken into small pieces. Add tomato soup to broth. Mix in chicken, pimento, grated cheese and olives. Cook noodles and drain. Stir noodles in chicken mixture. Pour into a 9 x 13-inch Pyrex dish. Cover well with broth. Cook 45 minutes in a 350 degree oven. Garnish with mushrooms. Can be made a day ahead and frozen for later use.
Mrs. James L. Pleitz (Margaret Ann)
Dallas, Texas

FREEZER YEAST ROLLS

2 packages dry yeast
1 cup water, boiling
¾ cup Crisco
¾ cup cold water
2 eggs

½ cup sugar
2 teaspoons salt
7 cups all-purpose flour, sifted
Melted butter

Dissolve yeast in 3 tablespoons warm water. Bring to boil 1 cup water. Add Crisco and let melt. Add ¾ cup cold water. Cool to lukewarm. Beat eggs, sugar and salt until smooth. Combine all three mixtures and add 5 cups sifted all-purpose flour and beat well. Pour 2 more cups flour on dough board. Knead this into mixture until satiny and easy to handle (add more flour if needed). Roll out to about ¼-inch thickness and cut with biscuit cutter. Brush back with melted butter and fold over and pinch edges together. Place on cookie sheets and freeze. When frozen place in freezer bags. Take out of freezer about 3 hours before serving and let rise. Bake in 425 degree oven until brown. Makes about 50 rolls.
Mrs. Wendell Price (Frances)
Nashville, Tennessee

GREEN BEAN BUNDLES

4 cans whole green beans, vertical pack	Toothpicks
Mushroom caps	Salt and pepper
Bacon strips	Butter

Drain beans; save liquid. Arrange beans in individual serving bundles. Wrap each in ½ strip of bacon. Fasten with toothpick. Top with mushroom cap. Place bundles in casserole dish. Almost cover with bean liquid. Salt and pepper to taste. Put dot of butter on each bundle. Cover. Bake at 350 degrees for 1 hour. Take cover off last 15 minutes for bacon to brown.
Mrs. Frank Gunn (Sandra)
Biloxi, Mississippi

LUSCIOUS CHEESE CAKE

CRUST

1 cup all purpose flour, sifted	½ cup butter or margarine, melted
¼ cup sugar	1 egg yolk, slightly beaten
1 teaspoon grated lemon peel	½ teaspoon vanilla

Mix flour, sugar and peel. Cut in melted butter. Mix egg yolk and vanilla and add to first mixture. Blend well. Pinch off and pat to bottom and sides of tall spring-form cheese cake pan. Heat oven to 500 degrees.

FILLING

4 8-ounce packages cream cheese	4 tablespoons flour
½ teaspoon vanilla	¼ teaspoon salt
1 teaspoon lemon peel, grated	5 eggs and whites left over
1¾ cups sugar	¼ cup cream or Pet milk

Mix cheese until fluffy. Add peel and vanilla. In separate bowl, mix sugar, flour and salt. Add to cream cheese. Add eggs one at a time. Stir in heavy cream and mix. Pour in crust. Bake in hot oven for 8 minutes. Reduce heat to 200 degrees and cook 1½ hours.

GLAZE

1 box frozen strawberries	¾ cup water
2 tablespoons cornstarch	½ to ¾ cup sugar
Lemon juice	Red food coloring

Bring strawberries to a boil. Mix lemon juice in berries. Make a paste of sugar, cornstarch and water. Add to berries. Stir in red coloring as desired. Serves approximately 15 people.
Mrs. W. L. Bennett (Doris)
Fort Smith, Arkansas

LUNCHEON

Fresh Shrimp With Louis Dressing
Polynesian Ham with Curried Rice
Cucumber Lime Jello Salad
No Fail Crescent Rolls
Butter

Maunaloa Volcano   **Coffee or Tea**
(Dessert)

FRESH SHRIMP WITH LOUIS DRESSING

1 pound fresh, clean shrimp, deveined
1 head lettuce

1 lemon
Louis dressing

Line small stemmed dishes with lettuce leaves. Fill dish with freshly cleaned shrimp. Serve with lemon wedge and Louis dressing. Serves 4.

LOUIS DRESSING

1 cup mayonnaise
¼ cup chili sauce
1 teaspoon Worcestershire

½ cup sour cream
1 teaspoon horseradish
Salt to taste

Combine ingredients. Add salt to taste. Chill.

POLYNESIAN HAM WITH CURRIED RICE

¼ cup sugar
¼ cup cornstarch
¼ teaspoon salt
1 pound cooked ham, cubed (canned ham is good)
1 11-ounce can mandarin oranges, drained

1 13½-ounce can pineapple tidbits, undrained
¾ cup seedless green grapes
1 cup pineapple juice
⅓ cup vinegar
⅓ cup orange marmalade

Combine first three ingredients in heavy fry pan. Mix well. Place over high heat. Stir in pineapple juice, vinegar and marmalade, stirring constantly until it thickens. Reduce flame to low and fold in ham. Heat slowly. Add fruit. Serve over curried rice. Serves 6.

Mrs. Gilbert E. Barrow (Barbara)
Montgomery, Alabama

CURRIED RICE

¼ teaspoon curry powder
½ cup diced celery

½ cup toasted slivered almonds
6 cups Minute Rice, cooked

Cook Minute Rice according to package directions. Add curry powder, celery and toasted slivered almonds.
Mrs. Gilbert E. Barrow (Barbara)
Montgomery, Alabama

NO-FAIL CRESCENT DINNER ROLLS

¾ cup milk, scalded
1 package dry yeast
¼ cup warm water
½ cup shortening

½ cup sugar
1 teaspoon salt
3 eggs, beaten
4¼ cups flour

Dissolve yeast in ¼ cup warm water. Set aside. Mix milk, shortening, sugar and salt until well blended. Cool to lukewarm. Add dissolved yeast. Stir. Add eggs and mix well. Add flour all at once. Mix well. Knead lightly on floured surface, about 8 times. Place dough ball into greased bowl and turn once. Cover and let rise 1 hour or until double in bulk. Punch down. Divide in fourths. Place ¼ on floured board and roll into circle ½ to ¼-inch thick. Brush with melted butter. Cut into 12 wedges. Roll each wedge from wide edge to point. Place on greased cookie sheet, point side down. Brush again with melted butter and let rise until double again (about 1 hour). Bake at 400 degrees for 10 to 12 minutes.
Mrs. Dale Allen (Anne)
St. Louis, Missouri

CUCUMBER LIME JELLO SALAD

1 small package lime-flavored gelatin
¾ cup hot water
¾ cup cucumber, shredded unpeeled

2 tablespoons onion, grated
1 cup cottage cheese
1 cup mayonnaise
⅓ cup slivered almonds

Dissolve gelatin in hot water. Cool. Add remaining ingredients. Chill until firm. Serves 6.
Mrs. Bill Carr (Dell)
Pensacola, Florida

MAUNALOA VOLCANO
Mrs. Sam Wilder King
(A dessert representing our volcano
on the Big Island – Hawaii)

Sponge cake
Vanilla ice cream
4 egg whites
½ teaspoon baking powder

6 teaspoons powdered sugar
1 teaspoon vanilla
Red jelly (strawberry or guava)
Maraschino cherries

Place a piece of sponge cake or French meringue sponge cake about ½-inch thick on each plate; a ball of vanilla ice cream on each, and cover with meringue made of 4 egg whites beaten stiffly with baking powder, powdered sugar and vanilla. Pile meringue into peaks to represent a volcano. Put red jelly on the top of each and have it run down the merginue to represent lava. Bake at 500 degrees until brown (just a few minutes), watching carefully. Put a cherry on the top of each before serving.
Mrs. Edmond Walker (Lurie)
Honolulu, Hawaii

LUNCHEON

Chilled Cantaloupe Balls En Compote
Chicken Cordon Bleu
Green Beans-Southern Style
Company Carrot Casserole
Blueberry Salad — Tasty and Pretty
All Bran Muffins
Lemon Tarts
Coffee or Tea

CHILLED CANTALOUPE BALLS EN COMPOTE

Select well-ripened meaty cantaloupes. Use melon ball scoop to shape cantaloupe balls. Refrigerate, covered, until serving time. Place in compotes and serve.

GREEN BEANS — SOUTHERN STYLE

1 quart green beans
2 or 3 strips bacon
1 teaspoon salt

2 or 3 cups warm water
Dash garlic salt

Snap and wash green beans. Cook bacon in heavy saucepan. Add beans to bacon and drippings. Marinate until beans are dark in color. Add salt and seasoning. Add 2 or 3 cups warm water and cover. Coook over medium heat about 40 minutes or until tender.
Mrs. Doyle B. Bledsoe (Mildred)
Pine Bluff, Arkansas

CHICKEN CORDON BLEU

3 whole chicken breasts, boned
3 slices boiled ham
3 slices Swiss cheese

3 eggs, beaten with 1 teaspoon water
Flour for dredging
Corn flake or Italian bread crumbs

Flatten chicken breasts by pounding between waxed paper. Place ½ slice ham and ½ slice Swiss cheese on chicken breast. Roll up and fasten with toothpick. Dip in beaten egg, then in flour, again in eggs and finally in corn flake or Italian bread crumbs. Place on lightly greased baking sheet or foil-lined pan. Bake in 350 degree oven 40 minutes. Brush with melted butter or margarine after 20 minutes baking time.

MUSHROOM SAUCE

1 tablespoon butter or margarine
2 tablespoons flour

1 can cream of mushroom soup
1½ cans milk
½ can water

Melt butter or margarine and add flour. Stir until creamy. Add cream of mushroom soup, milk and water. Cook, stirring constantly, until creamy and bubbly. Pour over chicken before serving.
Mrs. Carl Bates (Myra)
Charlotte, North Carolina

COMPANY CARROT CASSEROLE

2 cups carrots, sliced
1 stick margarine
1 cup sugar
3 tablespoons flour

1 teaspoon baking powder
3 eggs, well beaten
Dash cinnamon

Cook carrots in lightly salted water until tender. Mash until smooth. Place carrots in mixing bowl. Add remaining ingredients. Mix well. Pour into casserole dish. Bake in 400 degree oven for 15 minutes, then 45 minutes in 350 degree oven.

Mrs. Milton Gardner (Nancy)
Thomasville, Georgia

BLUEBERRY SALAD — TASTY AND PRETTY

1 large package raspberry-flavored gelatin
1 cup boiling water
2 cups juice drained from blueberries and pineapple
1 Number 2 can crushed pineapple

1 Number 2 can blueberries
1 cup nuts, chopped
½ pint whipping cream or Dream Whip

Dissolve gelatin in boiling water. Add fruit juice and chill. Add fruit and nuts and refrigerate until mixture begins to set. Fold in whipped cream. This is nice in individual molds. Serves 8 to 12.

Mrs. James Landes (Irene)   *Mrs. Ken Carter*
Dallas, Texas   *Riverdale, Georgia*

LEMON TARTS

1 cup sugar
3 tablespoons flour
¼ cup lemon juice
¼ cup butter, melted
3 egg yolks

1 cup milk
1 carton sour cream
Whipped cream for topping
Stemmed cherries for topping
Tart shells

Combine first 5 ingredients in saucepan; stir in milk. Cook over medium heat, stirring until thick. Cool. Fold in sour cream. Chill. Serve in pastry shells. Serves 6 to 8 dessert-size shells. More in smaller shells. Nice for coffee or tea when using tiny bite size shells.

Mrs. William K. Weaver, Jr. ("B")
Mobile, Alabama

ALL BRAN MUFFINS

½ cup shortening
½ cup boiling water
½ cup all bran
¼ cup sugar
1 egg

1 yeast cake
¾ teaspoon salt
½ cup lukewarm water
3½ to 4 cups all purpose flour
(sift before measuring)

Mix shortening, boiling water, sugar, all bran and salt. Stir until melted. Let stand until lukewarm. Add 1 egg, well beaten, and yeast cake that has been soaked in lukewarm water. Add flour and mix thoroughly. Place in ice box, covered, and let stand until ready for use. Roll out and dip in melted butter. Place in pan and let rise about 2 hours before cooking. Bake at 350 degrees to 400 degrees. Makes about 35 rolls.

Mrs. W. E. Darby (Mary)
Jefferson City, Tennessee

Mrs. Orvind Dangeau (Freddie Ann)
Franklin, Tennessee

LUNCHEON

Cream of Watercress Soup

Crabmeat au Gratin
Coke Salad

Buttered English Peas
Sour Cream Biscuits
With Butter

Ice Cream Fudge Pie
Coffee or Tea

CRABMEAT AU GRATIN

1 stalk celery, chopped fine
1 cup onion, chopped fine
¼ pound margarine or butter
½ cup all-purpose flour
1 can evaporated milk
2 egg yolks

1 teaspoon salt
¼ teaspoon black pepper
½ teaspoon red pepper or to taste
1 pound white crabmeat
½ pound grated Cheddar cheese

Sauté onions and celery in butter until onions are wilted. Blend flour in well with this mixture. Pour in the milk gradually, stirring constantly. Add egg yolks, salt, red and black pepper. Cook for 5 minutes. (Sauce is very thick.) Put crabmeat in a bowl suitable for mixing and pour cooked sauce over crabmeat. Blend well. Transfer into lightly greased casserole and sprinkle with grated cheese. Bake at 375 degrees for 10 to 15 minutes or until lightly brown. Serves 6.

Mrs. Paul B. Leath (Marita)
La Palma, California

CREAM OF WATERCRESS SOUP

4½ cups fresh watercress leaves and tender stems, washed and dried with paper towel
6   green onions, minced
3   tablespoons butter or margarine
2   egg yolks

¾ cup heavy cream
½ teaspoon salt
3   tablespoons flour
5   cups chicken broth, heated
Pepper to taste
1   cup watercress leaves for garnish

Place onions and butter in saucepan. Add ½ cup water and heat to boiling; reduce heat and simmer until onions become translucent in color. Add salt and watercress. Cover and cook until watercress leaves become tender. Make a flour paste by adding a little water to flour. Gradually stir in the hot broth. Simmer about 5 minutes. Place mixture, a small amount at a time, in electric blender and puree. Return to saucepan. Season to taste. Combine egg yolks with heavy cream. Using a whip, beat until thoroughly mixed. Take one cup hot soup and gradually beat into egg mixture. Add to soup, beating constantly, very slowly. Place soup over medium heat until hot through. Do not allow mixture to reach boiling point. Chill in refrigerator. If you prefer thinner soup, add more cream at serving time. Scald watercress leaves then refresh in cold water. Drain. Sprinkle on top of soup as a garnish.

BUTTERED ENGLISH PEAS

Buy tiny frozen English peas. Cook according to directions given until just tender. Add salt to taste. Toss gently with butter.

SOUR CREAM BISCUITS

2   cups all-purpose flour
½ teaspoon salt
½ teaspoon baking soda

3   teaspoons baking powder
½ cup sour cream

Mix together dry ingredients. Add sour cream and mix to a soft dough. Roll on floured board and cut with floured cutter. Bake in hot 450 degree oven for 12 minutes.
Mrs. Earl Pounds (Esther)
St. Louis, Missouri

COKE SALAD

1 can sour cherries	1 can crushed pineapple
1 cup sugar	1 cup pecans, chopped
2 regular packages cherry-flavored gelatin	1 10-ounce bottle cold Coca-Cola

Mix cherries with 1 cup sugar. Bring to a boil. Add gelatin. When cool add remaining ingredients. Pour into mold to chill. Great to take to church dinners. Good with turkey or fish meals.
Mrs. Ted E. Francis (Glenda)
Malden, Missouri

ICE CREAM FUDGE PIE

1 box vanilla wafers	1 cup white marshmallows
½ gallon vanilla ice cream	1 can evaporated milk
1 package chocolate chips	½ cup walnuts, chopped

Melt chocolate chips, marshmallows and evaporated milk together in double boiler on low heat. Add walnuts. Line bottom and sides of pie pan with whole vanilla wafers to make crust. Layer vanilla ice cream on crust, then fudge sauce, then ice cream, then more fudge sauce until pan is full. Freeze.
Mrs. Denise George
Chelsea, Massachusetts

Dinner

CHRISTMAS DINNER

Roast Turkey   Oyster Stew   Giblet Gravy
Cornbread Dressing
Broccoli Spears   Baked Party Rice
Sweet Potato Casserole   Festive Cranberry Salad
Parkerhouse Rolls   Butter
Georgia Pecan Pie
Coffee   Tea

ROAST TURKEY

Prepare turkey: Wash 12 pound turkey carefully and scrape off all pin-feathers. Remove inedible parts which have been left in cavity. Rinse inside and out with cold water. Pat dry with paper towel. Place turkey in shallow roasting pan breast-side up. Add salt and pepper and seasonings to taste. Tie drumsticks to tail of turkey with string and press wings to sides of breast. Brush turkey with melted butter or margarine. Cover roasting pan loosely with heavy duty foil and roast at 325 degrees for 4 to 4½ hours. Test for doneness by moving drumstick up and down. Meat thermometer should register 190 degrees when turkey is tender.

PREPARE GIBLETS

Place gizzard, heart and liver in saucepan. Add 2 quarts salted water, 1 bay leaf, and celery tops. Boil gently until tender, about 2 to 3 hours. Test liver for doneness after the first half hour. Remove from pan. Cool. Cut cooked meat into small pieces for giblet gravy. Store in refrigerator, covered, until ready for use.

GIBLET GRAVY

4 tablespoons margarine	4 cups turkey broth
4 tablespoons flour	Minced turkey giblets

Place 4 tablespoons margarine in saucepan and heat until melted. Add flour and blend. Cook over medium heat until light brown in color, stirring constantly. Remove from fire and cool slightly. Stir in 4 cups chicken broth. Return to burner and blend until smooth. Cook until partially thickened. Stir in giblets and cook until desired consistency. Season to taste. If mixture gets too thick, add more broth.

OYSTER STEW

1 pint oysters	¼ cup butter
4 cups milk	1 teaspoon paprika
1 teaspoon celery salt	Salt and pepper to taste

Heat butter in saucepan. Add oysters, paprika, celery salt, salt and pepper to taste. Cook oysters until edges begin to curl slightly. Add milk and heat until milk comes to boiling point. Do not boil. Serves 4.

BAKED PARTY RICE

1 cup chopped onions	1 can mushrooms
1 stick butter or margarine	1 can Swanson's chicken broth, or 2
1 cup long grain rice	cans Campbell's beef broth

Sauté onions in butter. Add rice and cook until it begins to change color. Add mushrooms and broth. Bake in covered casserole for 1 hour at 350 degrees. Serve with broiled chicken or roast beef. For a main dish, stir in 1½ to 2 cups chopped chicken before baking.

Mrs. Joe Spirakis (Terry)　　　　　*Mrs. Billy J. Turner (Lucille)*
Pensacola, Florida　　　　　*Stearns, Kentucky*

Mrs. Leon Johnson (Louise)
Greenville, South Carolina

BROCCOLI SPEARS

2 packages frozen broccoli spears	Salt to taste
	Butter to taste

Buy frozen broccoli spears. Cook according to directions on package. Season to taste with salt and butter.

CORN BREAD DRESSING

6 cups corn bread, crumbled
6 cups dry bread crumbs
4 mediun onions, chopped
½ cup celery, cut small
1 teaspoon poultry seasoning
   or to taste

3 cups chicken broth or more
1 tablespoon Worcestershire
2 eggs, beaten
1 pound sausage, fried
   (optional)

Sauté onions and celery until just tender. Mix with bread crumbs. Add poultry seasoning. Stir in beaten eggs, chicken broth and Worcestershire. Add fried sausage, if desired. Bake at 425 degrees for 30 minutes or until done.
Mrs. Bryce Myers (Jenny Lynn)
Charleston, South Carolina

PARKERHOUSE ROLLS

1 cup milk, scalded
3 tablespoons shortening
3 tablespoons sugar
1 teaspoon salt

1 egg, well beaten
3½ cups flour
1 package granular yeast

Melt shortening in boiler and add milk. Let heat to lukewarm. Add sugar and salt. Pour this mixture in a large bowl and gradually stir in flour. Add egg. Beat vigorously, adding all of flour. Cover and let rise in warm place till double in bulk, about 2 hours. Turn out on lightly floured board or cloth. Roll out and cut with biscuit cutter. Fold in half and let rise again, about 1 hour. Cook in 400 degree oven until nicely browned.
Mrs. Robert Ledbetter (Katherine)
North Augusta, South Carolina

FESTIVE CRANBERRY SALAD

2 small packages cherry-flavored
   gelatin
2 oranges
2 apples, unpeeled
1 lemon (juice of)

1 cup nuts, chopped
1 cup sugar
2 cups fresh cranberries
1 cup hot water

Mix gelatin with 1 cup hot water. Cool. Grind up oranges, apples and cranberries. Mix ground fruit and chopped nuts into gelatin. Add lemon juice. Pour into individual molds. Chill until firm. Delicious!
Mrs. Charles Allman (Lillie Mae)
Marion, North Carolina

SWEET POTATO CASSEROLE

1 large can sweet potatoes	¼ teaspoon cinnamon
¾ cup brown sugar	2 tablespoons butter
½ cup white sugar	¼ teaspoon salt
1 can pie-sliced apples	½ cup broken pecans
1½ tablespoons cornstarch	Miniature marshmallows

Combine sugars, salt, cornstarch and cinnamon. Stir 1 cup water into dry mixture. Place in saucepan over medium heat. Cook to boiling. Continue cooking approximately 2 minutes. Add apples. Place sweet potatoes in baking dish. Pour syrup mixture over potatoes. Push apple slices in between potato wedges. Sprinkle pecans over potatoes, blending in potato mixture. Bake at 350 degrees for 1 hour. Just before baking time is over, remove casserole from oven. Sprinkle miniature marshmallows on top; return to oven and brown at 375 degrees.

GEORGIA PECAN PIE
(Has a delightful maple flavor)

¾ cup brown sugar (packed)	Dash of salt
1 tablespoon butter	1 teaspoon vanilla
1 cup Karo Pancake & Waffle Syrup	1 cup pecans, coarsely chopped
3 eggs, well beaten	1 unbaked pie shell

Mix well, adding pecans last. Pour into unbaked pie shell. Bake at 325 degrees about 1 hour or until pie is set.
Mrs. John J. McMillan (Arrie)
Cordova, South Carolina

Every good tree bringeth forth good fruit. Matt. 7:17

VALENTINE'S DINNER

Cream of Mushroom Soup
Roast Sirloin of Beef   Gravy
Green Beans Almondine
Macaroni and Cheese Soufflé
Lemon-Lime Congealed Salad
Potato Refrigerator Rolls   Butter
Cherry-Cheese Pie
Coffee — Tea

CREAM OF MUSHROOM SOUP

2 8-ounce cans mushrooms, minced
1 can chicken stock
3 cups milk
¼ teaspoon celery seed

1½ tablespoons onion, minced
1 teaspoon salt
⅛ teaspoon pepper
3 tablespoons flour
2 tablespoons butter or margarine

Sauté mushrooms in 1 tablespoon butter or margarine. Melt the other tablespoon butter in saucepan. Add flour and stir until smooth. Add seasonings. Slowly add milk, stirring constantly. Add onion. Add chicken stock and mushrooms. Continue to stir until mixture reaches boiling point. Serves 6.

GREEN BEANS ALMONDINE

2 cans French Style Green Beans
½ teaspoon sugar

Salt to taste
Butter
Toasted slivered almonds

Place green beans with juice in saucepan. Season with sugar and salt to taste. Cook until beans are practically free of liquid. Toss with butter. Sprinkle with toasted slivered almonds.

ROAST SIRLOIN OF BEEF

1 6 pound sirloin tip beef roast   Garlic salt to taste
Salt and pepper to taste

Season meat with salt, pepper and garlic salt to taste. Place meat on rack in roasting pan. If there is no fat on roast, ask butcher to give you extra fat for roasting. Place fat on top side of roast. Place meat thermometer in center of roast, making sure it does not touch bone. Roast meat uncovered at 300 degrees for about 3 hours, or until meat thermometer reaches 170 degrees. If roast is desired medium rare, roast to 160 degrees.

GRAVY
3 tablespoons flour   3 cups Campbell's beef broth or 2
3 tablespoons margarine   cups broth and 1 cup water

Place margarine in saucepan over medium heat. Let margarine get hot but not brown. Stir in flour; continue stirring until medium brown in color; remove from heat. Stir in beef broth and blend until smooth. Cook slowly until thickened.

POTATO REFRIGERATOR ROLLS

1 medium Irish potato   1 tablespoon salt
2 cups potato liquid   2 eggs, slightly beaten
2 packages active dry yeast   ⅔ cup shortening
½ cup sugar   6½ cups all-purpose flour, sifted

Boil potato reserving 2 cups liquid. Allow potato water to cool to 115-120 degrees. Dissolve yeast in ½ cup of potato liquid. To remaining 1½ cups liquid, add sugar, shortening and yeast. Let stand 1 hour. Add eggs and 3 cups flour. With electric mixer at high speed, beat just until smooth. Add 2 cups flour, beating with wooden spoon until flour is incorporated. Add remaining flour, mixing with hands until smooth. Brush with 1 tablespoon melted butter. Cover. Let rise in refrigerator 2 hours. Punch down. Cover and refrigerate up to 3 days. Punch down daily. About 2 hours before serving, remove dough from refrigerator. Shape rolls as desired. Let rise 1 hour. Preheat oven to 400 degrees. Brush rolls with butter. Bake 12 minutes.
Mrs. Kenneth D. Emerson (Cleta)
Wichita, Kansas

LEMON-LIME CONGEALED SALAD

1 3-ounce package
lemon-flavored gelatin
3 3-ounce packages lime-
flavored gelatin
1 cup hot water
1 cup cold water

1 cup mayonnaise
1 can condensed milk
1 large can crushed pineapple
1 large container cottage cheese
½ cup pecans, chopped

Dissolve gelatin in hot water. Cool. Add remaining ingredients. Pour into large mold and let congeal.

Mrs. Bobby Moore (Joyce)
Memphis, Tennessee

Mrs. Bennie Oliver (Dorothy)
Hamilton, Alabama

BAKED MACARONI & CHEESE

2 cups homogenized milk
½ cup canned milk
1 cup elbow macaroni
2 eggs

1 pound Cheddar cheese, or more
Salt and pepper to taste
Margarine

Cook macaroni according to directions. Drain. Beat eggs in 2 quart casserole dish. Add the milk and season with salt and pepper. Mix in the cooked, drained macaroni and fill with the Cheddar cheese, using more or less according to preference. Dot with margarine. Bake at 350 degrees for 30 to 40 minutes or until done. Serves 8 to 10.

Mrs. Joe Hewitt (Mary Etta)
Cordova, South Carolina

CHERRY CHEESE PIE

2 cans cherry pie filling
1 6-ounce bar cream cheese,
softened
1 envelope Dream Whip
2 bananas

3—4 tablespoons lemon juice
½ cup cold milk
½ teaspoon vanilla
Vanilla wafers, crushed
1½ sticks margarine, melted

Crush enough vanilla wafers to line bottom and sides of 2—9-inch pie plates. Mix with 1½ sticks margarine which has been melted, and press into pie plates. Set aside. Place Dream Whip, milk and vanilla in mixing bowl. Beat as directed on package. In separate mixing bowl beat softened cream cheese until fluffy and smooth. Combine the two mixtures. Blend well. Slice bananas. Marinate in lemon juice to keep from turning dark. Place banana slices in pie plates on top of vanilla wafer crust. Spread one half cream cheese mixture over bananas in each pie plate. Spoon 1 can cherry pie filling over top of each. Chill. Pies are better if refrigerated overnight.

CELEBRATION SPRING FEAST

Baked Oysters in Half Shell
Michigan Baked Fish
Beaumont Chicken-Shrimp Gumbo
With White Rice
Avocado Spring Salad
Petite Brioche Bread
Almond Crunch Ice Cream With Ruby Fruit Sauce
Coffee   Tea

BEAUMONT GUMBO

1 large onion, chopped   ½ cup flour
½ cup bacon drippings

In large pot cook onion in bacon drippings until onion is clear; remove onion with slotted spoon and set aside. To remaining drippings add ½ cup flour and cook at medium high heat, stirring constantly, till flour turns brown. (This is called a "Roux.") Remove from fire and add to Roux:

2 cans chicken broth   1 cup diced celery
2 cans water   ¼ cup minced parsley
1 clove garlic, minced   1 can minced crabmeat
Cooked onion   1½ pounds cleaned raw shrimp or 2
1 package cut frozen okra (1 box)   cans shrimp (chicken may be
1 tablespoon salt and pepper   substituted for shrimp)

Cook 30-45 minutes. Serve spooned over rice, in bowls. Sprinkle top with *Gumbo Filé* seasoning. This is an authentic recipe gained by watching a French speaking black woman cook her gumbo. She never wrote it down.
Mrs. Browning Ware (Corrine)
Austin, Texas

BAKED OYSTERS IN HALF SHELL

Grind together *finely:*
Onions   Celery
Green peppers   Parsley

Cook in margarine and season with garlic, Worcestershire sauce, and lemon juice. Break up fine crisp bacon and add to the mixture. Sprinkle on top of oysters in half shell and bake.
Mrs. James Monroe (Laura)
Fort Walton Beach, Florida

MICHIGAN BAKED FISH

Prepare fish: Cut in half. Remove back bone and side bones. Remove skin if desired. Pour boiling water over fish and let stand 1 or 2 minutes. Skin will peel off.

1 5-6 pound fish	½ cup margarine, melted (less if
2 medium onions, chopped	fatty fish)
1 egg, beaten	Salt and pepper to taste
¾ cup milk	Sage
1-2 tablespoons lemon juice	Bread crumbs

Lightly grease 12 x 13-inch pan. Cover bottom of pan with bread crumbs and sprinkle with onions and sage. Mix beaten egg and milk together. Dip fish in milk mixture. Salt and pepper fish on both sides. Place in pan. Cover with bread crumbs and sprinkle with onions and sage. Sprinkle lightly with salt and pepper. Drizzle remaining milk mixture and margarine mixed with lemon juice over fish. Cover pan and place in refrigerator over night. Remove from refrigerator about 2 hours before baking. Bake, uncovered, at 350 degrees for 1 hour and 15 to 30 minutes or until done. Bread crumbs serve as a dressing.
Mrs. Roland Miljevich (Cecelia)
Wakefield, Michigan

AVOCADO SPRING SALAD

1 package lime-flavored gelatin	1 teaspoon onion juice
1 cup hot water	2 ripe avocados
1 large package cream cheese	¾ cup celery, minced
½ teaspoon salt	¼ cup green pepper

Dissolve gelatin in hot water. Cool slightly. Mash cheese with the avocados. (I add a little mayonnaise.) Put in blender with a little of the cool gelatin liquid and blend until smooth. Add the rest of the gelatin, then the celery, pepper and onion juice. Refrigerate and serve on a bed of shredded lettuce.

TOPPING

1 clove garlic, crushed	2 tablespoons lemon juice
1 egg yolk	¼ cup mayonnaise

Blend ingredients together in blender then fold gently into ¾ cup additional mayonnaise. Spread on Avocado Spring Salad. Make salad at least the day before you plan to use it.
Mrs. Forest H. Siler (Evelyn)
Lawton, Oklahoma

PETITE BRIOCHE
(The lemon hint is lovely!)

1 cup milk	¼ cup water
½ cup butter or margarine	4 eggs, beaten
1 teaspoon salt	1 teaspoon grated lemon peel
½ cup sugar	5 cups flour, sifted (about)
2 packages active dry or comp.	Butter, melted
yeast	

Scald milk; stir in butter, salt and sugar. Cool until lukewarm. Sprinkle dry yeast over warm (110 degrees) water or crumble compressed yeast over lukewarm (85 degrees) water. Let stand 5 minutes. Add eggs and lemon peel; mix well. Combine with cooled milk mixture. Add flour gradually to make a soft dough. Knead lightly until dough is smooth and satiny. Place in greased bowl; cover with cloth and let rise in warm place until doubled in bulk, about 2 hours. Punch down and turn out on lightly floured board. Knead lightly. Shape ⅔ of dough into smooth balls about 2-inches in diameter. Shape other ⅓ into smaller balls, about 1-inch in diameter. Place large balls in greased muffin-cup pans; set one small ball firmly on top of each of larger ones. Brush surface with butter; let rise until doubled in bulk. Bake in hot oven at 425 degrees for about 10 minutes. Remove from pans at once. Cool on rack. Makes about 3 dozen. Wrap rolls, as soon as they are cool, in moisture proof material or place in plastic bags. Seal and freeze if desired.
Mrs. Robert E. Hall
Huron, Ohio

ALMOND CRUNCH ICE CREAM
WITH
RUBY FRUIT SAUCE
(Recipe copied from Alabama Sunday magazine)

1 cup natural almonds, sliced	Ruby Fruit Sauce
½ cup sugar	
6 scoops pistachio or vanilla ice	
cream	

Stir almonds in buttered skillet over medium heat until light golden brown. Stir in ½ cup sugar and continue cooking a few minutes, stirring constantly, until sugar coats almonds in a granular crust and just starts to melt; spread out on foil and cool, breaking up if necessary. Drop scoops of ice cream onto almonds and roll to coat. Place in shallow pan and freeze. Wrap pan if freezing balls overnight or longer. Serve with Ruby Fruit Sauce. Serves 6. Prepare double or triple if desired (do almonds in two or three batches).

RUBY FRUIT SAUCE

6 to 8 red or green apples
½ cup lemon juice
2 cups seedless grapes or red grapes halved, seeded
1 1-pound can whole cranberry sauce
1 10-ounce package frozen raspberries
⅛ teaspoon salt
1 tablespoon grated orange rind
6 cups sugar
½ 6-ounce jar liquid pectin

Pare, core and cube apples to get 6 cups; coat with the lemon juice in large kettle and add all remaining ingredients except pectin. Bring to full boil and boil vigorously 1 minute. Stir in pectin and remove from heat. Continue stirring, skimming off foam, for 5 minutes. Pour into sterilized jars, clean off rims and seal with melted paraffin or special screw tops. Store in cool, dark place. Makes 10 to 11 half-pint jars. NOTE: I buy red grapes when they are at lowest price and freeze by pints. I also put up sauce and process in hot water bath for 10 minutes. Almonds can be kept in tin or jar after they are carmelized and can be sprinkled over ice cream for "unexpected" company instead of ice cream being rolled in the almonds.
Mrs. George E. Bagley (Helen)
Montgomery, Alabama

EASTER DINNER
Vichyssoise
Pineapple Glazed Ham
Fresh Asparagus With Almonds
Old Virginia Corn Pudding
Delicious Three-Layer Salad
Buttermilk Rolls   Butter
Fresh Strawberry Pie
Demitasse

VICHYSSOISE

3 leeks, minced (or onions)
2 cups chicken broth
1 teaspoon salt
½ cup milk
3 tablespoons butter or margarine
3½ cups boiling water
1 cup heavy cream
4 cups potatoes, sliced finely
¼ teaspoon pepper
Dash paprika
1 sprig parsley, chopped fine
2 tablespoons chives, finely minced

Cook leeks or onion, minced, in butter or margarine until tender. Do not brown. Cook potatoes in boiling water until tender. Press potatoes with water through a very fine sieve. Return to saucepan. Add chicken broth, milk, cream, butter, parsley, salt, pepper, leeks, and dash of paprika. Return to fire and heat to boiling point. Serve in individual bowls topped with minced chives. Serves 4 to 6.

PINEAPPLE GLAZED HAM

6 to 8 pound ham, fully cooked
1 large can sliced pineapple
1 cup brown sugar

Whole cloves
Maraschino cherries

Place ham on trivet in shallow roasting pan, skin side up. Roast ham approximately 20 minutes per pound at 325 degrees in preheated oven. About 1 hour before ham has finished cooking, take ham out of oven and remove rind. Use knife to aid in trimming off stubborn portions. Using sharp knife, score top of ham by cutting diagonally across ham about ¼-inch deep. Cut another line across ham about 1-inch from first line. Repeat until entire ham has been scored. Cut ham in opposite lines all the way across top 1-inch apart as before. Continue until all of ham has small rectangular sections. Place whole cloves in intersecting lines over top of ham. Mix juice drained from pineapple and 1 cup brown sugar. Stir until thoroughly blended. Pour over ham. Return to shallow roasting pan and cook until done, basting frequently. Garnish by placing pineapple slices on top of ham with maraschino cherries in centers. Secure with tooth picks. Serves 8 to 10.

FRESH BUTTERED ASPARAGUS WITH ALMONDS

2 to 3 pounds fresh green
  asparagus spears
1 teaspoon salt or to taste

Butter
Toasted slivered almonds

Carefully wash and clean asparagus spears. Remove scales by scrubbing gently with brush. Snap off tough portion, reserving only tender part of spears. Bring about 1 cup water to boil in a tall saucepan or coffee pot. Add salt. Gently tie asparagus spears in bundles. Stand, tip ends up, in wire basket or make an anchor with crumpled foil in tall pan or coffee pot. Cover and steam about 15 minutes or until tender. Do not overcook. Gently remove from pot. Add butter. Divide into serving portions and sprinkle with toasted slivered almonds.

OLD VIRGINIA CORN PUDDING

2 cups corn
2 or 3 eggs
1 cup milk
¼ cup sugar

¼ cup butter, melted
Salt & pepper to taste
1 tablespoon flour

Mix dry ingredients. Add corn. Beat eggs; add milk and stir into corn mixture. Pour into buttered casserole. Bake in 350 degree oven for ½ hour. Serve hot.

Mrs. J. H. Cates (Hilda)
Fredericksburg, Virginia

Mrs. Bernes K. Selph (Tommie)
Benton, Arkansas

Mrs. William M. Halliburton
Willoughby, Ohio

DELICIOUS THREE-LAYER SALAD

LAYER 1

1 small package lemon-flavored gelatin
1 small package orange-flavored gelatin
2 cups hot water
1½ cups cold water

1 No. 2 can crushed pineapple, drained (reserve juice)
4 cups colored miniature marshmallows
2 bananas, diced

Dissolve both packages gelatin in 2 cups hot water. Add 1½ cups cold water. Mix in remaining ingredients. Chill till firm.

LAYER 2

½ cup sugar
2 tablespoons flour

1 egg, beaten
1 cup pineapple juice

Combine the sugar and flour. Mix beaten egg and pineapple juice. Add to first mixture. Cook over low heat until thickened, stirring constantly. Cool; spread over first layer.

LAYER 3

½ pint cream, whipped or Cool Whip

3 ounces cream cheese
Sharp cheese, shredded

Blend together the whipped cream and cream cheese. Pour over second layer. Sprinkle top with sharp shredded cheese.

Mrs. Franklin Owen (Sue)
Middletown, Kentucky

BUTTERMILK ROLLS

1 package yeast	¼ teaspoon soda
1 cup warm water	1 teaspoon salt
½ cup sugar	4 teaspoons baking powder
½ cup Wesson oil	6½ cups flour
2 cups buttermilk	

Dissolve 1 package yeast in 1 cup warm water. Add remaining ingredients. Mix together and chill. Pinch off small balls and place on a greased pan. Bake at 350 degrees for 20-30 minutes.
Mrs. Bob Woods (Ann)
Muskogee, Oklahoma

FRESH STRAWBERRY PIE
(Delicious!)

2 cups sugar	6 tablespoons cornstarch
1 small package strawberry gelatin	2 cups water
	Whipped cream or Cool Whip

While 2 pie shells are baking, wash, drain and slice 1 carton fresh strawberries. In saucepan mix together 2 cups sugar, 1 small package strawberry gelatin and cornstarch. Add 2 cups water and stir in well. Bring to a boil; stir as it simmers until thickened. Cool. Fill shells with sliced berries. Pour mixture over, and refrigerate until set. At serving time, spread whipped cream or Cool Whip over top.

Mrs. John R. Riddle (Tommye)
Birmingham, Alabama

Mrs. J. Norman Griffith (Mimi)
Athens, Georgia

Mrs. W. E. Pettit
Winston-Salem, North Carolina

Mrs. C. Wray Ivey
Swainsboro, Georgia

Mrs. C. E. Hall
Hickman, Tennessee

Mrs. Jimmie E. Harley (Gayle)
Greenville, South Carolina

Mrs. Thomas Knotts (Jeanne)
Belvedere, South Carolina

Party Fare-
Appetizers

*Wait on the Lord: be of good courage
and he shall strengthen thine heart:
wait, I say, on the Lord. Ps. 27:14*

PARTY PIZZA

Combine:

1 5 ounce jar sharp cheese spread (Old English)
¼ cup margarine

1 teaspoon caraway seed
1 teaspoon Worcestershire sauce
⅓ cup tomato paste

Let cheese and margarine set at room temperature until ready to use. Mix all ingredients well and spread on Ritz crackers or party rye bread. Sprinkle with oregano. Put on cookie sheet and bake at 350 degrees for 6 to 7 minutes. May be served as appetizers for a spaghetti dinner.

Mrs. Charles M. Becton (Janie)
Monroe, North Carolina

Mrs. Gayle Alexander
Alamo, Tennessee

Mrs. Brock Watson
Fayetteville, Arkansas

Mrs. Ralph M. Smith (Bess)
Austin, Texas

PIZZA BITES

Top crisp crackers with cheese spread, a small amount of chili sauce, and slice of frankfurter. Bake at 350 degrees for 10 minutes. Great for young people.

Mrs. R. F. Smith, Jr. (Faye)
Hickory, North Carolina

HAM 'N CHEESE BALL

2 8-ounce packages cream cheese
½ pound sharp Cheddar cheese, shredded
2 teaspoons onion, grated (optional)
2 teaspoons Worcestershire Sauce
1 teaspoon lemon juice
1 teaspoon dry mustard

½ teaspoon paprika
½ teaspoon seasoned salt
¼ teaspoon regular salt
1 2¼-ounce can deviled ham (don't use potted ham)
2 tablespoons drained pimento, finely chopped
2 tablespoons parsley, chopped or
⅔ cup nuts, chopped

Soften cream cheese and beat with mixer; add Cheddar cheese and next eight ingredients. Stir in pimento. Cover and place in refrigerator for several hours until firm enough to handle. Shape into 2 balls and roll in nuts or parsley.

Mrs. A. F. Tuck
Champaign, Illinois

SWEET-SOUR CHEESE RING

1 pound longhorn cheese	½ cup mayonnaise
1 onion	Strawberry preserves
1 cup nuts	Crackers

Grind together cheese, onion and nuts. Mix in mayonnaise. Shape into a ring on large plate. Fill center with preserves. To eat, dab a little of both on a cracker.
Mrs. James G. Harris (Tunis)
Fort Worth, Texas

CHEESE BALL

2 8-ounce Philadelphia cream cheese	1 tablespoon onion, grated
1 8-ounce Cracker Barrel sharp Cheddar cheese	1 teaspoon Worcestershire sauce
1 tablespoon pimento, chopped	1 teaspoon lemon juice
1 tablespoon green pepper, grated	Dash salt and pepper
	Nuts, finely chopped

Combine cheeses. Mix well until blended. Add other ingredients and mix well. Shape into ball or long roll. Roll in chopped nuts. Refrigerate.
Mrs. Ray W. McClung (Faye)
Little Rock, Arkansas

OYSTER ROLLS

2 8-ounce packages cream cheese	½ small onion, grated
2 cans smoked oysters	2 to 3 tablespoons mayonnaise
2 teaspoons Worcestershire sauce	½ teaspoon salt

Mix cheese and enough mayonnaise to hold together. Add Worcestershire and onion. Add salt. Combine well. Divide mixture in ½ and spread on waxed paper about ½-inch thick to make 4 x 8-inch rectangles. Chop oysters and spread over cheese mixture. Roll as for jelly roll, using knife to help start. Chill for at least 12 hours. Serve with crackers.
Mrs. Barry Landrum (Charlotte)
Greenville, Mississippi

A lover of hospitality . . . sober, just, holy, temperate. Titus 2:8

RED DEVIL BALLS

1 4½-ounce can deviled ham	1 cup pecans, chopped
1 large bar cream cheese	Red coloring (optional)

Blend ham, cream cheese and red coloring. Chill. Make into balls. Roll in chopped pecans.
Mrs. E. Harmon Moore
Indianapolis, Indiana

CHIPPED BEEF BALL

3 8-ounce packages cream cheese	1 medium onion, chopped
3 packages chipped beef	2 tablespoons Accent
	2 tablespoons Worcestershire sauce

Chop 2 packages beef finely. Mix with cheese and other ingredients. Make into balls and roll in the remaining package of chopped beef. Makes 1 large or 2 small balls.
Mrs. R. F. Smith, Jr. (Faye)
Hickory, North Carolina

BROCCOLI DIP

3 stalks celery, chopped	1 medium onion, chopped
1 can mushroom pieces	1 package frozen chopped broccoli
1 can golden mushroom soup	1 roll Kraft garlic or bacon cheese

Sauté celery, onion and mushroom pieces in butter. Cook broccoli as directed and drain. Add to soup and cheese. Heat to melt. Serve warm in chafing dish with Fritos.
Mrs. Bobby Perry (Sue)
Moss Point, Mississippi

AVOCADO DIP

3 tablespoons salad dressing	1 teaspoon lemon juice
1 teaspoon grated onion	¼ button garlic, grated
¼ package cream cheese	3 dashes hot sauce
1 avocado	Salt and pepper

Peel and mash avocado. Add remaining ingredients. Whip.
Mrs. C. S. Maynard
Little Rock, Arkansas

CHEESE DIP

1 can cream of mushroom soup
1 Nippy cheese roll
1 cube beef bouillon
1 teaspoon Worcestershire sauce

Melt in double boiler. Serve warm for dip. Use cauliflower, carrot stick or celery.
Mrs. Bruce H. Price (Eva)
Newport News, Virginia

HOT CHEESE DIP

4 tablespoons butter
2 cups celery, finely chopped
½ cup green peppers, finely chopped (optional)
1 large onion, finely chopped
2 pounds Kraft Old English Cheese
1 small can Ro-tel green chiles and tomatoes

Sauté celery, onion and bell pepper in butter. Add cheese, green chiles and tomatoes. Use double boiler, serve in chafing dish with large Fritos and Tostados. This is a favorite with teenagers.
Mrs. Tommy R. Jones (Dian)
Macon, Georgia

JALAPENO PEPPER DIP

2 12-ounce packages cream cheese
1 can Rotel tomatoes
1 Jalapeno pepper, chopped fine (more or less according to how hot you want it)

Mix all ingredients and heat until creamy. Beat and serve or refrigerate and serve cold. Serve with all kinds of chips and crackers. Texans love this recipe!
Mrs. Travis Berry (Bernice)
Plano, Texas

QUICK TUNA DIP

1 pint sour cream
2 tablespoons prepared mustard
½ cup chili sauce or catsup
1 envelope dehydrated onion soup mix
2 6½-ounce cans tuna

Blend together sour cream, mustard and catsup. Stir in onion soup mix and tuna; mix well. Chill until ready to serve. Serve with cucumber wedges, corn chips, cherry tomatoes, potato chips and celery pieces. Makes 1 quart.
Mrs. Billy D. Allen (Elray)
Springfield, Illinois

RAW VEGETABLE DIP

1 teaspoon lemon juice
1 cup mayonnaise
½ cup whipped cream
⅛ teaspoon curry powder
2-4 teaspoons minced onion

¼ cup parsley flakes
Dash of garlic powder
Dash of paprika
Chopped chives or minced
green onions

Mix and refrigerate. Serve with broccoli, cauliflower, cherry tomatoes, celery, carrots, etc.
Mrs. R. F. Smith, Jr. (Faye)
Hickory, North Carolina

VEGETABLE DIP

1 8-ounce package cream cheese
½ cup catsup
½ cup mayonnaise

1 teaspoon Worcestershire sauce
1 onion, finely chopped

Put all in blender to mix. Serve with raw vegetables.
Mrs. R. F. Smith Jr. (Faye)
Hickory, North Carolina

FAVORITE LOW-CAL VEGETABLE DIP

1 12-ounce carton cottage cheese
1 8-ounce carton plain yogurt
1 8-ounce carton sour cream or
cream cheese
Salt and pepper

2 tablespoons dehydrated onion
flakes
1 tablespoon steak sauce, or more
if desired

In mixer, beat smoothly the cottage cheese. Add either 2 (yogurt and sour cream or cream cheese) and mix well. Add onion, steak sauce, seasonings and mix only until blended. Store in refrigerator until firm; overnight if possible. Serve on a platter with raw vegetables of your choice, especially broccoli and slices of cucumber.
Mrs. Thomas W. Downing, Jr. (Sue)
Baltimore, Maryland

And he took the seven loaves and the fishes, and gave thanks, and brake them, and gave to his disciples, and the disciples to the multitude. Matt. 15:36

SHRIMP DIP

4 teaspoons Worcestershire sauce
¼ teaspoon hot sauce
1 tablespoon onion, grated

¾ pint Kraft mayonnaise
Boiled shrimp

Mash shrimp with fork. Add other ingredients except mayonnaise. Gradually add mayonnaise till mixture can be dipped.
Mrs. Tilman C. Burks (Quinnie)
Pensacola, Florida

HAM BALLS

1 pound ground ham
1 pound ground pork
2 eggs

1 cup milk
1 cup oatmeal —
   form into balls

Bake in shallow pan at 300 degrees for 1 hour. Pour off juice.

SAUCE
⅔ cup brown sugar
¼ teaspoon cloves
1 cup fruit juice
2 tablespoons flour

1 teaspoon dry mustard
2 tablespoons vinegar
⅓ cup Karo

Pour sauce over meat balls. Bake 30 minutes at 300 degrees.
Mrs. W. L. Bennett (Doris)
Fort Smith, Arkansas

CHEESE-SAUSAGE BALLS

1 pound pork sausage
1 pound sharp Cheddar cheese,
   grated

3 cups Bisquick

Mix this together until crumbly. Form into small biscuits. Bake on cookie sheet for 10 minutes at 400 degrees.
Mrs. Larry Rose
Waco, Texas

Mrs. Betty Powell
Jasper, Alabama

Mrs. George L. Kerr
Fairview Heights, Illinois

Mrs. R. Earl Allen (Joyce)
Fort Worth, Texas

COCKTAIL MEATBALLS

2 pounds chuck (beef, venison, antelope, elk)
1 envelope onion soup mix
1 egg
2 tablespoons butter
2 teaspoons monosodium glutamate

¼ cup bread crumbs
1 10- ounce jar currant or apple jelly
2 14-ounce bottles pizza or plain catsup

Brown bite-sized meat balls. 30 minutes before, mix catsup and jelly. Simmer 25 minutes until hot.
Mrs. Henry A. Parker (Virginia)
Orlando, Florida

HAWAIIAN MEATBALLS

1½ pounds ground beef
⅔ cup cracker crumbs
½ cup onion, chopped
⅔ cup evaporated milk

1 teaspoon seasoned salt
⅓ cup flour
3 tablespoons shortening

Combine first 5 ingredients; mix lightly until blended. Shape meat mixture into small balls. Roll in flour. Brown meat balls in shortening. Drain excess fat. Meanwhile prepare sweet and sour sauce. After sauce is cooked, pour over meat balls. Simmer covered for 15 minutes.

SWEET AND SOUR SAUCE
1 can (13½ ounces) pineapple chunks
2 tablespoons cornstarch
½ cup vinegar
½ cup brown sugar

2 tablespoons soy sauce
2 tablespoons lemon juice
1 cup green bell pepper, chopped
1 tablespoon pimento, chopped

Drain pineapple; reserve pineapple syrup. Add water to make 1 cup liquid; blend with cornstarch until smooth. Stir in next 4 ingredients. Cook until thick and clear. Add pineapple, green pepper and pimento; mix well. Cover. Simmer over low heat 15 minutes. Add meat balls and simmer.
Mrs. R. Paul Caudill (Fern)
Memphis, Tennessee

DEVILED HAM PUFFS

1 8-ounce package cream cheese, at room temperature
2 teaspoons onion juice
2 teaspoons onion, finely minced
1 teaspoon baking powder
2 egg yolks, beaten
½ teaspoon garlic salt
2 4½-ounce cans deviled ham
1 loaf extra thin sliced bread, crust trimmed
Butter
Paprika

Cut bread into 4 triangles per slice. Place small amount of butter in skillet and toast 1 side of bread triangle in butter until brown. Blend cream cheese and remaining ingredients except paprika. Spread on untoasted side and sprinkle with paprika. Bake 10 to 12 minutes at 375 degrees. Makes about 80. (These may be frozen before baking on a cookie sheet. Then store in freezer in smaller containers until ready to use.) Let thaw 5 to 10 minutes, then bake as directed.
Mrs. Charles H. Beal (Winona)
Sarasota, Florida

PARTY MEATBALLS

4 pounds ground beef
1 egg, beaten
1 large onion, finely chopped
1 21-ounce bottle chili sauce
1 12-ounce jar grape jelly
Salt
Juice of 1 lemon

Blend together meat, egg, onion, and salt. Form into 100 small meatballs and arrange in electric skillet. Combine chili sauce, jelly and lemon juice. Pour over meatballs and simmer for 1 hour. Serve in heated chafing dish.
Mrs. Gilbert E. Barrow (Barbara)
Montgomery, Alabama

SALMON BALL

1 pound salmon
1 8-ounce package cream cheese
1 tablespoon lemon juice
2 teaspoons onion, grated
1 teaspoon horseradish
½ teaspoon salt
½ teaspoon liquid smoke
½ cup nuts, chopped
3 tablespoons parsley

Blend salmon that has been drained and deboned with cream cheese, lemon juice, onion, horseradish, salt and liquid smoke. Roll into 1 big ball and cover with nuts. Sprinkle with parsley. Surround with raw vegetables or crackers.
Mrs. Milton Ferguson (Betty)   *Mrs. William C. Lamb (Miriam)*
Kansas City, Missouri   *Raleigh, North Carolina*

CLAM-POTATO NIBBLER

1 package instant mashed potatoes (enough for 2 servings)	Dash white pepper
1¼ teaspoons Worcestershire or soy sauce	½ 6-ounce can minced clams, drained (reserve liquid)
⅛ teaspoon garlic powder	1 egg, slightly beaten
	½ cup fine dry bread crumbs

Prepare potatoes according to package directions, using liquid from drained clams in place of water. Add instant onion to water using 2 table-spoons less milk than called for. Stir in Worcestershire (or soy) sauce, garlic powder, and dash of white pepper. Add minced clams and cover dish. Place in refrigerator 30 minutes or until mixture has cooled and become firm. Remove from refrigerator and shape into bite-size balls; dip into beaten egg, then roll in crumbs. Fry in deep hot fat at 375 degrees for about 1 minute or until golden brown. Drain and serve with tartar sauce. Makes about 30 to 36 balls.

Mrs. Pete Bradfield (Lois)
Throckmorton, Texas

PENNY PUFFS

1 cup flour	½ pound sharp cheese, grated
½ cup margarine	⅛ teaspoon salt

Mix and work with fingers, Form into marble-sized balls. Place about 2 inches apart on greased cookie sheet. Bake at 425 degrees for 10 minutes. (Do not brown.) Good on tea table or with apple or tomato juice before dinner. Makes about 50.

Mrs. Chester C. O'Brien, Jr. (Bonnie)
Albuquerque, New Mexico

BETTY'S THIS AND THAT

1 8-ounce package cream cheese	Butter (approximately 1 stick)
½ cup sugar	Cinnamon and sugar
1 egg	Bread
Vanilla	

Remove crust from bread. Roll bread slices flat with rolling pin. Mix the cream cheese, sugar, egg, and vanilla. Blend well and spread on bread. Dip in melted butter and roll in sugar and cinnamon mixture. Store in deep freeze until ready to bake. Cut each roll into 3 pieces and bake at 350 degrees for 10 to 15 minutes. Makes 72 pieces. This is excellent for a coffee.

Mrs. Doug Watterson (Jan)
Dallas, Texas

MINIATURE PECAN TARTS

SHELLS

1 3-ounce package cream cheese   1 cup all purpose flour
1 stick butter or margarine

Combine ingredients, blending well. Refrigerate overnight. Shape into 24 small balls and press into muffin tins in the shape of tart shells.

FILLING

¾ cup brown sugar   1 egg
1 teaspoon vanilla   ⅔ cup pecans, chopped
1 tablespoon butter or margarine   Pinch of salt

Combine sugar, vanilla, butter, egg and salt. Fill tart shells with mixture; sprinkle with nuts. Bake at 350 degrees for 25 minutes. Yield: 24 servings.
Mrs. Patricia Allison
Springville, Tennessee

PARTY CHEESE TARTS

SHELLS

1 3-ounce package cream cheese   1 cup all purpose flour
1 stick butter

Combine ingredients, blending well. Place in refrigerator overnight. Divide into small balls and press into miniature muffin tins in the form of shells.

FILLING

1 cup sugar   1 cup nuts, chopped
2 egg yolks   1 cup white raisins
2 egg whites   1 teaspoon vanilla

Cream sugar and butter. Add beaten egg yolks, nuts, raisins, and vanilla. Blend well. Fold in beaten egg whites and bake at 350 degrees for 20 minutes. Very good!
Mrs. Bryce Myers (Jenny Lynn)
Charleston, South Carolina

SWEET AND SOUR SAUSAGE

1 pound hot ground sausage	½ cup apple jelly, melted
2 pounds regular ground sausage	6 tablespoons apple cider
1 cup cracker crumbs	4 tablespoons soy sauce
2 or 3 eggs, slightly beaten	14 ounces catsup

Mix sausage, eggs, and crumbs. Roll into ¾-inch balls and brown in skillet. Drain on paper towels.

SAUCE
Combine jelly, cider, soy sauce and catsup. Return sausage balls to skillet and pour sauce over. Simmer until heated through, about 15 minutes. Serve. This is good served from a food warmer.
Mrs. John A. Moore (Julia)
Greenville, North Carolina

BUTTERMILK FONDUE

2 tablespoons cornstarch	1 pound natural Swiss cheese,
Dash ground nutmeg	shredded (4 cups)
½ teaspoon salt	2 cups buttermilk
Dash pepper	

In mixing bowl, combine cornstarch, salt, nutmeg and pepper. Toss Swiss cheese with cornstarch mixture. In saucepan carefully heat buttermilk. When warm gradually add cheese; stir constantly until cheese melts and mixture thickens. Transfer to fondue pot; place over fondue burner. Spear dipper with fondue fork; dip in fondue, swirling to coat. Serves 6 to 8.
Mrs. Bill Hickem (Billie)
Jacksonville, Florida

Soups

SPLIT PEA SOUP

1 small package split peas	1 bay leaf
1 ham bone	Salt and pepper to taste
1 clove garlic	Grated celery and carrots (optional)
2 large onions, chopped	

Cover ham bone with water and cook approximately 1 hour. Take out ham bone and cool. Keep liquid cooking and add split peas. Add chopped onions, garlic and bay leaf. Salt and pepper to taste. Cook slowly for at least 1 hour. Add water to thin. Add ham pieces from the bone. May add grated celery and carrots if desired. Beat with mixer. Keep in refrigerator. Yields less than a quart.

Mrs. Sam Friend (Donna)
Bothell, Washington

CLAM CHOWDER

1½ quarts chicken broth (May use ½ water)	½ cup celery, diced
1 pint clams, chopped	4 cups milk
2 cups potatoes, diced	Salt, pepper, and seafood seasoning to taste
½ cup onion, diced	

Cook vegetables in broth until tender. Add clams and milk. Thicken with a white sauce if desired. Salt, pepper, and seafood seasoning to taste. Sprinkle with chopped chives before serving.

Mrs. Sam Friend (Donna)
Bothell, Washington

ANN'S CORN CHOWDER

¾ cup celery, chopped	1 can cream of chicken soup
¼ cup butter	½ teaspoon basil
1¾ cups milk or half & half	½ teaspoon salt
1 cup whole kernel corn	Pepper to taste

Sauté celery in ¼ cup butter. Combine all ingredients and allow to simmer 30 to 45 minutes. Serve hot with cheese and crackers.

Mrs. Robert S. Scales (Ann)
Oklahoma City, Oklahoma

ADA'S TOMATO SOUP

1 medium can tomatoes	1 cup milk
2 cans water	2 tablespoons flour
1 can beef consommé	Wesson oil or bacon drippings (about
1 teaspoon sugar	1½ tablespoons)
1 medium onion, chopped	Salt to taste (about 2 tablespoons)

On low heat cook onion in oil until slightly tender. Add tomatoes and liquid. Salt to taste and add sugar. Allow to boil slowly for 30 minutes or longer. Place milk and flour in a jar with lid, and shake well to mix. Slowly add to soup, stirring well. Cook slowly a few minutes longer.
Mrs. Lamar Crocker (Rachel)
Louisville, Mississippi

BEEF-VEGETABLE SOUP

1 pound beef stew meat, chopped	1 quart home canned tomatoes or 1
2 strips celery, chopped	large can tomatoes
3 medium potatoes	Macaroni or spaghetti (optional)
1 onion, chopped	Salt and pepper
3 carrots	

Boil beef until almost tender, about 45 minutes. Add chopped vegetables, salt and pepper to taste. Cook about 20 minutes. Add tomatoes and macaroni and simmer a few minutes more.
Mrs. Doyle B. Bledsoe (Mildred)
Pine Bluff, Arkansas

HOTEL ROANOKE PEANUT SOUP

2 quarts chicken broth	3 tablespoons flour
1 small onion, diced	1 pint peanut butter
¼ pound butter	½ cup ground peanuts
2 stalks celery, diced	2 teaspoons celery salt
1 teaspoon lemon juice	1 teaspoon salt

Melt butter in cooking vessel. Add onion and celery and sauté for 5 minutes, but do not brown. Add flour and mix well. Add hot chicken broth and cook for 30 minutes. Remove from stove. Strain; add peanut butter, celery, salt, and lemon juice. Sprinkle ground peanuts on soup just before serving. Serves 8.
Mrs. Helen Horne
Richmond, Virginia

CHOWDER RANCHERO

2 slices bacon, chopped
1 medium onion, chopped
½ pound ground beef
1 can tomatoes
3 teaspoons instant beef bouillon
3 cups water

½ teaspoon salt
⅛ teaspoon pepper
1 teaspoon chili powder
1 can red pinto beans
3 cups rice, hot cooked

Cook bacon till crisp in heavy Dutch oven. Remove and drain. Add onion to bacon drippings. Sauté. Add beef; cook until evenly browned. Stir in tomatoes, beef broth, water, salt, pepper, chili powder and pinto beans. Cover. Simmer 15 minutes. Put ½ cup rice in bowls. Ladle in chowder. Sprinkle with bacon. Serves 6. One of our family's favorite dishes, especially while camping.
Mrs. Elbert L. Smithen (Jo)
Midland, Texas

Sandwiches

CUCUMBER-SHRIMP SANDWICHES

HERB MAYONNAISE
1 cup mayonnaise
1 tablespoon vinegar
¼ teaspoon salt
¼ teaspoon paprika
1 teaspoon crushed oregano
and dill

1 tablespoon onion, grated
⅛ teaspoon garlic salt
1 tablespoon chives, chopped
⅛ teaspoon curry powder
½ teaspoon Worcestershire sauce

Blend all ingredients well.

Bread
Shrimp

Cucumbers

Cut bread with biscuit cutter. Place on cookie sheet; put into plastic bag and freeze. Slice cucumbers the night before and put in bowl of ice. Spread mayonnaise mixture on bread. Place cucumber slice on each piece of bread. Garnish with a shrimp.
Mrs. E. T. Vinson (Katherine)
Scotland Neck, North Carolina

OLIVE-PECAN SANDWICH SPREAD

1 8-ounce package cream cheese,   ½ cup pecans, chopped
   softened   1 tablespoon olive juice
½ cup mayonnaise   Dash pepper
1 cup chopped salad olives

Mash cream cheese with fork. Add mayonnaise. Mix well. Add remaining ingredients and blend together. Refrigerate for at least 24 hours. Delicious on snack crackers.
Mrs. E. Harmon Moore
Indianapolis, Indiana

CORNED BEEF SANDWICHES

1 can corned beef   ⅓ cup mustard
2 cups sharp Cheddar cheese,   1 stick margarine
   grated   1 loaf fresh bread

Melt margarine and cheese. Add mustard and chipped up corned beef. Mix. Put heaping tablespoon of mixture on slice of bread. Roll from corner to corner. Wrap in waxed paper. Freeze. To serve, brown in oven 20 minutes at 350 degrees.
Mrs. Charles Powell (Betty)
Jasper, Alabama

SUPREME HAM SANDWICHES

8 large split hamburger buns   8 slices Swiss cheese
¾ pound shaved or chipped
   cooked ham

SAUCE FOR BUNS

2 sticks butter   1 teaspoon Worcestershire sauce
3 tablespoons prepared mustard   1 medium onion, finely chopped
1½ teaspoon poppy seed

Mix sauce and spread generously on each side of bun. Put ham on buns and top with cheese. Wrap each sandwich in foil and warm in 400 degree oven for 10 minutes. Serve hot. Can make several hours ahead and refrigerate. Heat just before serving.
Mrs. Ted Sisk (Ginny)
Lexington, Kentucky

HAM-ASPARAGUS-SOUP SANDWICH

4 slices buttered toast	⅓ cup milk
4 slices cooked ham	¼ cup mayonnaise
1 can asparagus spears	½ tablespoon pimento, chopped
1 can cream of chicken soup	

Place toast on cookie sheet; top each with sliced cooked ham and cooked asparagus spears. Blend cream of chicken soup, milk, mayonnaise and pimento. Spoon over open face sandwiches. Broil until hot.

Mrs. Bruce H. Price (Eva)
Newport News, Virginia

VEGETABLE SANDWICH SPREAD

1 large ripe tomato	1½ teaspoons salt
1 cucumber	½ teaspoon mustard
1 green pepper	1 cup mayonnaise
1 carrot	1 package plain gelatin
½ small onion	¼ cup cold water
1 teaspoon Worcestershire sauce	

Grind together the tomato, cucumber, green pepper, carrot and onion. Drain. Add Worcestershire sauce, salt, paprika, mustard and mayonnaise. Next add the gelatin dissolved in ¼ cup cold water. Mix all ingredients together and refrigerate. Spread will keep for several days.

Mrs. J. L. Bryson, Jr. (Dottie)
Mt. Airy, North Carolina

RAISIN LEMON-NUT SANDWICH FILLING

1 egg	1 cup raisins
¾ cup sugar	1 cup pecans, chopped
¾ cup mayonnaise	Juice of 1 lemon and grated rind

Beat egg. Add sugar and cook thoroughly on low heat. After cooking several minutes, add raisins and mayonnaise. Continue to stir. Let cook slowly until raisins plump up and soften. Add nuts. Use without extra mayonnaise on bread for sandwiches. Use Teflon or stainless steel pot and spoon, as aluminum discolors the mixture.

Mrs. Ted Callahan
Jackson, South Carolina

BAKED TUNA-CHEESE SANDWICH

12 slices sandwich bread
6 slices cheese
1 can tuna
1 can cream of mushroom soup
1 can milk

2 tablespoons minced onion
1 tablespoon pimento, chopped
2 eggs
Salt and pepper to taste
1 cup Ritz cracker crumbs, buttered

Remove crusts from bread. Grease a 7½ x 11½-inch baking dish and place 6 slices of bread on bottom of pan. Crumble tuna over 6 slices of bread. Place cheese over tuna. Arrange remaining bread on top, forming 6 sandwiches. In mixing bowl, beat 2 eggs, mushroom soup, milk and onions. Add salt and pepper, then pimento. Pour well-beaten mixture over sandwiches. Let stand overnight in refrigerator. Take out an hour before placing in oven. Cover with buttered cracker crumbs. Bake at 350 degrees for 45 minutes to 1 hour or until set.
Mrs. Bill Carr (Dell)
Pensacola, Florida

HOT DOG CHEESE ROLLS

½ pound chunk bologna, or ham, cut in ¼-inch cubes
½ pound American or Cheddar cheese, cut in ¼-inch cubes
⅓ cup green onion, chopped or sliced

2 hard boiled eggs, chopped
½ cup sliced stuffed olives
3 tablespoons salad dressing
½ cup chili sauce
8 or 10 hot dog buns

Combine bologna and cheese cubes with green onion, boiled eggs and olives. Toss mixture with salad dressing and chili sauce. Mix well. Spread into hot dog buns. Wrap in foil tightly. Bake 10 minutes at 400 degrees or until cheese begins to melt. Nice for after church snacks.
Mrs. Robert N. Hammons (Ella)
Clinton, Oklahoma

Beverages

CROSBY PUNCH

1 small package lime-flavored gelatin
1 cup hot water
2 cups sugar
1 large bottle Real Lemon juice
1 large can pineapple juice
1 bottle almond extract
7½ cups water
1 large bottle ginger ale

Pour 1 cup hot water over gelatin and stir until dissolved. Stir in remaining ingredients except ginger ale. Put in large plastic jug, but do not fill to the top. Freeze. Approximately 3 hours before serving time, remove from the freezer and let begin to thaw to mushy stage. Pour in punch bowl. Mix in 1 large bottle ginger ale and serve. Yield: 50 cups.

NOTE: This recipe is adaptable to the occasion and color wanted. For golden punch just substitute orange-flavored gelatin for the base gelatin. Use one can apricot juice along with all other ingredients to give color or add a few drops yellow food coloring. For red punch, substitute strawberry-flavored gelatin for base. Use one can Hawaiian punch, etc.

Mrs. Kenneth L. Henson (Loriene)
Grove Hill, Alabama

Mrs. Cecil Little (Lanette)
Maplesville, Alabama

Mrs. J. D. Grey (Lillian)
New Orleans, Louisiana

Mrs. W. Eugene Spears, Jr. (Lillian)
Beaufort, South Carolina

OPEN HOUSE PUNCH

2 cups water
2 cups sugar
1 46-ounce can apricot nectar
1 46-ounce can unsweetened pineapple juice
1½ cups lemon juice
1 small can frozen orange juice, mixed according to directions on can
2 quarts ginger ale

Combine sugar and water; heat until dissolved. Cool and chill. Add other juices. Chill until ready to serve. Gently combine with cold ginger ale in punch bowl. Garnish. Serves 50.

Mrs. Ted Sisk (Ginny)
Lexington, Kentucky

PARTY PUNCH

2 cups lemon juice
6 cups sugar
2 packages pre-sweetened
  Kool-Aid (Choice of color)

6 quarts water
3 48-ounce cans pineapple juice
1 large bottle ginger ale (optional)

Mix all ingredients. Freeze in wide-mouth containers. Thaw 2 or 3 hours before serving until it is slush. Serves 50.
Mrs. John R. Riddle (Tommye)
Birmingham, Alabama

RED PUNCH

6 cups water
4 cups sugar
1 small package cherry-flavored
  gelatin

1 large can pineapple-orange juice
1 12-ounce can lemon concentrate
1 gallon water

Heat 6 cups water with 4 cups sugar. Add gelatin and pineapple-orange juice. Mix in lemon concentrate. Add 1 gallon water. Yield: 12 gallons. Inexpensive, but good!
Mrs. Glen G. Waldrop (Anne)
Atlanta, Georgia

STRAWBERRY SPARKLE PUNCH

2 cups fresh strawberries, hulled
1 cup water, boiling
3 cups cold water
1 28-ounce bottle ginger ale,
  chilled

1 3-ounce package strawberry
  gelatin
1 6-ounce can frozen lemonade
1 quart bottle cranberry juice
  cocktail, chilled

Put strawberries in blender container; cover and blend on low speed until fruit is pureed. Dissolve gelatin in boiling water. Stir in lemonade concentrate till melted. Add the cold water, cranberry juice and the strawberry puree. Pour over ice in large punch bowl. Slowly pour in chilled ginger ale. Makes about 30 servings.
Mrs. Bobby Perry (Sue)
Moss Point, Mississippi

My soul thirsteth for God, for the living God . . . Ps. 42:2

PINEAPPLE PUNCH

2 20-ounce cans crushed
  pineapple with juice
2 6-ounce cans frozen lemonade
  concentrate

¼ cup sugar
1 28-ounce bottle club soda
1 tray ice cubes

About 10 minutes before serving, place crushed pineapple with its liquid in blender container. Blend one can at a time at high speed 15 to 20 seconds until thick. Stir blended pineapple in chilled punch bowl. Add undiluted lemonade and sugar. Add the club soda. Serve at once. Serves 18 to 20.

Mrs. Gary Payne (Doda)
Syracuse, Missouri

BANANA CRUSH PUNCH

4 cups sugar
1 14-ounce can pineapple juice
1 can frozen lemonade
7 28-ounce bottles ginger ale

6 cups water
2 12-ounce cans frozen
  orange juice
6 bananas, crushed

Dissolve sugar in water. Add juices and bananas. Mix well and freeze in milk cartons. Place frozen block into punch bowl and pour in the ginger ale. Punch will be slushy. Serves 60.

Mrs. Bobby Perry (Sue)
Moss Point, Mississippi

Mrs. James P. Craine (Ruth)
Anderson, South Carolina

Mrs. Roy B. Dunn (Gladys)
Gulf Breeze, Florida

Mrs. C. R. Graham (Carolyn)
Amarillo, Texas

Mrs. Vernon H. Mitchell (Ruth)
Pueblo West, Colorado

Mrs. Rodrick Turner (Mary)
Toccoa, Georgia

ORANGE JULIUS

½ 3-ounce can frozen orange juice
½ cup milk
½ cup water

½ teaspoon vanilla
¼ cup sugar
8 ice cubes

Mix in blender. Serve immediately. Great with hamburgers. Serves 4.

Mrs. Glen G. Waldrop
Atlanta, Georgia

Whosoever drinketh of the water that I shall give him shall never thirst . . . John 4:14

CHRISTMAS PUNCH

4 cups cranberry juice
2 cups pineapple juice
3 quarts ginger ale, cold
1 tablespoon almond flavoring

½ cup sugar
1 teaspoon red food coloring
  (optional)

Combine all ingredients. Stir until sugar is dissolved and thoroughly mixed.

DECORATIVE ICE RING
Freeze 1 inch of water with halves of red cherries and green holly leaves arranged attractively in the bottom of a bundt baking pan. (This gives a Christmas wreath effect.) After this has frozen, add more water and freeze. Enough water may be added to make a 2 or 3-inch ice ring. The ice ring will be white in color.
Mrs. John T. Davis, Jr. (Georgia)
Monroe, North Carolina

HOT APPLE PUNCH

½ cup sugar
2 cups water
1 3-inch cinnamon stick
5 whole cloves

1 teaspoon ground allspice
2 cups orange juice
½ cup lemon juice
1 quart apple juice

Boil sugar and water 5 minutes. Remove from heat and add spices. Let syrup stand covered 1 hour. Strain. When ready to serve, combine sugar mixture and fruit juices and bring to boil quickly. Makes 2 quarts.
Mrs. R. William Dodson (Janelle)
Martin, Tennessee

WASSAIL

2 quarts apple juice
2 Number 2 cans pineapple
  juice
1 cup lemon juice

1 teaspoon cloves
2 cups orange juice
1 stick cinnamon
Sugar to taste

Combine ingredients. Bring to a simmer and serve hot.
Mrs. James W. Parker
Santa Ana, California

HOT CHOCOLATE MIX

1 16-ounce can Quick or
   Hershey's Instant Chocolate mix
1 11-ounce jar Pream or
   Cremora

1 8-quart box powdered
   instant milk
½ pound powdered sugar

Mix ingredients together in large container. Store in tightly covered jars. To serve, use ½ cup mix. Fill cup with boiling water. Marshmallows may be added if desired.

Mrs. John McClanahan (Rosalind)
Pine Bluff, Arkansas

Mrs. J. T. Ford (Mary Helen)
Carrollton, Georgia

Mrs. Pete Bradfield (Lois)
Throckmorton, Texas

Mrs. Billy Hickem (Billie)
Jacksonville, Florida

FRUIT SHAKES

½ cup milk
½ cup orange juice

1 banana, sliced
2 to 3 scoops vanilla ice cream

Put all ingredients in blender. Mix at medium speed. Puree until banana is well blended. Pour into tall glass and enjoy.

VARIATIONS
1. Use all or part chocolate ice cream.
2. Use ½ to 1 cup strawberries instead of banana or add a few strawberries to banana.
3. Use ½ to 1 cup peach slices instead of banana.
4. Use ½ to 1 cup blueberries instead of banana.

Mrs. Joe Burnette (Ann)
Charlotte, North Carolina

RUSSIAN TEA

12 cups water
4 tea bags
2 cups sugar
2 cups orange juice

2 cups pineapple juice
6 or 8 whole cloves
1 stick cinnamon
Juice of 2 lemons

Boil water. Add tea bags. Let stand in covered saucepan until dark in color. Remove tea bags. Mix in remaining ingredients. Heat to boiling or store in refrigerator and heat as desired.

Mrs. John A. Grant (Lois)
Charlotte, North Carolina

INSTANT RUSSIAN TEA

12-ounces Wyler's Lemonade
Mix (dry)
1½ cups plain instant Nestea
1 teaspoon cloves

1 teaspoon ginger
1 pound 2-ounce jar Tang
½ cup sugar
1 teaspoon cinnamon

Pour ingredients into 3 pound coffee can and shake until well mixed. Place about 2 teaspoons per cup of hot water.
Mrs. William M. Hinson (Bettye)
New Orleans, Louisiana

CRAN-APPLE TEA

1 pint cranberry juice cocktail
3 pints apple cider

3 sticks cinnamon
1 teaspoon cloves

Combine all ingredients and bring to a boil. Boil for 10 minutes. Strain and serve.
Mrs. Charles E. Myers (Bea)
Jackson, Mississippi

MOCHA

4 gallons double-strength coffee
(gallon is 24 cups water, 2 cups coffee)

3 gallons chocolate ice cream
1 quart half and half cream

Make coffee one day ahead of time. Then before serving, work in ice cream and lastly pour in half and half. Makes 150 6-ounce servings.
Mrs. Landrum Leavell (Jo Ann)
New Orleans, Louisiana

HOT CIDER

1 quart cider
1 lemon, sliced thinly
Peel of 1 orange and 1 lemon
1 stick cinnamon

1 whole nutmeg, crushed
6 cloves
1 tablespoon sugar

Mix ingredients in large sauce pan. Bring to a boil. Turn down heat and let simmer for 10 minutes. Strain and serve hot. (Can be made a day ahead and chilled, then reheated to serve.)
Mrs. Barnwell Gibson (Lita)
Bamberg, South Carolina

Breads

"O Taste And See
That The Lord Is Good" Ps. 34:8

62

DENVER BISCUITS

1 quart milk, scalded, cooled	1 tablespoon sugar
1 cup sugar	1 teaspoon baking powder
1 cup shortening	1 teaspoon soda
1 cup mashed potatoes	2 tablespoons salt
1 package yeast	5 pounds all-purpose flour
1 cup warm water	

Put sugar, shortening and potatoes in a large bowl. Pour scalded milk over this and stir until dissolved. Cool to lukewarm. Place yeast and sugar in bowl and pour warm water over this. Let set until milk mixture is cool. Mix together and add enough flour to make a batter. Set aside to rise, then add soda, baking powder and salt; then more flour to make a stiff dough. Put out on board and knead. Place dough in refrigerator; cover with a damp cloth. Pinch off enough dough to make a big bun. Put on greased cookie sheet. Place far enough apart so they have room enough to rise and not touch. Bake in 400 degree oven for 20 minutes or until done. Dough will keep several days in the refrigerator.
Mrs. Byron Atkinson
Independence, Missouri

SOUR DOUGH BISCUITS

1 package dry yeast	4 teaspoons baking powder
1 cup warm water	¼ teaspoon soda
2 cups buttermilk	1½ teaspoons salt
¾ cup salad oil	7 cups all-purpose flour, sifted
¼ cup sugar	

Combine yeast and water. Add remaining ingredients. Beat well until blended. Turn onto well-floured board and knead until smooth. Refrigerate. Roll out and cut as needed.
Mrs. Henry Chiles
Pierre, South Dakota

And Jesus answered him saying, It is written, That man shall not live by bread alone, but by every word of God. Luke 4:4

BRAN MUFFIN MIX TO SHARE

6 cups Bran cereal	1 quart buttermilk
2 cups water, boiling	3 cups raisins (optional)
1 cup oil	5 cups plain flour
3 cups sugar	2 teaspoons salt
4 eggs, well beaten	5 teaspoons baking soda

Mix 2 cups bran in boiling water, letting water absorb. Stir in oil. Mix remaining 4 cups bran with buttermilk and beaten eggs. Combine bran mixtures; add flour, soda, sugar, salt and raisins. Store in airtight container in refrigerator until ready to cook. May be kept for six weeks. Bake at 400 degrees in greased muffin tins for 20 minutes. This makes a generous amount; plenty to share with others.

Mrs. H. Edwin Young (Jo Beth)
Columbia, South Carolina

Mrs. Kenneth Chafin (Barbara)
Houston, Texas

Mrs. Robert M. McMillan (Jane)
Tallahassee, Florida

Mrs. Lee Morris (Gerry)
Oak Ridge, Tennessee

JALAPENO PEPPER CORN BREAD

1 cup corn meal	1 medium onion, chopped
1 cup buttermilk	3 peppers
2 eggs	½ can cream style corn
½ cup bacon drippings	¾ cup cheese, cut up
(may add less)	½ pound ground meat, cooked
¾ teaspoon soda	(optional)
½ teaspoon salt	

Mix all ingredients, except cheese. Pour ½ of the batter in greased iron skillet that has been heated. Sprinkle ground meat over it then cheese. Add rest of the batter. Don't let cheese touch side of pan or the corn bread will stick.

Mrs. Wallace Mitchell (Faye)
Gonzalez, Florida

Mrs. Howard Golden
Phenix City, Alabama

Mrs. Bobby Waggoner (Brenda)
Louisville, Mississippi

Mrs. W. E. Darby
Jefferson City, Tennessee

Mrs. Ronald D. Rhodus (Virginia)
Mt. Zion, Illinois

Mrs. Travis Berry (Bernice)
Plano, Texas

64

COMPANY CORN BREAD

1½ cups self-rising corn meal
1 cup sour cream (8-ounce carton)
1 small can creamed corn

2 eggs
1 small onion, chopped (optional)
¾ cup salad oil

Pour enough of the oil in skillet to cover the bottom and heat while mixing all ingredients in a bowl. Pour into heated skillet and bake at 350 degrees for 30 to 40 minutes or until done.

Mrs. John R. Riddle (Tommye)
Birmingham, Alabama

Mrs. Howard Knight (Joyce)
Moorehead City, North Carolina

OLD FASHIONED CORN BREAD

1½ cups corn meal
1½ cup self-rising flour
¼ teaspoon soda
½ teaspoon salt

1 teaspoon baking powder
2 tablespoons shortening, melted
1 cup buttermilk
¼ cup water

Melt shortening in 5-inch iron skillet. Mix all ingredients in mixing bowl and add melted shortening leaving enough in the skillet to grease pan. Cook in 400 degree oven for about 40 minutes or until golden brown.

Mrs. John A. Grant (Lois)
Charlotte, North Carolina

CORN LIGHT BREAD

1 cup sugar
1 cup all-purpose flour
2 cups corn meal
1 teaspoon salt

1 teaspoon soda
2 cups buttermilk
3 tablespoons shortening, melted

Mix together dry ingredients. Add buttermilk and shortening. Pour into greased loaf pan. Bake in 350 degree oven about 50 to 60 minutes. This is good served hot or cold. Wrap leftovers tightly in foil and refrigerate.

Mrs. Wayne Dehoney (Lealice)
Louisville, Kentucky

Mrs. Orvind Dangeau (Freddie Ann)
Franklin, Tennessee

HUSH PUPPIES

2 cups corn meal
1 cup all-purpose flour
4 teaspoons baking powder
4 teaspoons sugar
Milk

1 teaspoon salt
1 nice-size onion, chopped
Red peppers (optional)
2 eggs

Mix dry ingredients. Add onion, peppers and eggs. Mix in enough milk to make paste, but not too thick. Let set 15 minutes. Drop by teaspoon into hot fat. Fry until brown.
Mrs. C. R. Graham (Carolyn)
Amarillo, Texas

HERB BREAD STICKS

1 stick butter or margarine
1 teaspoon marjoram
1 teaspoon basil

½ teaspoon thyme
1 package weiner buns

Cut weiner buns lengthwise in four pieces. Soften margarine and add spices. Spread cut sides of buns with mixture. Bake in 250 degree oven for 1 hour. Turn off heat and leave in oven for another hour.
Mrs. Bobby C. Perry (Sue)
Moss Point, Mississippi

BUTTER ROLLS

2 cups all-purpose flour, sifted
3 teaspoons baking powder
½ teaspoon salt
4 tablespoons shortening
¾ cup milk

1 pint whipping cream
1 cup milk
Cinnamon (optional)
Sugar

Sift flour with baking powder and salt; cut in shortening till mixture resembles coarse crumbs. Add milk all at once and mix. Turn out on lightly floured surface; knead gently. Divide into 8 to 10 balls of dough. Pat into circles ⅛-inch thick. Cover each circle with soft butter; sprinkle each with 2 teaspoons of sugar. If desired, sprinkle cinnamon over the sugar. Roll into very loose rolls and place in a 9 x 12-inch baking dish. Pour over the rolls a mixture of 1 pint of whipping cream and 1 cup of milk. The rolls need to be almost covered with the liquid. Bake 40 to 50 minutes at 350 degrees.
Mrs. W. C. Carpenter (Fannie)
Portland, Oregon

SOURDOUGH ROLLS

SOURDOUGH STARTER

3½ cups flour, unsifted	1 package dry yeast
1 tablespoon sugar	2 cups warm water

Combine flour, sugar and dry yeast in a large bowl. Gradually add warm water, and beat until smooth. Cover with transparent wrap. Let stand in a warm place for 2 days to use in bread recipe as directed. To replenish starter, add to the remaining starter 1½ cups flour and 1 cup warm water. Beat until smooth, cover and keep in warm place. Stir before using. If not used in one week, remove 1½ cups starter and follow directions for replenishing.

SOURDOUGH BREAD

1½ cups Sourdough starter	¼ cup warm water
¾ cup milk	1 package dry yeast
3 tablespoons sugar	5 to 6 cups all-purpose flour,
1 teaspoon salt	unsifted
2 tablespoons margarine	

Prepare Sourdough starter. Scald milk. Stir in sugar, salt and margarine. Cook to lukewarm. Measure warm water into large warm bowl. Sprinkle in yeast and stir until dissolved. Add milk mixture, starter and 2½ cups flour. Beat until smooth. Stir in enough additional flour to make a stiff dough. Turn out onto floured board. Knead until smooth and elastic, 8 to 10 minutes. Place in greased bowl and cover. Let rise until double in bulk (about 1 hour). Punch dough down. Divide into 3 equal parts. Form each piece into a smooth round ball or a tapered roll. Place on a greased baking sheet. With a sharp knife, cut dough in a crisscross fashion on top. Cover and let rise until double in size (about 1 hour). Bake at 400 degrees for 25 minutes. Cool on wire racks. Makes 3 loaves.
Mrs. W. D. Sherman
Lufkin, Texas

QUICK DELICIOUS ROLLS

2 cups self-rising flour	2 tablespoons mayonnaise
2 tablespoons sugar	1 cup milk

Sift flour and sugar together. Mix ingredients together. Place in greased muffin pan. Spread butter on top. Bake at 450 degrees for 10 to 15 minutes.
Mrs. Robert K. Davis (Pat)
Elba, Alabama

MERINGUE ROLLS

4 cups flour, sifted
½ teaspoon salt
1 package dry yeast
1¼ cups butter (2½ sticks)
3 egg yolks, slightly beaten

½ cup commercial sour cream
1 teaspoon vanilla
Confectioners' sugar, sifted
Chopped nuts
Meringue filling

In large mixing bowl thoroughly stir together the flour, salt, and undissolved yeast. With pastry blender cut in butter until particles are fine. Add egg yolks, sour cream, and vanilla. Mix thoroughly by hand. Divide into 6 equal portions, forming each into a ball. Refrigerate while you prepare meringue filling.

MERINGUE FILLING Beat 3 egg whites until stiff. Gradually beat in 1 cup sugar; continue to beat, if necessary, until meringue holds into straight peaks. Beat in vanilla to taste.

Sprinkle a board or clean pastry cloth with sifted confectioners' sugar. Keeping remaining dough refrigerated, roll out 1 ball at a time into a 9-inch round; cover with 1/6 of the meringue filling and sprinkle with nuts; cut each round into 8 wedges. Begin at wide end and roll up each wedge, neither too tight nor too loosely. Place point-side-down several inches apart on an ungreased cookie sheet. Bake in a 350 degree oven for 25 minutes until lightly browned and meringue showing at ends of rolls is firm. Remove and sprinkle with confectioners' sugar.
Mrs. George L. Karr
Fairview Heights, Illinois

SPOON ROLLS

1 package dry yeast
2 cups very warm water
1½ sticks butter, melted

¼ cup sugar
1 egg
4 cups self-rising flour

Place yeast in water. Cream melted butter with sugar in large bowl. Add beaten egg and dissolved yeast to creamed mixture. Stir in flour until well mixed. Place in airtight bowl and keep in refrigerator. To bake, drop by spoonfuls into well greased 2½-inch muffin tins. Bake in a 350 degree oven for about 20 minutes. Mixture keeps for several days.
Mrs. John Dunaway (Jayne)   *Mrs. A. B. Coyle (Joan)*
Corbin, Kentucky   *Memphis, Tennessee*

HONEY-GLAZED SWEET POTATO BUNS

3¾ cups all-purpose flour
2 packages active dry yeast
½ cup water
¼ cup granulated sugar
3 tablespoons butter or margarine
1 teaspoon salt
1 8-ounce can sweet potatoes,
  drained and mashed (¾ cup)

2 eggs
1 teaspoon vanilla
5 tablespoons butter
½ cup honey
¾ cup brown sugar, packed
½ cup walnuts, chopped

In large mixing bowl, combine 1½ cups of the flour and the yeast. Heat together water, granulated sugar, 3 tablespoons butter and salt just until warm, stirring constantly until butter almost melts, about 115 degrees. Add to flour mixture along with sweet potatoes, eggs, and vanilla. Beat at low speed with electric mixer for ½ minute, scraping sides of bowl constantly. Beat 3 minutes at high speed. By hand, stir in enough of the remaining flour to make a moderately stiff dough. Knead until smooth and elastic, 8 to 10 minutes. Place in a greased bowl. Cover; let rise in warm place until almost double, about 1 hour. Punch down. Let rest 10 minutes. In small saucepan, melt the remaining butter; remove 2 tablespoons and set aside. Stir honey, ½ cup of the brown sugar and ¼ cup of the nuts into remaining butter in saucepan. Heat and stir until bubbly. Pour into a 13 x 9 x 10-inch rectangle. Brush with the reserved 2 tablespoons butter. Sprinkle with remaining brown sugar and nuts. Roll up jelly roll fashion beginning at long edge. Cut into 15 1-inch rolls. Place, cut-side-down, in pan. Cover and let rise in warm place till almost double, about 1½ hours. Bake in 375 degree oven for 25 minutes. Immediately invert pan onto wire rack. Makes 15 rolls.
Mrs. Orvind Dangeau (Freddie Ann)
Franklin, Tennessee

QUICK STICKY BUNS

1 can refrigerated biscuits
2 tablespoons butter, melted
  and cooled slightly
½ cup brown sugar, firmly packed

1 teaspoon cinnamon
2 tablespoons dark corn syrup
¼ cup chopped pecans or coconut,
  if desired

Cut each biscuit in half and form each piece into a ball. Combine sugar, cinnamon and pecans in small bowl. Dip each biscuit half into butter, then into sugar mixture. Place in greased 8-inch cake pan. Mix remaining butter and sugar and spoon over biscuit balls. Drizzle corn syrup over all. Bake at 450 degrees for 10 to 12 minutes. Serve warm.
Mrs. Kenneth Chafin (Barbara)
Houston, Texas

APPLE PANCAKE

4 medium apples
5 tablespoons butter
6 tablespoons sugar
½ teaspoon cinnamon
¼ teaspoon nutmeg
2 eggs

¼ teaspoon salt
½ cup milk
½ cup flour
1 tablespoon butter
2 tablespoons confectioners' sugar

Peel and slice apples. Melt butter in skillet. Add apples. Cook over medium heat for 5 minutes. Mix sugar, cinnamon and nutmeg. Sprinkle over apples. Continue cooking, covered, over low heat for 10 minutes. Set aside. Place eggs in blender. Mix at low speed. Add milk and salt. Add flour and blend until smooth. Pour into a 10-inch round, deep pie plate. Bake at 450 degrees for 15 minutes. Prick batter with fork when it rises in center. Reduce heat to 350 degrees and bake for 10 minutes. Spread with melted butter and sprinkle with confectioners' sugar. Place apple mixture on half and fold.

Mrs. Allen E. Schmidt (Catherine)
Surrey, British Columbia, Canada

SOUR DOUGH PANCAKES

SOUR DOUGH STARTER

1 cup all-purpose flour
1 cup water

1 package dry yeast

Mix in a quart jar and let stand 24 hours, stirring occasionally. Keep in refrigerator after the first 24 hours. The night before you want to serve the pancakes add to the starter:

1 cup water
¼ cup sugar

1½ cups all-purpose flour
½ teaspoon salt

Mix and let stand in a warm place overnight.

1 egg
¼ cup vegetable oil

1 teaspoon baking powder
½ teaspoon soda

Dissolve baking powder and soda into ½ cup water. Add egg and vegetable oil and stir into mixture. Cook on hot griddle as you would any other pancakes. CAUTION! Save starter for next pancakes before the last 4 ingredients are added. Refrigerate.

Mrs. W. C. Carpenter (Fannie)
Portland, Oregon

PANCAKES

2 cups all-purpose flour
1¼ cups milk
2 eggs
4½ tablespoons sugar

4 teaspoons baking powder
1 stick butter or margarine
1 teaspoon salt

Sift dry ingredients together. Add eggs and milk that have been beaten together. Stir only enough to mix well. Add melted butter last. Bake on preheated grill. Keep airtight in refrigerator, if desired, for later use. To vary, chop up bananas in batter.

Mrs. Bernes K. Selph (Tommie)
Benton, Arkansas

WAFFLES

2 cups all-purpose flour
2 eggs
1¼ cups sweet milk
4 teaspoons baking powder

1 teaspoon salt
6 tablespoons melted fat or
½ cup Wesson oil

Sift together dry ingredients; gradually add milk mixed with well beaten egg yolks and melted fat. Fold in stiffly-beaten egg whites. Bake on hot waffle irons. Enjoy with your preference of toppings.

Mrs. John T. Tippet, Jr. (Elise)
Savannah, Georgia

"MAMA CILE'S" CINNAMON TOAST

8 slices white bread
½ cup sugar
2 teaspoons ground cinnamon

¼ cup butter (½ stick)
2 tablespoons water

Toast bread lightly under the broiler on both sides. Mix together remaining ingredients. Cook briefly until sugar is melted and syrup is thick. Spread on the toasted bread and return to a 350 degree broiler for 3 to 5 minutes.

Mrs. Malcolm B. Knight (Joyce)
Jacksonville, Florida

PUFFY FRENCH TOAST

4 slices day old bread, cut
   diagonally
½ cup milk

1 egg
¾ cup Bisquick
½ cup shortening

Mix together the milk, egg, and Bisquick. Dip bread slices in batter. Heat ½ cup shortening in iron skillet. Sauté bread slices two at a time until golden brown and puffy, about 3 minutes on each side. Serve with warm maple syrup. Serves 2.
Mrs. Jess Baker (Nita)
Yuma, Arizona

APPLE-NUT BREAD

3 cups all-purpose flour
2 teaspoons baking soda
2 teaspoons baking powder
2 teaspoons cinnamon
2 cups sugar

1½ cups salad oil
4 eggs
2 cups apples, chopped
1 cup nuts, chopped

Mix together flour, soda, baking powder, cinnamon and sugar. Start mixer at low speed and add to above ingredients the salad oil, eggs, chopped apples and nuts. Bake in two medium sized loaf pans or square pan for 1 hour at 350 degrees.
Mrs. J. E. Hewlett (Mildred)
St. Louis, Missouri

BATTER BREAD

2 packages yeast
2 cups warm water
1 egg

1 stick margarine, melted, cooled
¼ cup sugar
4 cups self-rising flour

Dissolve yeast in lukewarm water. Mix together dry ingredients. Combine all ingredients, mixing well in large bowl. Refrigerate at least 3 hours before baking. Pinch off a good-size ball and drop onto greased muffin tins. Bake in 400 degree oven about 15 minutes until brown. Batter can be kept in refrigerator several days.
Mrs. J. O. Wade (Linda)
Plant City, Florida

Moses gave you not that bread from heaven; but my Father giveth you the true bread from heaven. John 6:32

EASY BANANA BREAD

1 cup sugar
½ cup butter or margarine
2 eggs, unbeaten
1½ cups bananas, mashed
1 tablespoon lemon juice

2 cups flour
3 teaspoons baking powder
½ teaspoon salt
1 cup nuts, chopped
1 teaspoon vanilla

Cream sugar with butter, add eggs one at a time, beating well after each addition. Stir in bananas and lemon juice. Sift flour with baking powder and salt; add and mix quickly. Stir in nuts. Bake in greased 9 x 5 x 3-inch loaf pan at 350 degrees about 1 hour or until done when tested. Cool on rack.

Mrs. James Penland (Arizona)
Tulsa, Oklahoma

Mrs. Lee Morris (Gerry)
Oak Ridge, Tennessee

Mrs. Bill Moore (Sue)
Houston, Texas

BISHOP'S BREAD

1½ cups all-purpose flour, sifted
1½ teaspoons baking powder
¼ teaspoon salt
½ cup chocolate morsels
2 cups walnuts, chopped

1 cup dates, chopped
1 cup candied cherries, chopped
3 eggs
1 cup sugar

Grease a 10 x 5 x 3-inch loaf pan and line with 3 layers of waxed paper. Set oven at 325 degrees. Into bowl sift flour, baking powder and salt. Stir in chocolate, walnuts and fruit. In another bowl, beat eggs well. Gradually beat in sugar. Fold in flour mixture. Pour into pan. Bake 1½ hours in preheated oven.

Mrs. James W. Parker
Santa Ana, California

JEW'S BREAD

1 pound dates
1 pound nuts (2 cups)
1 cup sugar
5 tablespoons flour

1 teaspoon baking powder
½ teaspoon salt
1 teaspoon vanilla
3 eggs

Sift together dry ingredients. Add slightly beaten eggs and vanilla. Stir in nuts and fruit. Pour into a 9 x 13-inch biscuit pan that has been greased and floured. Bake 20 minutes in a moderate oven.

Mrs. Bill Wilson (Marie)
Mobile, Alabama

MONKEY BREAD

2 packages yeast	1 cup Crisco
1 cup water, boiling	½ cup sugar
1½ teaspoons salt	6 cups flour
2 eggs, beaten	1½ pounds butter, melted

Dissolve yeast in 1 cup lukewarm water. Mix shortening, sugar and salt. Add boiling water and stir until shortening dissolves. Add eggs, flour and yeast alternately to shortening mixture. Beat. Let rise until double in bulk. Roll out 1½-inches thick. Cut in squares. Dip in melted butter. Layer in tube pan till ½ full. Let rise until it reaches top of pan. Bake at 350 degrees for 1 hour.

Mrs. Elbert L. Smithen (Jo)
Midland, Texas

HIGH PROTEIN BREAD
(Low in Fat and Sugar)

1 package granulated yeast	1½ teaspoons salt
1 cup lukewarm water	2 teaspoons sugar
2 tablespoons vegetable oil	3 tablespoons soya flour
2½ cups unbleached flour	3½ tablespoons powdered sugar

Dissolve yeast in lukewarm water; add oil. Measure dry ingredients into a bowl; add yeast mixture and stir vigorously until dough is smooth (may use your hands for this). Turn into oiled bowl and cover. Let rise for 1½ hours. Punch dough down and fold over edges in a kneading action. Cover and let rise again for 15 minutes. Turn out and knead until smooth and elastic. Shape into loaf; place in oiled pan. Cover and let rise until it fills pan, about 1 hour. Bake at 375 degrees for 35 minutes or until done. This bread freezes well and keeps well.

VARIATION
Substitute the 2½ cups unbleached flour with:

1¼ cups unbleached flour
1¼ cups whole wheat flour
or

1 cup unbleached flour	½ cup corn meal
1 cup whole wheat flour	

Mrs. Charles H. Ashcraft (Sarah)
Little Rock, Arkansas

Give us this day our daily bread. Matt. 6:11

CINNAMON YEAST BREAD

2 packages active dry yeast
½ cup warm water (105-115 degrees)
⅔ cup sugar
1 tablespoon salt
¼ cup shortening

2¼ cups warm water
6 to 7 cups all-purpose flour
Soft butter or margarine
⅔ cups sugar
2 tablespoons cinnamon

Dissolve yeast in ½ cup warm water. Stir in sugar, salt, shortening, 2¼ cups warm water and 3½ cups flour. Beat until smooth. Mix in enough remaining flour to handle dough. Turn dough on lightly floured board. Knead 10 minutes. Place in a greased bowl. Cover to let rise until double in bulk, about 1 hour. (Thumb impression remains when ready.) Punch down. Divide in half. Roll into 18 x 9-inch rectangles. Make a mixture of ⅔ cup sugar and 2 tablespoons cinnamon. Brush rectangles generously with very soft butter. Sprinkle with sugar and cinnamon mixture and roll and seal ends. Place seam side down in well greased pan. Cover and let rise in warm place until double, 1 hour. Preheat oven to 375 degrees and bake 40 to 45 minutes. Brush with soft butter when done.
Mrs. Bobby L. Eklund (Janis)
Hurst, Texas

DILLY BREAD

1 cake yeast
¼ cup warm water
1 cup creamed cottage cheese, heated lukewarm
2 tablespoons sugar
¼ teaspoon soda

2¼ to 2½ cups all-purpose flour
1 teaspoon salt
1 tablespoon dill seed
1 tablespoon dried onion flakes
1 egg, unbeaten
1 tablespoon butter, melted

Soften yeast cake in ¼ cup warm water. Combine all ingredients except flour in mixing bowl. Stir in flour, beating well after each addition. Grease the ball of dough. Cover and let rise in a warm place (85-90 degrees) about 45 minutes or until double in bulk. Punch down. Shape into a greased round or place in a bread pan. Grease, cover and let it rise again about a half hour or until double in bulk. Bake at 350 degrees for 25 to 30 minutes. While it is still hot, butter the crust and sprinkle with salt. Makes 1 loaf.
Mrs. Lee Morris (Gerry)
Oak Ridge, Tennessee

PRISCILLA'S EASY HONEY BREAD

2 packages yeast
½ cup honey
1 cup dry milk solids
2½ cups warm water
½ cup oil

1 tablespoon salt
2 packages unflavored gelatin
6 to 7 cups all-purpose flour,
   unbleached (may use whole
   wheat flour)

In large mixer bowl combine the yeast, honey, dry milk solids and lukewarm water. Mix well and let set 10 minutes. Add salt, gelatin and 3 cups flour. Mix well with mixer, then add ½ cup oil. Add 3 to 4 cups unbleached flour or to consistency that is easily handled when turned out on a floured counter top. Knead well. Place in a clean well-oiled bowl, turning once to bring oiled side up. Cover and let rise in warm place until double in size. Punch down and let rise at least once more, then punch down again. Shape into loaves or rolls. Place in greased pans. Let rise until less than doubled in size. Place in a 350 degree oven and bake until golden brown. Remove from pans to cooling rack and rub with butter or oil. This seals in the moisture. Slice with electric knife, butter and eat.

Mrs. Randall Thetford (Priscilla)
Coeur D' Alene, Idaho

Mrs. Ronald P. Liesmann (Eunice)
Bloomington, Indiana

PUMPKIN BREAD

2⅔ cups sugar
2 cups pumpkin
2½ cups all-purpose flour
⅔ cup oil
4 eggs
⅔ cup water

2 teaspoons baking powder
2 teaspoons soda
1⅓ teaspoons salt
1 teaspoon cinnamon
1 teaspoon ginger
1 teaspoon cloves

Combine all ingredients in a large bowl. Mix with electric mixer approximately 2 minutes. Prepare 2 loaf pans by greasing and lightly dusting with flour. Pour mixture in pans and bake at 350 degrees for approximately 1 hour.

Mrs. E. M. Adams (Marjorie)
Fredonia, New York

Mrs. Glenn Cox
Webbers Falls, Oklahoma

Mrs. H. T. Finch, Jr. (Judy)
Rock Hill, South Carolina

SURPRISE ZUCCHINI BREAD

3 large eggs, well beaten	2 teaspoons baking powder
1 cup oil	1 teaspoon cinnamon
2 cups sugar	3 cups zucchini squash
2 teaspoons vanilla	1 cup nuts, chopped
3 cups flour	1 cup coconut
1 teaspoon soda	

Add oil, sugar and vanilla to well-beaten eggs and mix well. Sift dry ingredients together and then add to the egg mixture alternately with 3 cups peeled and grated green zucchini squash. Stir in nuts and coconut. Pour into greased loaf pans and bake at 325 degrees for 1 hour and 15 minutes. Recipe makes 1 large loaf or 3 small ones.

Mrs. S. A. Qualls   *Mrs. Harry Foley*
Holt, Missouri   *Mesa, Arizona*

Mrs. Everett Lemay
Mt. Vernon, Illinois

SWEDISH LIMPA BREAD

(A great recipe, especially for holiday time)

1 cake compressed yeast	1½ teaspoons fennel seed
1 tablespoon lukewarm water	½ teaspoon anise seed
2 cups milk	¾ cup Wesson oil
2 cups lukewarm water	8 cups rye flour
6 cups white flour	1 tablespoon salt
1 cup dark corn syrup	Grated rind of 2 oranges
½ cup molasses	

Dissolve yeast with lukewarm water. Scald milk and allow it to cool to lukewarm. Combine the lukewarm milk with 2 cups water, the yeast and 6 cups of white flour and beat well. Allow this sponge to double in bulk. Combine syrup, molasses, fennel seed and anise seed in a saucepan and boil for 1 minute. Strain the mixture through a fine sieve to remove the seeds. Add Wesson oil to strained syrup and allow mixture to cool. Add this to the light sponge with 8 cups of rye flour, salt and grated orange rind. Mix dough well, turn onto lightly floured board and knead until smooth and elastic. Place in lightly greased large bowl, cover and let rise until double. Shape into loaves. Put into greased 9 x 4-inch aluminum foil loaf pans. Allow to double in bulk. Bake in 400 degree oven for 15 minutes, then reduce heat to 350 degrees and continue to bake for about 20 minutes or until done. Makes 6 loaves.

Mrs. George L. Karr
Fairview Heights, Illinois

Guest Section

Train up a child in the way he should go:
and when he is old,
he will not depart from it. Proverbs 22:6

"PLAINS SPECIAL" CHEESE RING

1 pound sharp cheese, grated
1 cup nuts, finely chopped
1 cup mayonnaise
1 small onion, finely grated
Black pepper
Dash cayenne
Strawberry preserves, optional

Combine all ingredients except preserves, season to taste with pepper. Mix well and place in a 5 or 6 cup lightly greased ring mold. Refrigerate until firm for several hours or overnight. To serve, unmold, and if desired, fill center with strawberry preserves, or serve plain with crackers.
Mrs. Jimmy Carter (Rosalynn)
Washington, D. C.

PUMPKIN CHIFFON PIE

3 beaten egg yolks
¾ cup brown sugar
1½ cups pumpkin, cooked
½ cup milk
½ teaspoon nutmeg
½ teaspoon cinnamon
½ teaspoon salt
1 envelope Knox gelatin
¼ cup cold water
3 egg whites, stiffly beaten
1 cup granulated sugar

Combine egg yolks, brown sugar, pumpkin, milk, salt and spice. Cook in double boiler until thick, stirring constantly. Soak gelatin in cold water; stir into hot mixture. Chill until partly set. Beat egg whites, add granulated sugar, and beat stiff. Fold into gelatin mixture. Pour into pie shell and chill until set. Garnish with whipped cream. Makes one big pie or 8 individual pies.
Mrs. Dwight Eisenhower (Mamie)
Gettysburg, Pennsylvania

Righteousness exalteth a nation . . . . Proverbs 14:34

BAKED TURKEY CASSEROLE

4 tablespoons butter or margarine
2 medium green peppers (cut in julienne strips)
6 tablespoons flour
3 cups hot chicken stock
1 pound cooked turkey (cut in julienne strips)
¼ pound smoked Virginia ham (cut in julienne strips)
1 tablespoon chopped parsley
½ tablespoon Worcestershire sauce
Salt to taste
¼ teaspoon ground white pepper
1 cup milk
10 ounces thin noodles
2 tablespoons grated cheese
6 saltine crackers, crushed

Melt butter or margarine in 3-quart saucepan. Add green pepper and simmer covered for 5 minutes. Add flour and stir well. Add chicken stock and bring sauce to boil. Cook sauce for 5 minutes or until smooth. Add turkey, ham, parsley, Worcestershire sauce, salt, and white pepper. Bring to a second boil and add milk gradually while gently stirring. Simmer 5 minutes. Cook noodles 7 minutes and drain. Place in a greased shallow casserole. Top with turkey mixture. Sprinkle with cheese and cracker crumbs. Bake in 375 degree oven for 20 minutes or until lightly browned.
Mrs. Gerald Ford (Betty)

BRAISED STEAKS

1 large onion, sliced
2 to 4 tablespoons corn oil
¼ teaspoon thyme
6 beef round steaks (8-ounces each)
Seasoned salt
Flour
1 cup V-8 vegetable juice
1 cup beef broth
1½ cups mixed julienne strips of carrots, leeks and celery
1 tablespoon chopped parsley

In a large ovenproof skillet, sauté onion in 1 tablespoon of oil until golden. Remove from heat and add thyme. Set aside. Sprinkle steaks on both sides with seasoned salt and flour. Heat remaining oil in an iron skillet and brown steaks on both sides. Transfer to pan with onions. Pour vegetable juice and broth over steaks. Cover and simmer very slowly 1 hour in the oven or on top of the stove. Turn steaks, sprinkle with the vegetable julienne and continue to cook 30 minutes longer. To serve, arrange steaks on a serving platter. Spoon sauce and vegetables over steaks and sprinkle with parsley.
Mrs. Richard Nixon (Pat)
San Clemente, California

POPOVERS

1 cup all-purpose flour, sifted	¼ teaspoon salt
1 cup milk	2 tablespoons shortening, melted
2 eggs, beaten	

Mix and sift flour and salt. Combine eggs, milk and shortening; gradually add to flour mixture, beating about one minute or until batter is smooth. Fill greased sizzling hot pans ¾ full and bake in very hot oven at 450 degrees about 20 minutes. Reduce heat to moderate, 350 degrees, and continue baking for 15 to 20 minutes.
Mrs. Lyndon B. Johnson (Lady Bird)
Austin, Texas

ESCALLOPED EGGPLANT

1 eggplant	Bread crumbs
1 green pepper, chopped	Grated cheese
1 cup celery, coarsely chopped	About ¼ pound butter
1 can tomatoes or 4 fresh	Chopped parsley
tomatoes	Salt and pepper to taste

Peel and dice eggplant. Boil eggplant and celery together until tender. Drain well. Sauté green pepper in butter. Put half of eggplant, celery mixture in bottom of casserole, then half of other ingredients. Add rest of eggplant, etc., and cover with bread crumbs and grated cheese. Cover and bake until all vegetables are tender.
Mrs. Harry Truman (Bess)
Independence, Missouri

NANCY'S SWEET & SOUR DRESSING
FOR FRUIT SALAD

½ cup sugar	1 teaspoon salt
2 level tablespoons flour	¾ cup oil
1 teaspoon paprika	1 teaspoon celery seed (soak in
½ cup vinegar	tablespoon water)
½ teaspoon onion, grated	

Mix sugar, flour and paprika; stir in vinegar; heat until thick in double boiler. Add onion and salt; cool. Add oil, a little at a time, while beating with a rotary beater. Add drained celery seed.
Mrs. Ronald Reagan (Nancy)
Los Angeles, California

SUKIYAKI

4 pounds eye of round, sliced paper thin	Mushrooms
	Bamboo shoots
1 head Chinese cabbage (celery cabbage), sliced diagonally	¼ cup sugar or to taste
	½ cup soy sauce or to taste
2 large Bermuda onions, sliced paper thin	

Place beef in heated skillet or Dutch oven. When lightly brown, add cabbage and other vegetables. Pour sugar and soy sauce over vegetables. Simmer just long enough for vegetables to cook slightly but still be crispy. Serve with rice, bowls, and chopsticks. (No forks or spoons allowed). If you have a "Wok" or electric skillet, its fun to cook on table and each person serve themselves directly from it.

Mrs. Billy Graham (Ruth)
Montreat, North Carolina

MARGARET CHILES' FRIED CORN

6 pieces bacon	Milk
10 ears fresh corn	Salt and pepper
3 tablespoons butter	

Fry bacon. Set aside. Leave fat from bacon in skillet. Prepare corn by holding ear perpendicular to cutting board. With a sharp knife, slice downward, cutting off tip ends of kernels. Scrape milk out of remaining kernels. Heat bacon fat in skillet. Add scraped corn and kernel tips. Fry lightly for three minutes, stirring constantly. Add enough milk to make creamed corn consistency. Add 3 tablespoons butter. Cook another 5 minutes. Add salt and pepper to taste. Pour into serving dish and sprinkle crushed bacon over all. consistency. Add 3 tablespoons butter. Cook another 5 minutes. Add salt and pepper to taste. Pour into serving dish and sprinkle crushed bacon over all. Serves 6.

Mrs. Lawton Chiles (Margaret)
Washington, D. C.

PAELLA AMIGOS

1½ pound lobster
6 cherrystone clams
6 mussels
½ pound crabmeat
1 frying chicken
¼ pound veal
¼ pound lean pork
¼ cup olive oil
1 clove garlic, minced
1 onion, finely chopped
2 teaspoons salt

¼ teaspoon freshly ground pepper
2 tomatoes, ripe (1 pound)
2 cups rice
4 cups water
1 sweet red pepper, chopped
1 package frozen peas
1 package frozen artichoke hearts
1 clove garlic
1 teaspoon saffron
12 asparagus tips, fresh or canned
Pimento

Remove meat from lobster. Scrub clams and mussels. Pick over crabmeat. Cut frying chicken into parts. Dice veal and lean pork. In a heavy deep skillet heat ¼ cup olive oil. Add chicken, veal and pork. Cook until chicken pieces are browned on all sides. Add garlic, and onion. Cook, stirring until onion is transparent. Add 2 teaspoons salt, ¼ teaspoon freshly ground pepper, and 2 ripe tomatoes, peeled and chopped. Cover and cook for 10 minutes longer. Add rice and 4 cups water. Stir to combine. Add 1 sweet red pepper, chopped, 1 package frozen peas and 1 package frozen artichoke hearts. Cover and cook over low heat for about 20 minutes. Mash in mortar 1 clove garlic and 1 teaspoon saffron. Add to paella. With large spoon turn rice from top to bottom to mix well. Add the crabmeat and the lobster meat; cover, and cook for 10 to 15 minutes longer.

GARNISH
Meanwhile, put mussels and clams in a heavy pot with ½ cup water. Cover and bring to a lively boil over high heat. Cook for 2 minutes, or until shells open. Cook 12 asparagus tips until tender in boiling salted water (or heat canned asparagus).

PRESENTATION
Arrange rice mixture in shallow paella dish or large shallow casserole. Place open mussels and clams in their shells on top of rice and garnish with the asparagus tips and strips of pimento.

Governor Edmund G. Brown, Jr.
Sacramento, California

Salads and Dressings

That they may teach the young women
to be sober, to love their husbands,
to love their children. Titus 2:4

 # Fruit Salads

GRAPE NUT WHIP SALAD

2 eggs, well-beaten
½ cup sugar
2 tablespoons lemon juice
1 cup heavy cream, whipped
½ cup nuts

1 cup pineapple tidbits, drained
1 cup red Tokay grapes, sliced
2 cups marshmallows, diced

Combine eggs, sugar and lemon juice. Cook until thickened. Cool. Fold in whipped cream. Fold in fruits and nuts. Chill 5 to 6 hours or overnight.

Mrs. Rollin Burhans (Delma)
Bowling Green, Kentucky
Mrs. Milton Baty
Novice, Texas

Mrs. Hugh L. Smith (Virginia)
Henderson, Texas
Mrs. Richard Brogan
Clinton, Missouri

HEAVENLY HASH SALAD

1 Number 2 can pineapple
   chunks
2 cups miniature marshmallows
⅓ cup well-drained maraschino
   cherries, cut in fourths

1 cup stiffly whipped cream
¼ cup slivered almonds or broken
   pecans
Shredded coconut

Drain pineapple, reserving ¼ cup syrup. Combine pineapple, marshmallows, cherries and syrup. Let stand 1 hour. Fold in the whipped cream. Spoon into salad bowl and chill. Sprinkle with coconut and nuts.

Mrs. Sam Friend (Donna)
Bothell, Washington

RASPBERRY-CHERRY FRUIT SALAD

1 can cherry pie filling
1 can mandarin oranges, drained
1 cup pineapple chunks, drained
1 box frozen raspberries, drained

Mix and keep chilled until served.
Mrs. Gary Cook
Sapulpa, Oklahoma

FRUIT SALAD

1 Number 2 can pineapple
   tidbits, drained
4 bananas
1 cup seeded grape halves
½ cup broken nuts
½ cup small marshmallows

SAUCE
½ cup sugar
1 egg, well beaten
1 tablespoon flour
1 cup pineapple juice

Cook over medium heat until thick, stirring constantly. Let cool and store in refrigerator. Pour sauce over salad just before serving.
Mrs. Dennis Lyle (Ressa)
Nashville, Tennessee

STIR AND GO SALAD

1 3-ounce package
   orange-flavored gelatin
1 8-ounce can crushed
   pineapple, drained
1 11-ounce can mandarin oranges,
   drained
1 pound cottage cheese
1 small carton Cool Whip

Empty gelatin powder into bowl. Stir in pineapple and cottage cheese. Mix until gelatin is dissolved. Carefully stir in mandarin orange slices to prevent breaking them. Gently fold in Cool Whip near serving time and refrigerate. Serves 6 generously. Delicious! NOTE: You may use strawberry-flavored gelatin and strawberries or cherry-flavored gelatin and cherries instead of orange-flavored gelatin and oranges.

Mrs. Jerry A. Kirkpatrick (Norma)
Glendale, Arizona

Mrs. C. R. Trammell (Beth)
North Little Rock, Arkansas

Mrs. Lloyd Conner (Catherine)
Alpine, Texas

Mrs. James P. Craine (Helen)
Anderson, South Carolina

PISTACHIO OR WATERGATE SALAD

1 small package instant pistachio
pudding mix
1 large can crushed pineapple,
undrained

2 cups miniature marshmallows
1 9-ounce carton Cool Whip
3 tablespoons nuts, chopped

Mix pudding with crushed pineapple until all is dissolved. Do not cook. Mix in marshmallows and nuts. Fold in Cool Whip. Chill and serve on a lettuce leaf. If used as a dessert, serve in compote.

Mrs. Carl Hudson (Dottie)
Bunkie, Louisiana

Mrs. A. O. Jenkins (Lucille)
Homer, Louisiana

Mrs. R. F. Smith, Jr. (Faye)
Hickory, North Carolina

Mrs. Dean Baxter (Eileen)
Columbia, Missouri

CHERRY SALAD

1 cup crushed pineapple, drained
1 can cherry pie filling
1 cup nuts, chopped

1½ cups miniature marshmallows
1 cup bananas, chopped
½ cup sugar

Drain pineapple and add sugar. Let set overnight. Drain pineapple the next morning if there is any liquid. Add remaining ingredients.

Mrs. Bill Moore (Sue)
Houston, Texas

FROZEN APPLE-CREAM SALAD

3 eggs, beaten
½ cup sugar
⅓ cup lemon juice
¼ teaspoon salt
½ cup crushed pineapple,
drained

½ cup carrots, shredded
½ cup walnuts, chopped
1 cup celery, diced
2 cups canned applesauce,
chilled
1 cup thick sour cream

Combine and thoroughly mix eggs, sugar, lemon juice, salt and juice from drained pineapple. Cook and stir over low heat until thick. Cool. Add pineapple, carrots, nuts and celery. Fold in chilled applesauce and sour cream. Spoon mixture into a 2-quart mold rinsed with cold water. Freeze about 4 hours or until firm. May be stored in freezer for a month.

Mrs. Bill Hickem (Billie)
Jacksonville, Florida

Blessed are they which do hunger and thirst after righteousness: for they shall be filled. Matt. 5:6

FROZEN SALAD

5 bananas
1 small can crushed pineapple
1 small package frozen
 strawberries
1 cup sour cream

½ cup lemon juice
1½ cups sugar
Chopped pecans
1 large carton Cool Whip

Blend all ingredients except Cool Whip in blender. Fold into Cool Whip.
Freeze.
Mrs. Landrum Leavell (Jo Ann)
New Orleans, Louisiana

FROZEN CRANBERRY SALAD

1 8-ounce package cream cheese
2 tablespoons mayonnaise
2 tablespoons sugar
1 can whole cranberry sauce

1 large can crushed pineapple,
 drained
1 large carton Cool Whip
1 cup nuts, chopped

Soften cheese; cream with mayonnaise and sugar. Add drained pineapple
and whole cranberry sauce. Fold in Cool Whip and nuts. Pour into 9 x
13-inch baking dish or baking cups. Place in freezer.
Mrs. John Wood (Pat)
Paducah, Kentucky

FROZEN FRUIT SALAD

1 small carton sour cream
½ cup sugar
2 tablespoons lemon juice
¼ cup cherries, chopped
½ cup nuts

1 can crushed pineapple,
 well drained
2 bananas, diced
1 cup Cool Whip

Stir together first three ingredients until creamy. Add remaining ingredients except Cool Whip. Fold in Cool Whip. Pour into mold and freeze.
Yummy!

Mrs. Adrian Rogers (Joyce)
Memphis, Tennessee

Mrs. Ellis Marks
Monroe, North Carolina

Mrs. John C. Frantz (Ruth)
Independence, Missouri

Mrs. Robert K. Davis (Pat)
Elba, Alabama

FROZEN WALDORF SALAD

2 eggs, slightly beaten
¼ cup sugar
⅛ teaspoon salt
½ cup pineapple juice
¼ cup lemon juice
½ cup celery, finely chopped

2 cups unpeeled apples, finely chopped
½ cup nuts, broken
1 cup heavy cream, whipped
½ cup crushed pineapple, drained

Combine eggs, sugar, salt and juices in top of double boiler. Cook, stirring until thick. Cool. Add nuts, fruit and celery. Fold in whipped cream. Freeze in large mold or 12 individual molds. Serve frozen on lettuce. Garnish, if desired, with mayonnaise.
Mrs. Dennis Lyle (Ressa)
Nashville, Tennessee

FROZEN SALAD DELIGHT

1 can strawberry pie filling
1 large carton Cool Whip
1 large can crushed pineapple, drained

1 can condensed milk
½ cup broken nuts

Mix together all ingredients. Put in large plastic container and freeze. Remove from freezer shortly before serving time so it can thaw slightly. Serve while still partially frozen. NOTE: Cherry pie filling may be substituted for the strawberry pie filling. Add 1 cup lemon juice and 1 cup nuts.

Mrs. Mike McGee
Columbia, South Carolina

Mrs. Ronald D. Rhodus (Virginia)
Mt. Zion, Illinois

Mrs. Wayne Dehoney (Lealice)
Louisville, Kentucky

Mrs. Clyde Hampton (Alice)
Hartwell, Georgia

FROZEN MINT SALAD

1 carton whipping cream
1 20½-ounce can crushed pineapple
1 tablespoon unflavored gelatin

1 10-ounce jar mint jelly
1 teaspoon confectioners' sugar
Dash salt

Heat pineapple juice and gelatin. Add jelly and gently heat until melted. Stir in pineapple. Chill until syrupy. Whip cream and fold into mixture. Pour into molds and freeze.
Mrs. Tom S. Brandon (Dolly)
Sherman, Texas

CINNAMON APPLE SURPRISES

1 large package cinnamon Red
  Hot candies
1½ cups water, boiling
6 to 8 small apples
⅓ package cream cheese

½ tablespoon mayonnaise
¼ cup pineapple juice (or any
  canned fruit juice)
Chopped walnuts and raisins

Melt cinnamon Red Hot candies in the boiling water. Peel and core apples. Simmer in cinnamon liquid, basting and turning, until apples are cooked but still firm. They should be dark pink in color. Cream together cream cheese, mayonnaise and fruit juice. Add walnuts and raisins as desired. Fill apples with cheese mixture. Place on lettuce leaf and serve. Especially good during Thanksgiving and Christmas holidays.
Mrs. Paul W. Thompson (Sue)
Jefferson City, Missouri

APRICOT CHEESE SALAD

2 Number 2½ cans apricots, cut
  and drained, reserve syrup
2 Number 2 cans pineapple
  tidbits, drained, reserve syrup
4 3-ounce packages orange
  gelatin

4 cups miniature
  marshmallows
1 cup sugar
2 tablespoons lemon juice

Mix juices, reserve 2 cups for topping. Use remaining juices for making jello. Mix gelatin; use juice and lemon juice. Add water to make 4 cups. Add sugar; bring to a boil. Let cool until syrupy. Add pineapple, apricots and marshmallows. Pour into pan to congeal before adding cheese topping.

TOPPING
1 cup sugar
6 tablespoons flour
2 eggs

2 cups juice
1 cup American cheese, grated
2 cups cream, whipped

Cook the above over low heat, except cream and cheese. Add to mixture when cold. Pour over gelatin mixture.
Mrs. Harry Foley
Mesa, Arizona

The fruit of the spirit is love, joy, peace . . . Gal. 5:22

APRICOT SALAD

1 large can crushed pineapple
½ cup sugar
2 3-ounce packages
  apricot-flavored gelatin
1 8-ounce package cream
  cheese, soft

1 cup ice water
1 cup celery, finely chopped
1 cup nuts, finely chopped
1 large can evaporated milk

Bring pineapple and sugar to rolling boil and stir all the time. Add gelatin and cream cheese. Heat until cheese melts. Add 1 cup ice water and cool. Add celery and nuts. Place in refrigerator until it starts to congeal. Chill evaporated milk. Whip and fold in salad mixture. Chill. Makes a large salad.

Mrs. Frank Campbell (Janet)
Statesville, North Carolina

AMBROSIA MOLD

1 package orange-pineapple
  flavored gelatin
1 teaspoon sugar
1 cup water, boiling
¾ cup cold water
1 to 2 cups Dream Whip or
  whipped cream

1 can mandarin oranges, cut up
  (reserve a few slices for
  decoration)
2 medium bananas
⅓ cup coconut
¼ cup pecans or walnuts

Dissolve gelatin and sugar in boiling water. Add cold water. Chill until thickened. Fold in Dream Whip or whipped cream and other ingredients. Chill until firm.

Mrs. Dan Stringer, Jr. (Harriet)
Tigard, Oregon

SYL'S FAVORITE JELLO

1 large package cherry-flavored
  gelatin
1 large can blueberry pie filling

1 small can crushed pineapple
1 9-ounce carton Cool Whip
1 3-ounce package cream cheese

Mix gelatin with 2 cups hot water until dissolved. Add ½ cup cold water. Next add the blueberry pie filling and the crushed pineapple. Place in refrigerator to congeal. Mix the Cool Whip and cream cheese together. Spread on top of the congealed salad. Refrigerate.

Mrs. V. Allen Gaines (Leila)
Newport News, Virginia

BLUEBERRY SALAD

2 small packages grape-flavored gelatin

2 cups water, boiling

1 small can crushed pineapple, well drained

1 can blueberry pie filling

Dissolve gelatin in boiling water. Add pineapple and blueberry pie filling. Mix well and congeal.

TOPPING

1 large package cream cheese

1 cup sour cream

½ cup sugar

1 teaspoon vanilla

½ cup nuts, chopped

Mix together the first 4 ingredients. Spread over congealed salad. Sprinkle chopped nuts on top.

Mrs. Jerry Warmath (Barbara)
Little Rock, Arkansas

Mrs. James Kirkpatrick (Loretta)
Waynesville, North Carolina

Mrs. Charles C. Coffee (Jewell)
Kannapolis, North Carolina

PHILLY TOPPED CRANBERRY SALAD

6 ounce package raspberry-flavored gelatin

1 cup hot water

16-ounce can whole cranberry sauce

1 13¼-ounce can crushed pineapple, undrained

⅔ cup orange juice

½ cup pecans, chopped

Dissolve gelatin in water. Mix all ingredients together. Put in refrigerator till firm.

TOPPING

2 3-ounce packages Philadelphia cream cheese

1 cup dairy sour cream

Beat together and spread on top of salad.

Mrs. George S. Munro (Eva)
Fort Thomas, Kentucky

Mrs. Lloyd Elder
Plano, Texas

GRAPEFRUIT SALAD

3 grapefruits	1 tablespoon sugar
2 small packages lemon-flavored gelatin	¾ cup water, boiling

Cut grapefruits in half the long way. Scoop out pulp and juice. Mix together the gelatin, sugar and boiling water. Add 3¼ cups grapefruit and juice. Congeal in the halved grapefruit cups and cut in halves after congealed. Serve with dressing.

DRESSING

1 tablespoon flour	Juice of 1 lemon
1 heaping tablespoon sugar	4 marshmallows
1 egg yolk, well beaten	⅓ cup pecans
⅓ cup pineapple juice	½ pint whipped cream

Mix together the flour and sugar. Add the beaten egg yolk, juice of 1 lemon and pineapple juice. Cook until thick. Add marshmallows, nuts and whipped cream. VERY DELICIOUS!
Mrs. W. C. Tribble (Mildred)
Social Circle, Georgia

EGGNOG CHRISTMAS SALAD

1 20-ounce can crushed pineapple	1 3-ounce package raspberry-flavored gelatin
1 tablespoon plain gelatin	1¾ cups water
3 tablespoons lemon juice	1¼ cups raw cranberry-orange relish
1½ cups dairy eggnog	
¾ cup celery, chopped	

Drain pineapple and heat juice to boiling. Use to dissolve gelatin which has been soaked in lemon juice. Cool to room temperature. Add eggnog, pineapple and celery. Pour into 6-cup mold and chill until firm. Dissolve raspberry gelatin in boiling water. Add cranberry relish and pour over firm portion.

CRANBERRY RELISH

2 pounds fresh cranberries	1 cup sugar
2 whole oranges	

Run cranberries and oranges through food grinder or blender. Sweeten with sugar. Chill for several hours to allow flavors to blend.
Mrs. W. E. Pettit
Winston-Salem, North Carolina

YOGURT-CRANBERRY MOLD

1 6-ounce package lime-flavored
   gelatin
1 cup walnuts

1 container low-calorie yogurt
1 cup cranberries, either canned
   or freshly prepared

Prepare gelatin as directed on package using only half water called for. Cool. Combine the remaining ingredients. Pour into mold. Refrigerate. This makes a nice dessert or salad with a lovely appearance because the nuts go right to the top. Also high in roughage if fresh cranberries are used.

Mrs. Lynn P. Clayton (Brenda)
Wichita, Kansas

CALIFORNIA CRANBERRY SALAD

2 cups raw cranberries
1 orange
1¼ cups miniature marshmallows
1 cup whipping cream, whipped
1 package orange-flavored gelatin

1 cup water, boiling
1 cup sugar
½ cup nuts
½ cup cold water

Grind cranberries. Add orange rind, grated. Dice orange and add sugar. Dissolve gelatin in 1 cup boiling water; add ½ cup cold water. Thicken and whip. Fold in whipped cream, orange-sugar mix and cranberries. Chill several hours. Serves 8 to 10.

Mrs. Sheldon H. Russell
San Jose, California

CHERRY SALAD

½ cup sour pie cherries
½ cup crushed pineapple,
   drained
½ cup nuts, chopped
¾ cup sugar

1 small package cherry-flavored
   gelatin
1 cup hot water
Juice of 1 orange
Juice of 1 lemon

Dissolve gelatin in 1 cup hot water. Add enough pineapple juice and cherry juice to the orange and lemon juice to make 1 cup. Boil sugar and all juices for 5 minutes, then add dissolved gelatin. Cool. Stir in fruit and nuts and chill several hours or overnight.

Mrs. Hoyt Welch (Bertha)
Clovis, New Mexico

PERFECTION SALAD

2 small packages lemon-flavored gelatin
1 pint whipped cream
1 small can pimentoes
1 cup pecans

1 pint hot water
1 small can crushed pineapple
1 large package cream cheese
8 or 10 maraschino cherries

Dissolve gelatin in 1 pint hot water. Place in refrigerator until partially set. Mix softened cream cheese, pimentoes, nuts, cherries and pineapple together. Add to the gelatin mixture. Fold in whipped cream. Pour into mold and chill until firm. NOTE: To serve 25 or 30 people, double recipe and add 1 can Royal Anne cherries. Serve on lettuce leaf.

Miss Mickey Mitchum
Marion, North Carolina

Mrs. R. William Dodson (Janelle)
Martin, Tennessee

LIME JELLO SALAD

1 3-ounce package lime-flavored gelatin
1 cup water, boiling
1 8-ounce package cream cheese, softened or 1 cup cottage cheese
1 cup miniature marshmallows

1 cup nuts, chopped
½ pint whipped cream
3 tablespoons mayonnaise
1 small can crushed pineapple, drained

Dissolve gelatin in 1 cup boiling water in top of double boiler. Add cream cheese and marshmallows. Stir until dissolved. Cool. Place in refrigerator till chilled. Add pineapple, mayonnaise, nuts and whipped cream. Pour into mold. Refrigerate and let set until ready to serve. Serves 6 to 8.

Mrs. Wallace Kent
Frankfurt, Kentucky

Mrs. C. E. Colton (Lois)
Dallas, Texas

Mrs. C. H. Sutherland (Aileen)
Greenville, South Carolina

Mrs. Bobby Barnett (Mary)
Bradford, Rhode Island

Mrs. Fred V. Brown (Norma)
Spartanburg, South Carolina

Mrs. L. D. Holt (Annie)
Raleigh, North Carolina

ANNE'S SALAD

1 large package lemon-flavored gelatin
1 small package orange pineapple-flavored gelatin
3½ cups hot water
Juice of 2 lemons
2 or 3 tablespoons pear vinegar or apple cider vinegar

1 jar Ocean Spray Cranberry-Orange Relish
1 small can crushed pineapple, undrained
2 tart apples, chopped
1 cup pecans, chopped

Dissolve gelatin in hot water. Add remaining ingredients. Let congeal in refrigerator. Serves 12.
Mrs. Searcy S. Garrison (Antionette)
Atlanta, Georgia

CONGEALED RED APPLESAUCE

1 small package cherry-flavored gelatin
1 cup hot water

1 cup applesauce
1 cup water
2 tablespoons Red Hots

Cook Red Hots in 1 cup water until melted. Dissolve gelatin in 1 cup hot water. Mix Red Hot mixture with gelatin. Cool. Add 1 cup applesauce. Place in refrigerator and let set until firm.
Mrs. Everett Smalts (Mary Ruth)
Duke, Oklahoma

LEMON-CHEESE JELLO SALAD

1 3-ounce package lemon-flavored gelatin
¼ cup sugar
1 small flat can crushed pineapple

1 cup cold water
½ cup broken nuts
1 cup Cheddar cheese, grated
1 9-ounce carton Cool Whip

Combine first 3 ingredients. Cook until all sugar is dissolved. Add 1 cup cold water and chill till it reaches syrupy stage. Fold in nuts, grated cheese and Cool Whip. Chill till firm.
Mrs. Keith Hamm
El Dorado, Kansas

BROKEN GLASS TORTE SALAD

1 small package
raspberry-flavored gelatin
1 small package lemon-flavored
gelatin
1 small package orange-flavored
gelatin
1 envelope plain gelatin
¼ cup cold water

¼ cup hot pineapple juice
¾ cup cold pineapple juice
2 cups graham crackers, crushed
½ cup butter, melted
½ cup brown sugar
1 cup whipped cream or Cool Whip
1 teaspoon vanilla
½ cup sugar

Separately dissolve each box of gelatin in 1¼ cups cold water. Chill until set in individual dishes. Pour cold water over plain gelatin. Heat ¼ cup pineapple juice and pour into gelatin mixture. Add remainder of pineapple juice and set aside to cool. Should begin to thicken before adding other ingredients. Mix together the graham crackers which have been crushed, melted butter and brown sugar. Line bottom of pan with ½ of mixture and save remainder for the top. Whip cream. Add sugar and vanilla. Fold in gelatin-pineapple mixture. Cut jello into cubes and fold into this. Use remainder of cracker crumb mixture on the top. Chill.
Mrs. Douglas Olive (Eileen)
Lebanon, Kentucky

ROSEMARY JELLO SALAD

1 small package lime-flavored
gelatin
1 small package cherry-flavored
gelatin
2 small packages cream cheese
1 cup mayonnaise

1 large can crushed pineapple
and juice
1 cup nuts, chopped
½ pint whipped cream
128 small marshmallows

Dissolve lime-flavored gelatin in 1 cup hot water. Add marshmallows and stir until melted. Add pineapple. Mix mayonnaise with cream cheese and stir until smooth. Fold into gelatin mixture. Cool. Fold in whipped cream and nuts. Make cherry jello as directed on box. Cool. Pour on top of first gelatin mixture. Chill until firm.
Mrs. Robert K. Davis (Pat)
Elba, Alabama

DAIRY ORANGE SALAD

1 small package orange-flavored gelatin
1 small package cream cheese
1 cup water, boiling
1 small can crushed pineapple
2 cups miniature marshmallows
1 small can frozen orange juice

2 bananas, mashed
1 small container cottage cheese
½ cup sugar
1 small can mandarin oranges
½ pint cream, whipped or Cool Whip

Pour the boiling water over the gelatin. Add the marshmallows and stir until gelatin is dissolved. Defrost the orange juice and stir in ½ cup sugar. Add to gelatin mixture. Cream the cheese and add the crushed pineapple to cheese. Add this to gelatin mixture. Mix in cottage cheese, bananas and orange sections. Stir until well blended. Fold in whipped cream. Pour into large container. Refrigerate at least 3 hours. Serves 15.
Mrs. Roger Shelton
Nashville, Tennessee

RIBBON SALAD

1 small package lime-flavored gelatin
1 cup hot water
1 cup cold water
1 small package lemon-flavored gelatin
1 cup hot water
12 large marshmallows, cut up
1 3-ounce package cream cheese, cut up

1 cup whipped cream or Dream Whip
½ cup salad dressing
1 small can crushed pineapple
1 small package cherry-flavored gelatin
1 cup hot water
1 cup cold water

Dissolve 1 package lime-flavored gelatin in 1 cup hot water and add 1 cup cold water. Pour in 13 x 9 x 2-inch pan to set. Dissolve 1 package lemon-flavored gelatin in 1 cup hot water. Place in double boiler. Add marshmallows and cream cheese. Stir until marshmallows and cheese are dissolved in the hot gelatin mixture. Remove from stove and cool. When it begins to congeal, add whipped cream and salad dressing beat into the whipped cream. Then add crushed pineapple. Pour this mixture over the set lime gelatin. Chill until firm. Mix cherry-flavored gelatin with 1 cup hot water and add 1 cup cold water. Cool. Pour on top of middle layer. Great for family get togethers.
Mrs. Donald V. Wideman (Marian)
Kansas City, Missouri

ORANGE-APRICOT SALAD

1 small package orange-flavored gelatin
½ cup hot water
12-ounces apricot nectar
1 small package orange-flavored gelatin
½ cup hot water

12-ounces apricot nectar
8-ounces package cream cheese, whipped
1 package Dream Whip, whipped
2 tablespoons last batch of gelatin mixture
Chopped pecans

Mix together first 3 ingredients. Put in square dish and chill until firm. Dissolve orange-flavored gelatin with ½ cup hot water. Add apricot nectar. Chill. Do not let get firm. Combine last 3 ingredients. Do not beat. Put ½ of Dream Whip mixture on top of first gelatin mixture in square dish. Sprinkle with chopped pecans. Carefully spoon last gelatin mixture on top of chopped pecans. Spread on rest of Dream Whip mixture. Sprinkle with chopped pecans. Congeal.
Mrs. Bonner C. Magness (Beth)
Liberty, Texas

MANDARIN ORANGE SALAD

2 small packages orange-flavored gelatin
1 pint orange sherbet

2 cups hot water
1 tall can pineapple tidbits
1 small can mandarin oranges

Mix gelatin with hot water. Add the sherbet, drained pineapple and half of the juice. Stir in 1 small can mandarin oranges, drained. Pour into mold. Chill until firm.
Mrs. R. Paul Caudill (Fern)
Memphis, Tennessee

Mrs. W. E. Pettit
Winston-Salem, North Carolina

RASPBERRY SALAD

3 small packages raspberry-flavored gelatin
3 cups hot water
3 packages frozen raspberries, unthawed

1 can crushed pineapple, undrained
3 bananas, sliced
1 package blueberries
1 cup sour cream

Dissolve gelatin in 3 cups hot water. Add remaining ingredients. Place ½ gelatin mixture in mold or casserole. Let set. Spread 1 cup sour cream on top. Add rest of gelatin. Serves 12.
Mrs. James H. Smith (Nona)
Springfield, Illinois

GOOSEBERRY SALAD

1 can gooseberries
2 small packages lemon or
  lime-flavored gelatin
½ cup sugar

2 cups orange juice
1 cup celery, chopped
½ cup walnuts

Drain gooseberries, reserve syrup. Add water to syrup to make 1¾ cups. Heat 1 cup syrup mixture to boiling. Add gelatin and sugar, stirring to dissolve. Add remaining syrup and orange juice. Chill until partially set. Stir in gooseberries, celery and walnuts. Pour into mold. Chill.
Mrs. Elwood G. Kelley (Betty)
Jefferson City, Missouri

STRAWBERRY SALAD

1 6-ounce package
  strawberry-flavored gelatin
1 cup water, boiling
2 10-ounce packages strawberries
1 13½-ounce can crushed
  pineapple

2 large ripe bananas, finely diced
1 cup dairy sour cream
½ cup nuts, if used for dessert

Dissolve gelatin in boiling water. Add the partially thawed strawberries, stirring till thawed. Add the crushed pineapple and bananas. Pour half of mixture into 8 x 8 x 2-inch pan or mold. Chill until firm. Chill remaining half until partially set. Spread first layer with sour cream and pour partially chilled gelatin atop. Chill several hours. Salad is especially good with roast or steak.

Mrs. Tal Bonham (Faye)
Yukon, Oklahoma

Mrs. Ray E. Roberts (Margaret)
Columbus, Ohio

Mrs. Ellis Marks
Monroe, North Carolina

Mrs. Harry Girtman
Taylors, South Carolina

Mrs. William M. Hinson (Bettye)
Fort Lauderdale, Florida

Mrs. Jerry A. Kirkpatrick (Norma)
Glendale, Arizona

Mrs. Charles M. Becton (Janie)
Monroe, North Carolina

Mrs. Charles W. Boling (Betty)
Pinckneyville, Illinois

Mrs. Mabel Ferrell
Belvedere, South Carolina

Mrs. Ronald D. Rhodus (Virginia)
Mt. Zion, Illinois

Mrs. Elbert L. Smithen, Jr. (Jo)
Midland, Texas

Mrs. Bobby Waggoner (Brenda)
Louisville, Mississippi

FIVE CUP SALAD

1 cup marshmallows
1 cup pineapple, crushed or chunk

1 cup sour cream
1 cup mandarin oranges
1 cup coconut

Mix all fruit together. Fold in sour cream. Chill and serve.

Mrs. Roy L. Head (Vonceil)
Belvedere, South Carolina

Mrs. Thurman Booth
Bogalusa, Louisiana

Mrs. W. E. Pettit
Winston-Salem, North Carolina

PATRIOTIC SALAD

1 small package strawberry-flavored gelatin
2 cups hot water
1 envelope unflavored gelatin
½ cup cold water
1 cup sugar
1 cup coffee cream

1 teaspoon vanilla
2 cups sour cream
1 small package raspberry-flavored gelatin
1 cup hot water
1 can blueberries, drained (reserve juice)

FIRST LAYER: Dissolve strawberry flavored gelatin in hot water. Pour into 13 x 9 x 2-inch round mold. Let set in refrigerator.

SECOND LAYER: Soak unflavored gelatin in cold water. Combine sugar and cream. Sitr over low heat until sugar is dissolved. Stir gelatin into hot mixture. Cool. Add vanilla and sour cream. Pour over first layer. Allow to set.

THIRD LAYER: Dissolve raspberry gelatin in hot water. Cool slightly. Add blueberries and juice. Pour over second layer. Refrigerate until well set. Serves 15.

Mrs. Harold Sutton
Alpharetta, Georgia

SCRUMPTIOUS STRAWBERRY SALAD

2 small packages
   strawberry-flavored gelatin
1 small package lemon-flavored
   gelatin
½ cup sour cream

1 8-ounce package cream cheese,
   softened
4 tablespoons confectioners' sugar
2 10½-ounce packages frozen
   strawberries

Make lemon jello and set aside. Beat well the sour cream, cream cheese and confectioners' sugar. Add mixture to lemon jello. Blend well. Pour into large jello mold and chill until firm. Drain 2 packages frozen strawberries. Add enough water to the juice from the strawberries to measure 2 cups of liquid. Boil the juice and water and add 2 packages strawberry gelatin and the frozen berries. Pour slowly on top of chilled lemon mixture and refrigerate until firm. Remove from mold to attractive platter.
Mrs. John Woodall (Carole)
Columbia, Maryland

PINK SALAD

1 large Cool Whip
1 pint sour cream
1 large can crushed pineapple,
   well drained
1 can mandarin oranges, drained

1 cup nuts, chopped
1 cup coconut
1 can cherry pie filling
½ cup powdered sugar
1 tablespoon vanilla

Mix together Cool Whip and sour cream. Add remaining ingredients. Refrigerate.
Mrs. Lloyd Elder
Plano, Texas

YUM YUM OR BAVARIAN SALAD

2 cups water, boiling
¾ cup sugar
1 large package orange-flavored
   gelatin

1 large can crushed pineapple
1 cup Cheddar cheese, grated
½ cup pecans, chopped
1 large carton Cool Whip

Add the sugar to boiling water. Mix in gelatin until dissolved. Cool. Add crushed pineapple. Chill until mixture becomes syrupy. Add grated cheese and nuts. Fold in Cool Whip. Pour into mold and refrigerate.
Mrs. John A. Grant (Lois)
Charlotte, North Carolina

Mrs. H. G. Edwards
Moberly, Missouri

Vegetable Salads

BLENDER TOMATO-VEGETABLE ASPIC

Tomato juice
1 small onion
1 carrot
1 rib celery
1 medium cucumber,
    peeled and seeded

2 tablespoons wine vinegar or
    lemon juice
2 small packages lemon-flavored
    gelatin

Put 1½ cups tomato juice in blender and add onion, celery and carrot which have been chopped into chunks. Blend until all is pureed. Strain mixture into a bowl, using back of wooden spoon. Mash until pulp is dry. Throw away pulp. To this liquid add vinegar. Measure what you have and add enough tomato juice to make 1¾ cups. Bring 2 more cups tomato juice to a boil and dissolve the lemon-flavored gelatin in it. Mix with other ingredients and put in mold. Refrigerate. Has an excellent flavor! Good with Guacamole dressing.
Mrs. Don Harbuck (Elizabeth)
El Dorado, Arkansas

CALIFORNIA SALAD

2 envelopes granulated gelatin
½ cup cold water
1 can condensed tomato soup
3 small packages cream cheese
1½ cups celery, chopped

2 cups green pepper, chopped
2 tablespoons onion, chopped
¼ cup green or ripe olives, chopped
¼ to ½ cup nuts, chopped
1 cup mayonnaise

Add gelatin to the cold water and let soak 5 minutes. Heat tomato soup to boiling and remove from heat. Add the softened gelatin and stir until smooth. When almost cool, fold in mayonnaise and vegetables. Turn into mold.
Mrs. Herschel Hobbs (Frances)
Oklahoma City, Oklahoma

HARVEST SALAD

2 small packages lemon-flavored gelatin
2 cups cider or apple juice
2 tablespoons lemon juice
⅓ cup sugar
⅛ teaspoon salt
⅓ cup dates, chopped
1 cup red apples, diced
1 cup fresh pears, or pineapple, diced
½ cup pecans, chopped
1 apple, grated
1 cup mayonnaise

Heat cider just to boiling; add lemon juice, sugar and salt. Stir until sugar dissolves. Add to gelatin; stir well. Add dates. Chill until thick. Fold in diced apples, pears and nuts. Pour into mold. Chill until firm. Combine grated apple with mayonnaise. Serve over salad. Serves 6 to 8.
Mrs. Bill Hickem (Billie)
Jacksonville, Florida

LETTUCE-CAULIFLOWER SALAD

1 head lettuce, chopped
1 head cauliflower, chopped
2 cups mayonnaise
1 medium onion, chopped
1 jar Bacos or 1 lb. bacon, fried crisp
⅓ cup Parmesan cheese
Less than ½ cup sugar

Place lettuce and cauliflower in layers. Seal with mayonnaise. Sprinkle remaining ingredients on top of mayonnaise in order given. Seal with plastic wrap. Let set in refrigerator 12 hours. Toss and serve.
Mrs. Everett Lemay
Mt. Vernon, Illinois

AVOCADO LAYERED SALAD

1½ to 2 heads lettuce
1 cauliflower
2 packages dry Italian Dressing Mix
1 avocado
1 small bunch green onions
1 package small frozen green peas, cooked and drained
1 pint Hellman's mayonnaise

Tear lettuce into salad bowl. Add chopped green onions and flowerets of cauliflower. Pour green peas into mixture and toss together. Sprinkle dressing mix on top of salad and seal with mayonnaise. Refrigerate 24 hours. Add diced avocado and toss just before serving.
Mrs. Bobby Perry (Sue)
Moss Point, Mississippi

THREE LAYER VEGETABLE SALAD

1 head lettuce, cut up and crisp
1 package frozen green peas,
   cooked and drained
1 tablespoon sugar
1½ cups celery, chopped
1 large onion, cut in rings

Salt and pepper to taste
1 pint mayonnaise
¼ cup sour cream
Parmesan cheese
Bacos

Cook frozen peas. Drain and cool. Add sugar. Spread lettuce, celery, onion and peas in layers in dish or glass cake pan. Mix mayonnaise with sour cream. Spread as you would a cake. Sprinkle with Parmesan cheese and Bacos or crisp bacon bits. Make night before serving.
Mrs. Virgil Clark　　　　　　　　　*Mrs. Franklin Owen (Sue)*
Terre Haute, Indiana　　　　　　　*Middletown, Kentucky*

THREE-CUP BEAN SALAD

1 cup green beans
1 cup wax beans
1 cup kidney beans
½ cup green pepper
½ cup onion, minced

½ cup salad oil
½ cup vinegar
½ cup sugar
1 teaspoon salt

Drain beans well. Mix all beans together. Combine remaining ingredients. Pour over bean mixture and let stand 24 hours in refrigerator.
Mrs. Sam Adkins　　　　　　　　*Mrs. Raymond Sanders (Jan)*
Somerset, Kentucky　　　　　　　*Alpine, Texas*

ENGLISH PEA 'N CHEDDAR CHEESE SALAD

2 cans small English peas
3 to 4 celery sticks, finely cut
½ onion, grated
4 dill pickles, grated
3 to 4 tablespoons pickle relish

½ green pepper, cut fine
1 cup Cheddar cheese, diced
Mayonnaise
Salt

Mix all ingredients. Chill in refrigerator. Serves 10.
Mrs. James E. Coggin (Carolyn)
Fort Worth, Texas

TWENTY-FOUR VEGETABLE SALAD

1 can French green beans,
   drained
1 can whole kernel corn, drained
1 onion, chopped
1 green pepper, chopped
1 red sweet pepper, chopped

2 stalks celery, chopped
1 cup sugar
⅓ cup vinegar
½ cup salad oil
2 tablespoons salt

Combine drained vegetables. Mix sugar, vinegar, salad oil and salt. Let set 24 hours in refrigerator.

Mrs. Harry Foley
Mesa, Arizona

BEAN-SPROUT SALAD

1 can bean sprouts, drained
1 can sauerkraut, drained
½ cup onions, chopped
½ bell pepper, chopped
2-3 celery stalks, chopped

1 small jar pimento
½ teaspoon salt
1 cup sugar
½ cup vinegar

Combine all vegetables into serving dish. Mix together the salt, sugar and vinegar. Boil 5 minutes. Pour over vegetables while hot. Place in refrigerator when cool. Serve cold.

Mrs. Orvind M. Dangeau (Freddie Ann)
Franklin, Tennessee

RAW CAULIFLOWER SALAD

1 cup salad dressing
1 cup sour cream
2 teaspoons caraway seeds

1 package garlic salad
   dressing mix

Mix all ingredients together.

PREPARE:

1 cup radishes, sliced
¼ cup green onions, sliced
1 head cauliflower, broken into
   small flowerets

½ cup watercress or parsley
½ cup almond slivers (optional)

Add all ingredients with the salad dressing mix. Let chill overnight.

Mrs. Wallace E. Jones (Laura Jo)
St. Ann, Missouri

Mrs. Kendall Hatton
Marlinton, West Virginia

FRENCH BEAN AND ENGLISH PEA SALAD

1 can French green beans
1 can small English peas

1 can red kidney beans
3 onions, sliced

MARINADE
1 cup sugar
½ cup cider vinegar
1 ½ cups oil
4 stalks celery, chopped

½ bell pepper, chopped
Salt and pepper to taste
Mayonnaise

Place vegetables in layers with sliced onions between each layer. Combine sugar, vinegar and oil. Pour this mixture over vegetables and leave out overnight. Next day, drain off liquid and discard. Add bell pepper, chopped celery, salt and pepper to taste. Stir in mayonnaise.

Mrs. Charles H. Beal (Winona)
Sarasota, Florida

Mrs. T. J. Fulk (Marilee)
Fayetteville, North Carolina

Mrs. Charles W. Boling (Betty)
Pinckneyville, Illinois

GOLD PENNY CARROT SALAD

2 pounds carrots, sliced
  and cooked
1 or more large green
  peppers sliced in rings
1 or more large onions, cut in
  rings and separated

1 cup celery, chopped
1 cup cauliflower, broken into
  flowerets
(May add 1 cup canned green beans,
  1 cup garbanzos or any other
  vegetables)

SAUCE
½ cup sugar
⅓ cup salad oil
1 tablespoon Worcestershire
1 can cream of tomato soup,
  undiluted

½ cup vinegar
1 tablespoon prepared
  mustard

Combine ingredients to make sauce. Pour over vegetables. Store in refrigerator.

Mrs. R. L. Johnson (Nelle)
Portland, Oregon

Mrs. Billy D. Allen (Elray)
Springfield, Illinois

FROZEN ENGLISH PEA SALAD

1 small head lettuce, shredded
1 layer celery, chopped
1 layer bell pepper
1 layer onion, chopped
1 package frozen English peas,
   cooked, drained and cooled

1 cup cottage cheese
1 cup mayonnaise
2 tablespoons sugar
Bac-o's

Place all ingredients in a large, deep bowl in the order given. Combine cottage cheese and mayonnaise; spread to edges. Sprinkle sugar on top. Sprinkle with Bac-o's. Tightly cover with Saran Wrap and refrigerate for 24 hours before serving.

Mrs. Charles E. Myers (Bea)
Jackson, Mississippi

Mrs. William E. Stiles
Marietta, Georgia

Mrs. Henry B. Stokes (Etta)
Buies Creek, North Carolina

FROZEN CABBAGE SLAW

1 large head cabbage (2½ to 3
   pounds)
1 large carrot

1 large green pepper
1 teaspoon salt

DRESSING

2 cups sugar
1 cup vinegar

1 teaspoon celery seed
1 teaspoon dry mustard

Shred cabbage. Add salt. Let stand in refrigerator for at least one hour. Squeeze out liquid. Boil together ingredients for dressing, only one minute after it comes to a rolling boil. Cool. Add the cabbage, grated carrot and pepper. Place in freezer containers. Will keep for at least 3 weeks in refrigerator or can be frozen and is delicious when thawed.

Mrs. Allen Graves (Helen)
Louisville, Kentucky

Mrs. Orvind M. Dangeau (Freddie Ann)
Franklin, Tennessee

Mrs. Albert Baumgartner (Frances)
Neosho, Missouri

Mrs. Carl Bailey (Louise)
Port Richey, Florida

Mrs. W. C. Tribble (Mildred)
Social Circle, Georgia

HOT CHICKEN SALAD WITH SOUR CREAM

4 whole chicken breasts, cooked and diced
1½ cups celery, finely diced
3 hard boiled eggs, sliced
1 cup mayonnaise
1 cup sour cream
2 teaspoons onion, diced
1 can water chestnuts, drained and diced
½ cup slivered almonds
½ can cream of mushroom soup
1 teaspoon salt
½ teaspoon pepper
2 teaspoons lemon juice
1 cup Cheddar cheese, grated
1 can onion rings
1 4-ounce can mushrooms, drained and diced

Mix all ingredients except cheese and onion rings. Place in 13 x 9 x 2-inch casserole. Top with cheese. Bake in 350 degree oven for 30 minutes. Sprinkle onion rings on top and bake 15 minutes longer. Let stand 10 minutes before serving.
Mrs. Albert Moore (Lorraine)
Whiting, Indiana

HOT CHICKEN SALAD

4 cups cooked chicken, chopped
2 onions, chopped
½ cup ripe olives, chopped
4 tablespoons lemon juice
2 cups celery, chopped
½ cup green pepper, chopped
1 cup almonds (or less)
1½ cups mayonnaise
8 boiled eggs, chopped
2 cups cream of chicken soup
Crushed potato chips
Grated Cheddar cheese

Mix all ingredients except potato chips and cheese. Place in large baking dish. Sprinkle with crushed potato chips and grated cheese. Bake about 30 minutes in a 400 degree oven. This dish is easily doubled or tripled. It can be prepared in advance. Sprinkle with crushed potato chips and cheese when ready to heat and serve.
Mrs. C. W. Rich
Nashville, Tennessee

OYSTER SALAD

2 eggs
1 tablespoon sugar
⅛ teaspoon salt or to taste
½ cup milk
1 tablespoon prepared mustard
2 tablespoons vinegar

1 can oysters, drained, cut-up
¼ teaspoon pepper
⅔ cup saltine crackers

Mix whole eggs, sugar, salt, milk, pepper and crackers. Cook till thick, stirring constantly. Add vinegar and mustard. Mix with cut up, drained oysters. Excellent for Thanksgiving or Christmas dinner.
Mrs. Paul Box (Pattye)
Moore, Oklahoma

CONGEALED SHRIMP SALAD

2 small packages lemon gelatin
2 cups hot water
2 cans cream of tomato soup
1 pound cooked shrimp, deveined or 2 cans shrimp

1 cup celery, chopped
½ cup green pepper, chopped
1 cup pecans, chopped

Dissolve gelatin in hot water. Add tomato soup and blend well. Stir in remaining ingredients. Pour into mold. Chill. Great for luncheons!
Mrs. Charles Richards (Katie)
Baltimore, Maryland

CHINESE SHRIMP SALAD

2 cups rice, cooked
1 can June peas
1 cup celery, chopped
½ cup mayonnaise
⅓ cup French dressing

1 tablespoon onion, chopped
½ teaspoon salt
¾ teaspoon curry powder
½ teaspoon dry mustard
1 small package frozen shrimp

Combine rice, peas and celery; mix with remaining ingredients. Fold in shrimp. Chill overnight.
Mrs. James L. Adkins (Bess)
Augusta, Georgia

HOT TUNA SALAD

2 7-ounce cans tuna,
   drained and flaked
1 cup celery, diced
1 cup green grapes,
   halved and seeded
¼ cup ripe pitted olives, sliced
½ cup whole toasted almonds
⅔ cup mayonnaise
1 tablespoon lemon juice

¼ teaspoon celery salt
1 tablespoon onion, grated
½ cup corn cereal, crushed,
   bite-sized, toasted
2 tablespoons American
   cheese, grated
1 tablespoon butter or
   margarine, melted
½ teaspoon salt

Heat oven to 350 degrees. Combine tuna, celery, grapes, olives and almonds in a mixing bowl. Blend mayonnaise, lemon juice, grated onion,
celery salt and salt. Mix all together and toss lightly. Turn into an ovenproof dish. Top with crushed corn cereal, butter and cheese. Heat 10
minutes. Serve hot. Serves 4 to 6.
Mrs. F. M. Dowell (Edith)
Nashville, Tennessee

SAUERKRAUT SALAD

2 cups sauerkraut
½ cup sugar
½ cup celery, thinly sliced
½ cup thin strips green pepper

½ cup carrots, shredded
½ cup onion, chopped
¼ cup pimento, cut in pieces

Cut sauerkraut in short pieces with kitchen scissors. Stir in sugar and let
stand ½ hour. Add remaining ingredients. Cover bowl tightly and chill in
refrigerator at least 12 hours before serving. Especially good with poultry
or pork.
Mrs. H. E. Alsup (Willie Lou)
Harpville, Kansas

Mrs. M. E. Gibson (Mary)
Wilmington, North Carolina

TACO SALAD

1 head lettuce, broken in bite-size pieces or shredded
½ pound Cheddar cheese, grated
1 15-ounce can chili or kidney beans, washed and drained
2 tomatoes, diced
½ cup onion, chopped

1 pound ground beef
Taco seasoning package
1 8-ounce bottle Catalina dressing
½ bag Fritos or similar chips
Taco spice
¾ cup water

Brown ground beef, drain and cool. Season with Taco spice. Add ¾ cup water, Taco seasoning package, and simmer 10 to 15 minutes. Layer ingredients. Sprinkle Fritos on top. Serves 6 to 8. NOTE: Omit hamburger meat, if desired.

Mrs. James H. Smith (Nona)
Springfield, Illinois

Mrs. Billy J. Chambers (Louise)
Grand Blanc, Michigan

Mrs. James E. Coggin (Carolyn)
Fort Worth, Texas

Mrs. Paul Harvey (Ruth)
Jefferson City, Missouri

Mrs. V. Allen Gaines
Newport News, Virginia

MACARONI SALAD

2 cups macaroni, cooked
1 cup celery, chopped
2 green onions, chopped
1 carrot, grated

1 small can English peas, drained
Grated cheese (optional)
Bell pepper (optional)

Mix together:

1 cup mayonnaise
1 teaspoon sugar
1 teaspoon dry mustard (no substitute)

3 tablespoons vinegar or lemon juice
Dash of Bacos
Salt and pepper to taste

Add mayonnaise mixture to above ingredients. Leave in refrigerator overnight, or make early in the morning before using at night. This is important!

Mrs. Fred Halbrooks, Jr.
Louisville, Kentucky

CURRIED RICE SALAD

1⅓ cups Minute Rice
1⅓ cups water
3 tablespoons onion, finely chopped
1 tablespoon vinegar
2 tablespoons salad oil

¾ teaspoon curry powder
2 teaspoons salt
1 10-ounce package frozen peas
1 cup celery, chopped
¾ cup mayonnaise

Cook Minute Rice in 1⅓ cups water. Remove from heat. While still hot stir in onion, vinegar, salad oil, curry powder and salt. Chill 3 hours or overnight. Cook 1 package frozen peas. Chill. Mix rice, peas, chopped celery and mayonnaise together.
Mrs. Elbert L. Smithen, Jr. (Jo)
Midland, Texas

RICE SALAD WITH ARTICHOKES

1 cup Minute Rice
2 cups chicken broth
½ cup celery, chopped
½ cup artichoke hearts
2 tablespoons onion, finely chopped

½ bell pepper, chopped
½ cucumber, chopped
Salt and pepper to taste
Mayonnaise

Cook rice in chicken broth as package directs. Cool. Add the chopped celery, artichoke hearts, then onion, bell pepper and cucumber. Season with salt and pepper. Add enough mayonnaise to hold mixture together; more if desired.
Mrs. Henry Chiles
Pierre, South Dakota

COOL VALLEY LETTUCE WITH HAM

1 large head lettuce
1 egg, beaten
1 teaspoon sugar

⅓ cup sour cream
1 tablespoon vinegar
1 cup ham

Pull lettuce leaves apart and wash. Dry on paper towel. Mix beaten egg, sugar and sour cream together. Stir into vinegar. Heat, but do not boil. Cut up ham in a pan and fry to a nice crisp brown. Add to lettuce when dry. Pour heated dressing over the lettuce and ham. This is much like wilted lettuce and is delicious!
Mrs. Archie E. Brown (Louise)
Vandalia, Illinois

MAIN DISH SALAD

1 head lettuce	1 cup meat (turkey or ham, etc.)
¼ cup cabbage, shredded	Mayonnaise to taste
½ cup apples, chopped	Salt and onion salt
½ cup filburts, walnuts	Pepper
or pecans	Dash lemon juice

Slice lettuce; cut slices in thirds. Mix cabbage, apples and nuts together. Add mayonnaise and other seasonings. Serve on lettuce leaf with crackers, rye krisp or biscuits. Great for ladies meetings! Serves 6 to 8.
Mrs. Fred King (Elaine)
Oregon City, Oregon

CORNED BEEF SALAD

1 can corned beef, shredded	1 tablespoon onion, chopped
1 teaspoon salt	2 tablespoons pickle relish
1½ cups celery, finely chopped	3 hard boiled eggs, cut up
Dash pepper	1 cup mayonnaise
2 tablespoons green pepper or	1 can consomme, chicken or beef
pimento, chopped	1 package plain gelatin

Mix gelatin with 2 tablespoons cold water. Set aside. Mix in large bowl: corned beef, celery, green pepper, onion, relish, eggs, mayonnaise, salt and pepper. Heat consomme. Add gelatin; heat until dissolved. Add to other ingredients. Stir until blended. Pour into salad mold (not aluminum) or greased 8 x 12-inch Pyrex. Place in refrigerator and chill.
Mrs. James G. Harris (Tunis)
Fort Worth, Texas

BACON AND EGG SALAD

1 head lettuce, broken-bite size	Salt and pepper
4 hard-boiled eggs, chopped	Mayonnaise
8 strips bacon	

Cook bacon till nice and crispy; crush. Combine broken lettuce, chopped eggs, bacon, salt and pepper. Mix lightly with just enough real mayonnaise to moisten. Serve as tossed salad.
Mrs. Ted Sisk (Ginny)
Lexington, Kentucky

114

BLACK POINT SALAD BOWL

3 small crisp heads lettuce (use
  any variety: Iceberg, Bibb,
  Endive, Romaine, etc.)
5 green onions, sliced
6 oranges, sectioned
  and drained
16 pitted ripe olives, sliced

⅓ cup salad oil
¼ cup black pepper
3 tablespoons tarragon-flavored
  vinegar
¾ teaspoon salt
1 grapefruit, sectioned and drained

Tear greens into pieces. Place in bowl with onions, oranges and olives. Combine dressing and pour over greens. Toss. Add grapefruit last. Serve at once. Serves 6 to 8.

Mrs. Wayne Ward (Mary Ann)
Louisville, Kentucky

WILTED LETTUCE

1 head Boston lettuce
3 tablespoons bacon grease
3 tablespoons vinegar
3 tablespoons water

1 tablespoon sugar
½ teaspoon salt
4 slices bacon
1 teaspoon onion, chopped

Clean and tear lettuce into bite-size pieces. Combine bacon grease, vinegar, water, sugar and salt and simmer a few minutes. Fry bacon until crisp and break over lettuce. Add onion. Mix well. Add hot liquid mixture and serve at once. Delicious!

Mrs. Earl L. Pounds (Esther)
St. Louis, Missouri

CONGEALED TUNA SALAD

1 9-ounce can chunk tuna
1 6-ounce package
  lemon-flavored gelatin
1 cup hot water
1 small can crushed pineapple

1 cup celery, diced
½ cup Miracle Whip salad dressing
1 cup Cool Whip or ½ cup
  whipping cream
1 cup pecans, chopped

Dissolve gelatin in 1 cup hot water. Let cool in refrigerator. Drain tuna. Wash lightly under warm water to remove oil. Sprinkle a little lemon juice over tuna. Add all ingredients, folding in the Cool Whip last to the gelatin mixture. Chill in a mold or in a square pan. This is a great main dish for luncheons.

Mrs. Travis S. Berry (Bernice)
Plano, Texas

GUACAMOLE SALAD OR DIP

1 soft avocado
1 soft tomato, finely chopped
1 small onion, finely chopped

1 teaspoon mayonnaise
Garlic salt to taste

Mash avocado with fork. Add chopped tomato, onion and mayonnaise. Sprinkle garlic salt to taste. Serve on lettuce leaf with Tortos, Fritos, chips, or crackers. To store, place avocado pit in mixture in refrigerator. Avocado turns black when kept out over an hour.
Mrs. Charles Casey (Jeanette)
Silver Spring, Maryland

Dressings

BLEU CHEESE DRESSING

4-ounces bleu cheese
1 tablespoon white vinegar
¼ cup salad oil
¼ cup buttermilk

1 cup mayonnaise
¼ teaspoon salt
¼ cup sour cream
1 teaspoon garlic

Crumble cheese into a large mixing bowl; add mayonnaise and salad oil. Blend thoroughly. Add sour cream; blend. Add buttermilk, vinegar and garlic. Blend well and add salt and pepper to taste. Yields 2 cups.
Mrs. J. L. Bryson (Dottie)
Mt. Airy, North Carolina

Mrs. James G. Harris (Tunis)
Fort Worth, Texas

COOKED SALAD DRESSING

2 cups sugar
3 tablespoons flour
1 teaspoon dry mustard
½ teaspoon salt
½ teaspoon pepper

3 or 4 eggs, well beaten
1 cup vinegar
2 tablespoons butter
3 tablespoons cold water

Add sugar to beaten eggs. Add butter, vinegar and water. Add other ingredients and cook in saucepan about 5 minutes or until thick. Can be thinned with sweet or sour cream. Can also be stored in glass jars in refrigerator for several weeks.
Mrs. E. Halliburton
Willoughby, Ohio

DIJON DRESSING

⅓ teaspoon salt
⅓ teaspoon black ground pepper
1 teaspoon Dijon mustard
1 whole dry shallot, chopped

3 tablespoons red wine vinegar
6 tablespoons olive oil
1 tablespoon sesame seed, crushed
Fresh parsley, chopped

Stir vigorously until emulsified. This dressing should be served only on Boston lettuce with fresh sliced mushrooms.
Mrs. John R. Bisagno (Uldine)
Houston, Texas

FRENCH DRESSING

1 14-ounce bottle catsup
1½ cups oil
1 cup powdered sugar
1 medium onion, grated
1 teaspoon powdered garlic
1 teaspoon salt

2 ribs celery, grated
Dash celery salt
1 tablespoon vinegar (put
   in catsup bottle and rinse
   out into mixture)

Beat on medium speed until creamy. Do not refrigerate. Makes ¾ quart. Good on meat, as well as salad.
Mrs. Wayne Ward (Mary Ann)
Louisville, Kentucky

HITCHING POST SALAD DRESSING

1 cup salad oil
1 cup catsup
1 cup hard boiled eggs, (3 grated)
1 cup parsley, chopped

1 cup very small white
pickled onions
1 cup broken pecan meats

Mix and let stand 24 hours. Excellent on grapefruit or lettuce.
Mrs. Hugh L. Smith (Virginia)
Henderson, Texas

KAY'S DRESSING

1 quart Miracle Whip
Salad Dressing
2 cups milk
1 small onion, finely chopped
1 jar pimento, finely chopped
½ teaspoon garlic salt

1 cup mild Cheddar
cheese, grated
Salt and pepper to taste
¼ cup sugar
½ cup vinegar

Mix ingredients and store in refrigerator. Great for tossed salads!
Mrs. Tom S. Brandon (Dolly)
Sherman, Texas

MARY'S SALAD DRESSING

1 can Campbell's Tomato soup
½ can water
½ can vinegar
½ can Wesson oil
½ cup sugar

½ teaspoon pepper
1 teaspoon salt
¼ teaspoon garlic salt
1 tablespoon Worcestershire
sauce

Mix ingredients in quart jar and store in refrigerator.
Mrs. W. E. Darby (Mary)
Jefferson City, Tennessee

OIL AND VINEGAR DRESSING

1 cup oil	1 teaspoon pepper
1 cup sugar	1 teaspoon paprika
1 cup tarragon vinegar	1 clove garlic, crushed
1 teaspoon salt	

Blend together. Serve over crisp green salad.
Mrs. William T. Penick (Ginger)
Hyattsville, Maryland

SALAD DRESSING

1 cup Wesson oil	1 tablespoon salt
1 cup sugar	1 medium onion
1 cup white vinegar	3-4 shakes garlic salt
1 cup catsup	1 teaspoon celery seed

Mix in blender.
Mrs. Howard Knight (Joyce)   *Mrs. J. L. Bryson (Dottie)*
Morehead City, North Carolina   *Mt. Airy, North Carolina*

THOUSAND ISLAND DRESSING

1 cup mayonnaise	1 tablespoon pimento, chopped
1 tablespoon green pepper, chopped	¼ teaspoon paprika
2 tablespoon olives, chopped	1 hard boiled egg
	⅓ cup chili sauce

Combine all ingredients and chill. Keeps up to two weeks in refrigerator.
Mrs. Ted Sisk (Ginny)
Lexington, Kentucky

Vegetables

*. . . Suffer little children,
and forbid them not, to come unto me:
for of such is the kingdom of heaven. Matt. 19:14*

ASPARAGUS CASSEROLE

2 cans cut green asparagus spears
2 cans cream of mushroom soup
½ can evaporated milk

4 hard boiled eggs, sliced
Buttered Ritz cracker crumbs

Layer asparagus, sliced eggs and cream of mushroom soup mixed with ½ can evaporated milk in casserole dish. Top with buttered creacker crumbs and bake 30 minutes at 350 degrees.

Mrs. Joe Spirakis (Terry)
Pensacola, Florida

Mrs. Wyatt M. Gilbert (Irene)
Clarksville, Georgia

ASPARAGUS SOUFFLÉ

¼ pound margarine or butter
3 heaping tablespoons flour
3 cups milk
2 cans extra long asparagus
  spears

Salt and pepper
Paprika
1 can slivered almonds
Grated Cheddar cheese

Melt butter in saucepan. Stir in flour, salt and pepper until well blended. Add milk and cook until thick and creamy. In a greased baking dish, alternate layers of asparagus and grated cheese. Sprinkle with almonds, then a layer of white sauce. Continue layering process until dish is filled. Finish with a layer of cheese topped with almonds. Sprinkle with paprika. Bake 30 minutes in 400 degree oven until cheese is light brown and almonds toasted. Serves 12 to 14.

Mrs. Margaret Randall
Pensacola, Florida

ASPARAGUS-PEAS CRUMB BAKE

1 Number 2 can asparagus
1 Number 2 can garden peas
1 can cream of mushroom soup
2 tablespoons butter

½ teaspoon salt
½ teaspoon pepper
1 cup cheese, grated
1 cup bread crumbs

Drain asparagus and peas well. Mix with cream of mushroom soup. Place in 1-quart casserole. Season with butter, salt and pepper. Place cheese on top and cook for 25 minutes at 350 degrees. Sprinkle buttered bread crumbs on top of cheese. Return to oven and cook another 5 minutes.

Mrs. John Woodall (Carole)
Columbia, Maryland

ASPARAGUS AND PEAS CASSEROLE

1 Number 2 can cut asparagus, well drained
1 Number 2 can garden peas, well drained
2 hard boiled eggs
½ cup butter
4 tablespoons flour
2 cups milk
½ cup or more sharp Cheddar cheese
½ cup toasted almonds
Dash salt and pepper

Assemble ingredients. Place a layer of asparagus in casserole. Next a layer of peas. Slice hard boiled egg over this. Repeat layering process. Make a cheese sauce by melting butter in saucepan, carefully mix in flour, then milk. Add cheese. Cook over low heat until slightly thickened and cheese melts. Season with salt and pepper. Pour cheese sauce over casserole. Sprinkle almonds on top. Bake 30 minutes at 325 degrees.
Mrs. Bruce H. Price (Eva)
Newport News, Virginia

PEA CASSEROLE

2 cans peas
1 can cream of mushroom soup
1 can onion rings
½ cup Cheddar cheese, grated
Butter to taste
Salt and pepper to taste

Layer peas, onion rings, soup, cheese, salt, pepper and butter in casserole dish. Bake at 350 degrees or 375 degrees for 20 to 30 minutes until bubbly and brown.
Mrs. Thomas Williams (Nancy)
Falmouth, Kentucky

LOUISIANA BAKED BEANS

1 21-ounce can pork and beans
½ cup brown sugar
1 bottle cap Louisiana hot sauce
1 to 2 teaspoons curry powder
1 small onion, chopped
¼ bell pepper, chopped
1 stalk celery, chopped
¼ 20-ounce bottle catsup
1 tablespoon bacon drippings

Mix all ingredients together. Place in casserole or bean pot. Cover. Bake in 250 degree oven for 3½ hours. NOTE: Frankfurters may be placed across top of beans for a different flavor, if desired.
Mrs. Damon Vaughn (Carolyn)
Bossier City, Louisiana

SWEET-SOUR BAKED BEANS

4 large onions, sliced
1 cup brown sugar
1 teaspoon dry mustard
½ teaspoon garlic powder
   or garlic salt

1 teaspoon salt (use ½ teaspoon
   if garlic salt is used)
½ cup cider vinegar

Mix in pan and cook covered for 20 minutes.

2 15-ounce cans dry lima beans
1 16-ounce can green lima beans
1 16-ounce can dark red kidney
   beans

1 New England-style baked
   beans (B & M Brick Oven baked
   beans are good)
8 slices bacon

Drain limas and kidney beans. Mix all beans with above ingredients. Bake in 350 degree oven 1 hour in 3-quart casserole or divide into 2 casseroles. Crisp-fry bacon; drain. Crumble bacon on top before serving. Serves 12.
Mrs. James H. Smith (Nona)
Springfield, Illinois

BAKED BEANS WITH HAMBURGER

1 pound hamburger
1 large onion, chopped
1 green pepper, chopped
¼ stick margarine
3 medium cans pork and beans

⅔ cup brown sugar
2 tablespoons prepared mustard
½ small bottle catsup
Dash Worcestershire sauce

Brown onions, pepper and hamburger in margarine. Add remaining ingredients. Pour into baking dish. Bake at 325 degrees for 2 hours.
Mrs. Barnwell Gibson (Lita)
Bamberg, South Carolina

Mrs. Ted Cotten (Dorothy)
Longview, Washington

Mrs. Cort R. Flint (Ilene)
Meadows of Dan, Virginia

B. WARE'S RED BEANS

½ pound dried pinto beans
½ pound dried kidney beans
1 onion, sliced
1 tablespoon chili powder

1 tablespoon salt
Garlic bud, sliced thin
1 tablespoon honey or sugar
Several sprigs celantra, if available

Wash pinto and kidney beans. Place in large covered pot; cover with water. Bring to boil and cook for 5 minutes. Cover and remove from fire. Let stand 1 hour. Add to pot remaining ingredients. Simmer about 4 hours. Add a little Tabasco and salt to taste. Serve with cornbread and fresh green onions.

Mrs. Browning Ware (Corrine)
Beaumont, Texas

GREEN BEAN 'N BEAN SPROUT CASSEROLE

1 can French green beans
1 can water chestnuts
1 can cream of mushroom soup

1 can bean sprouts
1 can French fried onions
Grated Cheddar cheese

Drain beans and spread in dish. Slice water chestnuts onto beans. Drain and add bean sprouts. Cover with soup and sprinkle wtih cheese. Cook in 325 degree oven approximately 45 minutes. Pour can of French fried onions over top during last 10 minutes.

Mrs. Marshall E. Sargent (Gloria)
Stony Point, North Carolina

GREEN BEAN CASSEROLE WITH SOUR CREAM

2 packages frozen French
  green beans
1 teaspoon salt
2 heaping teaspoons sugar
3 tablespoons margarine
2 heaping tablespoons flour
½ pint sour cream

2 heaping teaspoons grated
  onion and juice
4-ounces medium Cheddar
  cheese, grated
1⅓ cups corn flakes, rolled
2 tablespoons margarine

Cook beans until tender without salt. In double boiler mix salt, sugar, 3 tablespoons margarine and flour to make thick paste. Remove from heat and stir in sour cream. Add grated onion and juice. Stir in Cheddar cheese. Drain beans and mix with sauce. Put in casserole. Coat corn flakes with 2 tablespoons margarine. Sprinkle mixture on casserole. Place in cold oven. Bake at 350 degrees for 20 minutes. Serves 6 to 8.

Mrs. E. T. Vinson (Katherine)
Scotland Neck, North Carolina

PARTY GREEN BEANS

3   packages frozen French   ½ cup half & half
     green beans   ¼ cup flour
2   tablespoons butter   ½ cup milk
1   medium can mushrooms   ⅛ teaspoon Tabasco sauce
1   cup slivered almonds, toasted   ⅛ teaspoon pepper
     slightly   ½ teaspoon salt
1   can water chestnuts, sliced   3   tablespoons Worcestershire
1   large jar Cheez Whiz   sauce
1   medium onion   1   can French fried onions

Cook beans until tender. Sauté minced onion and mushrooms in butter.
Make a cheese sauce by mixing flour, salt and pepper with milk and cream
slowly, then cheese. Add remaining ingredients except beans and onions.
Add beans last. Place in casserole dish. Bake 30 minutes in 325 degree
oven. Sprinkle French fried onions on top. Serves 12.

Mrs. Wendell Price (Frances)   *Mrs. Roy Ladd (Hazel)*
Nashville, Tennessee   *Houston, Texas*

GREEN BEAN CASSEROLE

2   1-pound cans cut green   1   can water chestnuts, sliced
     beans, drained   1   stack pack Ritz crackers,
1   cup Cheddar cheese, grated   rolled to fine crumbs
1   large onion, chopped   Melted butter
1   can cream of mushroom
     soup, undiluted

Grease 1 2-quart baking dish liberally with butter. Cover sides and bottom
of buttered dish with half of the Ritz crumbs. Place in layers: Beans,
cheese, onion and water chestnuts. Makes 2 layers. Cover with mushroom
soup. Top with remaining Ritz cracker crumbs. Drizzle 3 or 4 tablespoons
melted butter over crumbs. Bake at 350 degrees for 1 hour. Serves 10 to 12
people.

Mrs. James B. Riley (Vera)
Gonzales, Louisiana

GREEN BEAN BAKE

2 cans French green beans	1 small carton sour cream
1 tablespoon margarine	3 slices American cheese, grated
1 can cream of mushroom soup	Salt and pepper

Drain beans; dot with margarine. Season with salt and pepper. Pour into 9 x 11-inch baking dish. Mix cream of mushroom soup and sour cream together. Pour over beans. Top with grated cheese. Bake at 350 degrees for 30 minutes or until bubbly.
Mrs. James R. Maples (Mary Jo)
El Paso, Texas

BUTTER BEANS WITH SOUR CREAM

2 medium cans baby lima beans	1 8-ounce carton sour cream
1 medium onion, chopped	Pimento
1 stick margarine	

Sauté onion in margarine. Add sour cream. Blend well. Drain limas and fold in. Chop pimento and add. Heat to piping hot and serve.
Mrs. V. Allen Gaines (Leila)
Newport News, Virginia

PARTY BROCCOLI

2 10-ounce packages frozen broccoli spears	1 can French fried onion rings or 1 package frozen onion rings
1 cup American cheese, grated	⅔ cup evaporated milk
1 can cream of mushroom soup	

Prepare broccoli as package directs, but cook only 5 minutes. Drain and put into a greased 2-quart baking dish. Sprinkle grated cheese over broccoli. Pour cream of mushroom soup mixed with evaporated milk over top. Bake in 350 degree oven for 25 minutes. Remove from oven. Top with onion rings. Bake 8 to 10 minutes more, until onions are crisp and golden brown. Yield: 6 to 8 servings.
Mrs. John Dunaway (Jayne)
Corbin, Kentucky

And God said, Behold, I have given you every herb bearing seed which is upon the face of all the earth, and every tree, in the which is the fruit of a tree yielding seed; to you it shall be for meat. Gen. 1:29

BROCCOLI SUPREME

1½ pounds fresh broccoli or
  1 10-ounce package frozen
    chopped broccoli
1 can cream of chicken soup
1 tablespoon all-purpose flour
½ cup dairy sour cream
1 tablespoon onion, grated

¼ cup carrot, grated
¼ teaspoon salt
⅛ teaspoon pepper
¾ cup herb-seasoned stuffing
  mix (½ box)
2 tablespoons butter or
  margarine, melted

Remove outer leaves of broccoli and tough part of stalks; discard. Cut remaining broccoli into 1-inch pieces. Cook stalk pieces in boiling salted water 5 or 6 minutes; add flowerets. Cook until tender, about 5 more minutes. (Or prepare frozen broccoli according to package directions.) Drain. Blend together soup and flour. Add sour cream, carrot, onion, salt, and pepper; stir in broccoli. Turn into 2-quart casserole. Combine stuffing mix and the melted butter. Sprinkle around edge of baking dish. Bake in 350 degree oven 30 to 35 minutes or until hot through. Makes 6 servings.
Mrs. Frank F. Norfleet (Virginia)
Kansas City, Missouri

TUNA-BROCCOLI CASSEROLE

2 packages frozen broccoli
2 cans tuna or crabmeat
2 cans cream of celery soup

½ package Kellogg's stuffing mix
Grated Cheddar cheese

Place broccoli on bottom of buttered casserole dish after it has been cooked according to package directions. Put tuna on top of broccoli. Alternate layers of moistened stuffing mix and cream of celery soup. Place grated cheese on top. Bake 1 hour at 350 degrees.
Mrs. Charles H. Beal (Winona)
Sarasota, Florida

MARINATED BROCCOLI-CAULIFLOWER

1 medium cauliflower
1 bunch fresh broccoli
1 bunch fresh green onions

1 large carton sour cream
1 cup mayonnaise
2 teaspoons Beau Monde seasoning

Wash and prepare vegetables. Separate cauliflowerets and broccoli flowerets into bite size pieces. Cook just until tender crisp. Drain. Chop onions very finely. Place in mixing bowl. Mix sour cream, mayonnaise, Beau Monde seasoning and salt to taste. Pour over vegetables. Mix well. Marinate overnight in refrigerator, covered.
Mrs. Tom S. Brandon (Dolly)
Sherman, Texas

BROCCOLI-CORN BAKE

1 16-ounce can cream style corn
1 10-ounce package frozen chopped broccoli, cooked and drained
1 egg, beaten
1 cup saltine cracker crumbs (12 crackers)

1 tablespoon instant minced onion
2 tablespoons margarine, melted
½ teaspoon salt
Dash pepper
½ cup cracker crumbs (6 crackers)
1 tablespoon margarine, melted

Combine corn, broccoli, egg, ½ cup crumbs, onions, 2 tablespoons melted margarine, salt and pepper. Turn into 1-quart casserole. Combine ½ cup crumbs and remaining margarine. Sprinkle over vegetable mixture. Bake, uncovered, at 350 degrees for 35 to 40 minutes. Serves 6.

Mrs. A. B. Coyle (Joan)
Memphis, Tennessee

Mrs. Abner V. McCall
Waco, Texas

BROCCOLI-RICE CASSEROLE

2 packages frozen chopped broccoli
1 tablespoon dried diced onion
1 can cream of chicken soup

2 cups cooked Minute Rice
1 jar Cheez Whiz or 1 can cheese soup
1 stick margarine

Melt margarine in skillet. Add broccoli and onion. Cook over low heat until broccoli thaws and stir gently. Add Cheez Whiz and cream of chicken soup. Mix with 2 cups cooked rice. Bake at 350 degrees until hot and bubbly. Freezes well to cook later.

Mrs. Rufus Sprayberry (Doris)
Vernon, Texas

Mrs. A. D. Norris
Corpus Christi, Texas

Mrs. Wallace E. Jones (Laura Jo)
St. Ann, Missouri

Mrs. Elbert L. Smithen, Jr. (Jo)
Midland, Texas

Mrs. Ralph M. Smith (Bess)
Austin, Texas

Mrs. Ray E. Roberts (Margaret)
Columbus, Ohio

Mrs. V. Allen Gaines
Newport News, Virginia

Mrs. Jerry DeBell (Lurline)
Columbus, Ohio

Mrs. Albert Moore (Lorraine)
Greenville, North Carolina

Mrs. Gary W. Cook
Salpupa, Oklahoma

Mrs. James L. Kinsey (Ruby)
Sweetwater, Texas

Mrs. Glen G. Waldrop (Anne)
Atlanta, Georgia

CABBAGE SOUFFLÉ

4 eggs	Salt and pepper to taste
3 slices buttered bread, cut in small pieces	½ teaspoon dill seed (optional)
	1½ cups Cheddar cheese, grated
2 cups milk	Paprika
1 large head cabbage, cooked	

Blend together eggs, bread and milk. Fold cabbage into liquid mixture. Add salt and pepper to taste, dill seed and Cheddar cheese. Pour into 2-quart casserole dish. Sprinkle with Cheddar cheese, then sprinkle paprika over cheese. Bake in 250 degree oven for 2½ hours.
Mrs. Henry B. Stokes (Etta)
Buies Creek, North Carolina

STUFFED CABBAGE ROLLS

1 large head cabbage	½ teaspoon poultry seasoning or thyme
1½ pounds ground beef	
2 teaspoons salt	2 tablespoons Wesson oil
½ teaspoon pepper	2 8-ounce cans tomato sauce
1 cup rice, cooked	1 tablespoon brown sugar
1 small onion, diced	¼ cup water
1 egg	1 tablespoon vinegar

Wash cabbage. Steam the whole head of cabbage a few minutes. Cool. Separate leaves. Brown ground beef. Add salt and pepper. Mix together meat, rice, onion, egg, poultry seasoning and Wesson oil. Spoon meat mixture into cabbage leaves and roll up. Place in baking dish. Mix tomato sauce, brown sugar, water and vinegar. Spoon over cabbage rolls. Bake in 350 degree oven for 45 minutes to 1 hour.
Mrs. Fred Hollomon (Pat)
Topeka, Kansas

JAY'S CABBAGE, CHINESE STYLE

1 medium head cabbage	¼ cup celery or cucumber
¼ cup bell pepper, chopped	1 tablespoon shortening
¼ cup onion	Salt and pepper to taste

Shred cabbage very fine. Add bell pepper, onion and celery. Melt shortening in skillet. Add vegetables; stir and cover. Steam 5 minutes, stirring occasionally. Season with salt and pepper.
Mrs. Edward L. Byrd (Nora)
Florence, South Carolina

CABBAGE CASSEROLE

1 medium head cabbage	Sharp Cheddar cheese, grated
½ cup cabbage broth	1 can French fried onion rings
1 can cream of celery soup or	(optional)
cream of mushroom soup	Onion to taste
Cracker crumbs	

Cook cabbage until tender. Season with salt, butter and onion. Drain cabbage and save broth. Place a layer of cabbage in casserole dish, a layer of cracker crumbs, then a layer of grated sharp Cheddar cheese. Repeat layers. Mix celery soup with cabbage broth and pour over casserole. Bake at 350 degrees until bubbly hot. Top with cracker crumbs or French fried onion rings.

Mrs. Milton Gardner (Nancy)
Thomasville, Georgia

CARROTS EN SAUCE

6 to 8 carrots, sliced	½ teaspoon salt
¼ cup water, or liquid from carrots	¼ teaspoon pepper
2 tablespoons onion, grated	¼ cup cracker crumbs
2 tablespoons horseradish	Butter or margarine
1 cup mayonnaise	

Cook carrots until just tender. Drain. Place carrots in baking dish. Mix all other ingredients. Pour over carrots. Sprinkle cracker crumbs over top. Dot with margarine. Bake in 375 degree oven for 20 to 30 minutes.

Mrs. Frank Gunn (Sandra)
Biloxi, Mississippi

CARROTS AND CHEESE

2 bunches carrots, sliced	1 cup buttered bread crumbs or
½ pound Velveeta Cheese	croutons
1¼ sticks margarine	

Cook carrots in lightly salted water until just tender. Drain. Melt together margarine and cheese over low heat. Pour over carrots. Top with buttered bread crumbs or croutons.

Mrs. Everett Lemay
Mt. Vernon, Illinois

HONEY GLAZED CARROTS

1 quart carrots, diagonally sliced	½ cup orange juice
1 cup water, boiling	2 tablespoons butter
¼ teaspoon salt	2 tablespoons honey
2 teaspoons cornstarch	Parsley (optional)

Place carrots in medium saucepan with water and salt. Cook rapidly, covered, until just tender (8 to 10 minutes). Into small sauce pan turn cornstarch. Gradually stir in orange juice to make a smooth paste. Add butter and honey. Stir constantly over moderate heat until thickened and clear. Drain hot carrots. Add honey glaze and mix well. Parsley may be added, if desired.
Mrs. Warren C. Hultgren (Wanda)
Tulsa, Oklahoma

CARROT CASSEROLE WITH VEGETABLES

1½ cups celery, cut up	⅛ teaspoon thyme
1½ cups carrots, sliced	2 tablespoons onion
2 cans cut green beans	2 tablespoons butter
2 tablespoons celery leaves	1 can cream of mushroom
Salt to taste	soup

Cook vegetables 15 minutes in bean liquid. Add salt and thyme. While cooking, cut celery leaves and onion; cook in butter until onions are clear. Drain vegetables and reserve liquid. Mix with cream of mushroom soup diluted with ¼ cup vegetable liquid.

TOPPING

2 cups Rice Checks, mashed	⅛ teaspoon thyme
2 tablespoons butter	

Brown lightly in skillet. Spread crumbs on vegetable mixture. Bake until bubbly, about 30 minutes at 350 degrees.
Mrs. Harold C. Bennett (Phyllis)
Jacksonville, Florida

Thou visitest the earth, and waterest it: thou greatly enrichest it with the river of God, which if full of water: thou preparest them corn, when thou hast so provided for it. Ps. 65:9

CARROTS LYONNAISE

1 pound carrots (6 medium)
1 chicken bouillon cube, dissolved in ½ cup boiling water
¼ cup butter or margarine
3 medium onions, sliced

1 tablespoon flour
¼ teaspoon salt
¾ cup water
Dash pepper
Pinch of sugar

Pare carrots and cut in julienne strips. Place in covered saucepan. Cook 10 minutes. Melt butter; add onions and cook, covered, 15 minutes. Stir occasionally. Add next 4 ingredients; bring to a boil. Add carrots and stock. Simmer, uncovered, 10 minutes. Season with pinch of sugar. Serves 6.
Mrs. C. H. Sutherland (Aileen)
Greenville, South Carolina

CAULIFLOWER CASSEROLE

1 10-ounce package frozen
  cauliflower
2 10-ounce packages frozen
  peas and carrots
1 cup sour cream

1 tablespoon instant minced onion
1 can cream of celery soup
1 to 2 peeled tomatoes, sliced
1 cup American cheese, grated

Cook vegetables separately according to package directions. Cook cauliflower only until tender crisp. Cook peas and carrots until barely done. Drain all vegetables. Combine and turn into a greased casserole. Blend sour cream, minced onion and soup with salt and pepper to taste. Do not oversalt vegetables. Top with sliced tomatoes; sprinkle with grated cheese. Bake, uncovered, at 325 degrees for 25 minutes or until bubbly. Can grate cheese and cook vegetables ahead if you wish. This gives a complete meal with a salad and dessert.
Mrs. J. L. Bryson, Jr. (Dottie)
Mt. Airy, North Carolina

CREAM CHEESE CORN

1 2-pound bag whole kernel
  frozen corn
1 8-ounce package cream cheese

Salt and pepper to taste

Cook corn in smallest amount of water possible until just tender. Drain off all excess water. Add cream cheese. Stir gently until melted and well mixed. Add salt and pepper to taste. Delicious!
Mrs. Robert Fling
Munich, West Germany

ITALIAN EGGPLANT
Make meat sauce earlier in day.

1 eggplant
1 egg, beaten

Cracker meal
Mozzarella cheese, sliced

Pare and slice eggplant. Dip in beaten egg and cracker meal and fry till golden brown in cooking oil. Set aside. Make layers in baking dish of eggplant slices, meat sauce and sliced Mozzarella cheese. Bake at 375 degrees about 40 minutes.

MEAT SAUCE

1 onion
1 large can tomatoes
2 6-ounce cans tomato paste
12-ounces water
1 teaspoon salt
½ teaspoon Italian seasoning

½ teaspoon pepper
¼ teaspoon garlic powder
1 tablespoon sugar
2 bay leaves
1 to 1½ pounds ground beef

Brown meat; add blended onion, tomatoes, paste and water to meat. Mix and add spices. Simmer about 2½ hours.
Mrs. Robert Post (Helen)
Tulsa, Oklahoma

SCALLOPED EGGPLANT

1 large or 2 small eggplants, diced
⅓ cup milk
1 can cream of mushroom soup
1 egg, slightly beaten
½ cup onion, chopped

¾ cup packaged herb-seasoned stuffing
½ cup stuffing, finely crushed
2 slices bread, crumbled
2 tablespoons butter, melted
1 cup sharp cheese, shredded

Cook eggplant in boiling water for 8 to 10 minutes until tender; drain. Blend all ingredients with eggplant except last 4. Toss crushed stuffing crumbs and bread crumbs with melted butter and sprinkle over casserole. Top with cheese. Bake in 350 degree oven 25 minutes.
Mrs. Charles Nanney (Rachel)
Newberry, South Carolina

EGGPLANT CASSEROLE

2 medium eggplants	½ stick butter
1 onion, chopped	⅓ cup cracker crumbs
1½ cups water	1 teaspoon salt
2 eggs	1 cup cheese, grated
⅔ cup milk	

Wash and dice eggplant. Place in saucepan. Boil with onion in salted water 10 to 12 minutes. Beat eggs. Add to milk. Mix with drained eggplant. Add butter, cracker crumbs, salt and pepper. Top with grated cheese. Bake in preheated 325 degree oven for 30 minutes.
Mrs. Henry Chiles
Pierre, South Dakota

SPINACH MADELINE

2 packages frozen chopped spinach	½ teaspoon black pepper
	¾ teaspoon celery salt
2 tablespoons butter or margarine	¾ teaspoon garlic powder or 1 clove garlic, crushed
4 tablespoons flour	½ teaspoon salt
2 tablespoons onion, finely chopped	6-ounce roll Jalapeno or Snappy Cheese
½ cup Pet milk, undiluted	1 teaspoon Worcestershire sauce
½ cup vegetable liquid	

Cook spinach according to package directions. Drain in strainer. Reserve liquid. Melt butter in saucepan over low heat. Add flour, stirring until blended, but not browned. Add onion and cook until soft. Add vegetable liquid and Pet milk combined, stirring constantly. Cook until smooth and thick. Add all seasonings and the cheese, cut in pieces. Stir until melted. Next add cooked, well drained spinach. Carefully blend all ingredients. Pour into buttered casserole and cover with fine buttered bread crumbs. Bake in 350 degree oven until hot through and bubbly. Serves 6 to 8. NOTE: Flavor is better if refrigerated overnight. If frozen, let thaw very little before baking.
Mrs. Don Harbuck (Elizabeth)
El Dorado, Arkansas

SPINACH CONTINENTAL

1 10-ounce package spinach, chopped	1 egg, well braten
¾ cup milk	2 slices bread, toasted and cut in cubes
4 slices American cheese	Parmesan cheese
2 tablespoons butter	Onion powder

Thaw spinach and squeeze out water. Heat milk, butter and cheese until cheese melts. Cool. Stir in well beaten eggs. Mix in spinach. Pour in buttered baking dish. Melt 4 tablespoons butter. Add toasted bread cubes. Stir until butter is absorbed. Sprinkle with Parmesan cheese and onion powder. Arrange over spinach. Bake in 350 degree oven until set.
Mrs. Buren Higdon (Polly)
Union City, California

SPINACH SOUFFLÉ

2 packages frozen spinach, thawed and drained	¼ cup butter or margarine
2 cartons small curd creamed cottage cheese	3 tablespoons flour
4 eggs, beaten	1 8-ounce package American cheese

Combine all ingredients in a 1½-quart baking dish. Bake in 350 degree oven for 1 hour or more until set. Top should be bubbly and golden brown.
Mrs. R. Earl Allen (Joyce)
Fort Worth, Texas

SWEDISH MUSHROOMS

3 tablespoons butter or margarine	¾ cup light cream
2 small onions, chopped	2 teaspoons salt
2 eggs	¼ teaspoon pepper
⅔ cup dry bread crumbs	1 pound fresh mushrooms, coarsely chopped
¾ cup milk	

Preheat oven to 350 degrees. Melt butter in skillet. Sauté onions until golden. Beat eggs in 1½-quart casserole. Add bread crumbs, milk, cream, salt and pepper. Mix until crumbs have absorbed liquid. Carefully fold in mushrooms and onions. Bake 60 to 70 minutes until golden and set. Yield: 6 large servings.
Mrs. John J. Wolf (Elizabeth)
Houston, Texas

STUFFED SUMMER SQUASH

8　medium yellow crooked
　neck squash
2　tablespoons tomato paste
¼　teaspoon salt
2　tablespoons paprika

Pinch cayenne
1　tablespoon onion, grated
2　tablespoons butter
½　cup sharp Cheddar cheese, grated
Buttered bread crumbs

Wash squash. Simmmer in small amount of salted water in covered pot until just tender. Cool. Cut off a slice horizontally. Scoop out centers and mix with tomato paste, onion, salt, butter, paprika, cayenne and cheese. Stuff shells with mixture and sprinkle with buttered bread crumbs. Bake in shallow casserole at 350 degrees for 20 to 25 minutes.
Mrs. Oscar McDougal (Sylvia)
Cordova, South Carolina

GOURMET SQUASH-CARROT CASSEROLE

2　pounds squash, cooked and
　drained
1　pound carrots, sliced and
　cooked
1　small onion, grated
1　can cream of chicken soup

2　4-ounce jars sliced pimentoes
½　pint dairy sour cream
1　8-ounce package herb seasoned
　stuffing mix
½　cup margarine

Melt margarine. Add herb stuffing mix. Line 9 x 13-inch baking pan with half of mixture. Mix squash, carrots, onion, soup, pimentoes and sour cream. Spoon over stuffing mix. Top with remaining herb stuffing mix and bake at 350 degrees for 45 minutes. Serves 10 to 12.

Mrs. Kenneth D. Emerson (Cleta)
Wichita, Kansas

Mrs. John J. Wolf (Elizabeth)
Houston, Texas

Mrs. J. R. White (Nell)
Montgomery, Alabama

Mrs. Kenneth Bailey (Faye)
Wake Forest, North Carolina

Mrs. Billy D. Allen (Elray)
Springfield, Illinois

Mrs. T. L. Cashwell (Helen)
Raleigh, North Carolina

SUMMER SQUASH BAKE

1 quart squash, sliced	1 green pepper, chopped
½ cup water	1 onion, chopped
1 teaspoon salt	½ cup bread crumbs
1 cup medium white sauce	½ cup Cheddar cheese, shredded
¼ teaspoon sugar	2 eggs, beaten

Grease a 1½-quart casserole. Cook squash in boiling salted water for 5 minutes. Drain. Mix with white sauce, eggs, sautéed onion and green pepper. Add sugar. Pour in casserole. Sprinkle with crumbs and cheese. Bake 25 minutes in a 350 degree preheated oven.

MEDIUM WHITE SAUCE

2 tablespoons margarine	2 tablespoons flour
¼ teaspoon salt	1 cup milk

Melt margarine in saucepan. Mix salt and flour. Stir slowly into melted margarine to make a smooth paste. Slowly add milk. Cook over medium heat, stirring constantly, until it begins to thicken.
Mrs. Bill Moore (Sue)
Houston, Texas

MIXED VEGETABLES WITH CHEESE

2 cans mixed vegetables, drained	1 cup celery, chopped
¼ cup onion, chopped	1 cup mayonnaise
½ cup cheese, grated	1 package Waverly Wafers
	1 stick butter

Mix all ingredients. Pour into casserole. Melt 1 stick butter. Crumble up 1 package Waverly crackers. Mix. Spread over casserole mixture. Place in 350 degree oven for 45 minutes.
Mrs. Joe Abrams
Sylacauga, Alabama

SPANISH SQUASH

9 yellow squash	4 slices toast, crumbled
4 slices bacon	Salt
1 onion, chopped	Grated Cheddar cheese
1 can chopped green chiles	

Cut up squash. Cook and drain well. Fry bacon till crisp; break into small pieces. Mix all ingredients together, reserving grated cheese for top. Bake at 400 degrees until brown.
Mrs. Gloria Singleton
Rankin, Texas

SQUASH CASSEROLE

3 pounds squash
¾ cup onion, chopped
¾ cup green pepper, chopped
¾ stick margarine
½ cup mayonnaise

¾ cup pimento, chopped
1½ tablespoons sugar
2 eggs, separated
1 cup Cheddar cheese, grated

Sauté onion in margarine. Cook green pepper with squash. Drain well. Separate eggs. Add beaten egg yolks, onion and other ingredients. Reserve some cheese for top. Add beaten egg whites. Turn into buttered dish. Sprinkle with remaining cheese. Bake at 300 degrees until firm. Serves 8 to 10.

Mrs. Page Kelley (Vernice)
Louisville, Kentucky

Mrs. Hugh L. Smith (Virginia)
Henderson, Texas

Mrs. J. R. White (Nell)
Montgomery, Alabama

Mrs. A. L. McGee
Castle Hayne, North Carolina

Mrs. Gilbert E. Barrow (Barbara)
Montgomery, Alabama

Mrs. Ray K. Hodge (Joyce)
Kinston, North Carolina

Mrs. Bill Hickem (Billie)
Jacksonville, Florida

Mrs. James L. Kinsey (Ruby)
Sweetwater, Texas

STUFFED TOMATOES WITH YELLOW RICE

1 package yellow rice
1 can beef consommé
1 tablespoon parsley, chopped

1 small can pimento, chopped
Sharp Cheddar cheese
Tomatoes

Cook rice according to package directions, adding at least ½ can beef consommé. Scoop pulp out of tomatoes and drain. Mix together, rice, cheese, parsley and pimento. Top with grated cheese. Place in baking dish with a small amount of water in bottom. Bake in 350 degree oven 15 to 20 minutes or until done.

Mrs. Bryce Myers (Jenny)
Charleston, South Carolina

COMPANY ZUCCHINI

3 cups diced zucchini, cooked
   and mashed
1½ cups soda cracker crumbs
3 eggs, beaten
½ cup butter, melted
1 cup milk

1 can Cheddar cheese soup or
   2 cups Cheddar cheese, grated
½ teaspoon salt
2 tablespoons onion flakes
¾ cup pimento (optional)

Mix all ingredients. Place in a greased casserole. Bake at 300 degrees for 40 minutes or until golden brown. Serves 6.
Mrs. Jerry DeBell (Lurline)
Columbus, Ohio

OUR FAVORITE ZUCCHINI

3 small zucchini, chopped
2 tablespoons onion
2 eggs, beaten
1 can cream of mushroom soup

¼ cup margarine
1 cup saltine crackers,
   crushed
1 cup Parmesan cheese

Boil squash and onion in salted water for 8 minutes. Drain. Mix eggs and mushroom soup. Add to squash. Melt margarine; mix with cracker crumbs and Parmesan cheese. Add ½ crumb mixture to the squash. Pour into buttered casserole. Spread remaining crumb mixture on top. Bake in 375 degree oven for 45 minutes.
Mrs. Fred Halbrooks, Jr.
Louisville, Kentucky

ZUCCHINI CASSEROLE

1 medium tender zucchini
½ cup onion, chopped
½ cup green pepper, chopped

1 6-ounce can tomato paste
⅔ cup water
1 cup Cheddar cheese, grated

Slice zucchini ¼-inch thick. Sprinkle with salt, pepper and flour. Fry on both sides, until brown, in bacon drippings or cooking oil. Take out of skillet and drain on paper towel. Sauté onion and green pepper in same drippings. Add tomato paste and water. Arrange squash in baking dish. Pour tomato mixture over squash. Sprinkle with grated cheese. Bake about 20 minutes in 350 degree oven. Serves 6.
Mrs. Cort R. Flint (Ilene)
Meadows of Dan, Virginia

GREEN VEGETABLE CASSEROLE

1½ cups water, salted, boiling
1 medium onion, chopped
1 package frozen baby lima beans

1 package frozen green peas
1 can French green beans, drained

Add chopped onion to boiling salted water. Cook 5 minutes or longer. Add lima beans. Cook 12 minutes. Next add green peas and cook 3 to 5 minutes. Drain green beans; stir in vegetable mixture.

TOPPING:
3 hard boiled eggs, mashed fine
1 cup mayonnaise

1 teaspoon prepared mustard
Several dashes Tabasco

Mix ingredients together. Spread on top of casserole. Bake 30 minutes in a 350-375 degree oven. Brown lightly on top.

Mrs. Frank Campbell (Janet)
Statesville, North Carolina

Mrs. Landrum Leavell (Jo Ann)
New Orleans, Louisiana

NEW ORLEANS RAGOUT

6 hard-boiled eggs

CREAM SAUCE
½ cup flour
1 stick margarine

1⅔ cup milk
Salt to taste

1 tablespoon Worcestershire sauce
1 cup cheese, grated
1 cup green peas, drained

1 can tomatoes, drained or stewed down and mashed up
Ritz cracker crumbs

Make cream sauce in double boiler. Mix flour and salt to taste. Gradually add ½ cup milk, making a smooth paste. Add remaining milk and margarine. Cook until thickened, stirring constantly. Add remaining ingredients except eggs to sauce. In 2 quart baking dish, place layer of sauce and diced eggs, repeating until used up. Cover with Ritz cracker crumbs. Cook 15 to 20 minutes at 375 degrees until bubbly hot.

Mrs. Robert Cuttino (Molly)
Lancaster, South Carolina

VEGETABLES 'N RICE CASSEROLE

1 cup rice, cooked	2 cans peas and carrots, mixed
1 can whole kernel corn, partially drained	1 jar Jalapeno Cheese Whiz

Mix rice and vegetables. Warm in saucepan. Put cheese on top in a lump. Turn off heat. Place lid on pan; let cheese melt to make liquid. Serve hot.
Mrs. Larry Rose
Waco, Texas

VEGETABLE MEDLEY

2 packages frozen lima beans	1 Number 2 can French green beans
2 packages or 2 cans frozen green peas	

Cook vegetables separately until tender. Drain and mix.

TOPPING:

1 cup sour cream	Dash Tabasco
1 cup mayonnaise	1 tablespoon onion, grated
2 teaspoons mustard	½ cup Wesson oil
1 teaspoon Worcestershire sauce	4 hard-boiled eggs, cut up

Mix; do not heat. Pour over hot vegetables. This is also delicious cold!
Mrs. Wayne Dehoney (Lealice)
Louisville, Kentucky

VEGETABLE-POTATO BAKE

1 envelope sour cream sauce mix	1 cup milk
1 10-ounce package frozen Parisian Style vegetables with sauce cubes	3 cups frozen Southern-style hash brown potatoes, thawed
1 envelope white sauce mix	½ of 3-ounce can French fried onions (1 cup)
¼ teaspoon salt	

Prepare the sour cream sauce mix using package directions. Set aside. In large saucepan, cook Parisian-style vegetables according to package directions. Do not drain. Stir in milk. Bring to boiling, stirring constantly. Stir in sour cream sauce and hash browns. Turn into 12 x 7½ x 2-inch baking dish. Bake in 350 degree oven 30 minutes or until hot. Top with onions. Bake 5 minutes. Yield: 10 servings.
Mrs. Wallace E. Jones (Laura Jo)
St. Ann, Missouri

Seafoods

For God so loved the world,
that he gave his only begotten Son,
that whosoever believeth in him
should not perish,
but have everlasting life. John 3:16

BAKED FISH AU GRATIN

1   pound fish fillets
1   can cream of celery soup
¼ cup sharp cheese, grated

Salt and pepper
Paprika
Herbs

Cut raw fish in serving size pieces and layer in a greased baking dish. Season to taste with salt, pepper, paprika and herbs of your choice. Spread over the fish other ingredients which have been mixed together. Bake at 350 degrees for 45 minutes. Serves with home fried potatoes. Serves 4.
Mrs. Thomas W. Downing (Sue)
Baltimore, Maryland

FISH MEAL A LA BALTIMORE

2   pounds fish fillets
2   tablespoons butter
2   medium carrots

2   medium onions
Salt, pepper
Herbs

Wipe fish with paper towel. Grease the center of piece of aluminum foil with the butter. Have a second piece of foil to place underneath the buttered foil, placing in opposite (perpendicular) direction to later reinforce and wrap airtight. Arrange fish on buttered foil. Season. Arrange over the fish the carrots which have been finely sliced crosswise, the onions (ringed if desired) and any other vegetable for flavor as a little chopped celery or green pepper. Wrap securely. Place on shallow pan. Bake at 450 degrees for 30 minutes. Serve with lemon. Serves 4.
Mrs. Thomas W. Downing
Baltimore, Maryland

And Jesus took the loaves; and when given thanks, he distributed to the disciples to them that were set down; and likewise of the fishes as much as they would. John 6:11

CATFISH STEW

2 pounds dressed catfish
2 pounds Irish potatoes
1 pound onions
½ pound lean salt pork,
  thinly sliced
1 stick butter

2 to 3 small cans tomato sauce
Worcestershire sauce to taste
  (optional)
Salt and pepper
4 hard boiled eggs

Boil catfish in slightly salted water until flesh leaves bones. Fry salt pork until very crisp. Remove from fat and mash with a fork. Cube Irish potatoes and put in separate sauce pan. Chop onions and boil with potatoes until done. Add to fish. Add salt pork, tomato sauce, Worcestershire, butter and salt and pepper to taste. Add water if needed. Allow to boil on medium heat at least an hour before serving. Slice hard boiled eggs and stir in stew just before it is served. Very good for men's suppers. They love it!

Mrs. Joseph P. DuBose, Jr. (Sybil)
Graceville, Florida

SALMON LOAF

1 large can salmon
½ cup celery, cut up
½ onion, finely chopped
½ cup tomato juice
Juice of ½ lemon
2 or 3 eggs, beaten

Salt and pepper to taste
2 teaspoons catsup
1 cup cracker crumbs
1 tablespoon flour
1-2 tablespoons butter, melted
2 teaspoons baking powder

Mix all ingredients together except baking powder. This is important: Just before putting salmon loaf in oven, stir in 2 teaspoons baking powder. Bake in a loaf pan or casserole at 350 degrees for a half hour or a little longer. Can be served with a white sauce having boiled eggs cut up in it, or eaten without the sauce.

Mrs. Charles H. Beal (Winona)
Sarasota, Florida

SALMON CROQUETTES

1 large can salmon, drained
2 cups soft bread crumbs
2 eggs, beaten
2 tablespoons butter, melted

1 tablespoon parsley, chopped
1 tablespoon onion, finely grated
2 tablespoons baking powder
Salt and pepper

Drain salmon. Remove skin and bones. Add beaten eggs, then seasonings, butter, bread crumbs and baking powder. Mix and roll into patties. Fry in hot fat until brown on both sides. Serves 4 to 6.

Mrs. James W. Parker
Santa Ana, California

TUNA NOODLE CASSEROLE

6 ounces (about 3 cups) medium noodles
1 can tuna, drained
½ cup mayonnaise
1 cup celery, sliced
⅓ cup onion, chopped
¼ cup green pepper, diced
¼ cup pimento
1 teaspoon salt
1 can cream of celery soup
½ cup milk
1 cup sharp cheese, shredded
½ cup slivered almonds, toasted

Cook noodles in boiling salted water until tender; drain. Combine noodles, tuna, mayonnaise, vegetables and salt. Blend together cream of celery soup and milk. Heat through. Add shredded cheese and heat, stirring until cheese melts. Add to noodle mixture. Turn into ungreased 1½-quart casserole. Sprinkle with toasted almonds. Bake in 425 degree oven about 20 minutes or till bubbly. Makes 6 servings.
Mrs. Charles H. Beal (Winona)
Sarasota, Florida

DEVILED CRABS

20 squares crackers, crushed
1 medium green pepper, grated
½ teaspoon to 1 tablespoon crushed red pepper
2 teaspoons prepared mustard
1 egg, beaten
1 tablespoon hot sauce or steak sauce
1 cup mayonnaise
1 cup crabmeat
1 onion, grated

Mix ingredients together. Form into patties or put into aluminum shells. Bake at 400 degrees until brown.
Mrs. V. Allen Gaines (Leila)
Newport News, Virginia

MOTHER'S CRAB CAKES

1 pound clean crabmeat
1 cup crumbs (2 slices soft bread without crusts)
¼ cup milk
2 tablespoons salad dressing or mayonnaise
2 eggs, beaten
1 tablespoon dry mustard
Salt and pepper to taste

Mix all ingredients together and make into cakes. Fry lightly in oil.
Mrs. Edward E. Garland (Ruth)
Oxford, Maryland

CRAB BAKE

(good for dinner party-buffet)

¼ cup butter	1 pound can crabmeat
4 tablespoons flour	1 small jar pimento, chopped
1 teaspoon salt	½ cup blanched slivered almonds,
2 cups milk	optional
⅛ teaspoon pepper	2 hard cooked eggs, chopped
¾ cup or more dry bread crumbs	
buttered generously	

Melt butter, add flour and blend. Add milk and cook until thick, stirring constantly. Add milk and cook until thick, stirring constantly. Add remaining ingredients. Pour into greased molds or into 1½-quart greased casserole. Top with buttered bread crumbs. Bake at 325 degrees for 20 to 25 minutes. Serves 8. Note: Serve with ham. Tuna could be substituted for crab, also chicken.
Mrs. William L. Self (Carolyn)
Atlanta, Georgia

CHICKEN-CRAB GUMBO

1 medium fryer	½ cup bacon grease
1 large onion, chopped	1 pint oysters
1 cup celery, chopped	2 cups fresh crabmeat or 2 7-ounce
1 16-ounce can tomatoes	cans
1 fresh tomato	2 teaspoons Worcestershire sauce
2 cups okra, sliced	Garlic salt to taste
Scant ½ cup flour	Salt and pepper to taste

Make Roux by browning a scant ½ cup flour in equal amount of bacon grease. Boil chicken until tender. Save broth. Cut chicken into small pieces. Place onion, celery, tomatoes and okra in broth and simmer for 1 hour. Add chicken pieces, Roux, oysters with liquid and crabmeat to broth. Bring to boiling point. Turn heat to low and cook 1 hour. Serve over fluffy white rice and sprinkle with Gumbo File.
Mrs. James L. Pleitz (Margaret Ann)
Dallas, Texas

CRABMEAT CASSEROLE

1 7½-ounce can King crabmeat, without tendons
4 hard boiled eggs, chopped
4 slices white bread, trimmed and pulled into pieces
1 teaspoon minced parsley
½ teaspoon onion, grated
1 cup mayonnaise
1 small can condensed milk
Buttered bread crumbs

Drain crabmeat and pull apart. Mix all ingredients except buttered bread crumbs. Fill buttered casserole and cover with buttered crumbs. Heat thoroughly at 350 degrees until crumbs are browned. Recipe will fill 6 to 7 shells.

Mrs. Herschel Creasman (Joanne)
Wauchula, Florida

CRAB MORNAY

½ cup butter
3 tablespoons flour
2 teaspoons white pepper
½ teaspoon salt
1 pint milk
1 pound white crabmeat
1 pound Monterey Jack cheese, grated
1 cup cheese, grated (for topping)

Melt butter. Add flour, pepper, and salt. Make a paste by adding milk slowly. Gradually stir in remaining milk. Cook over low heat, stirring constantly to make a thick white sauce. Into greased baking dish layer:
1 pound white crabmeat
1 pound grated cheese
White sauce
Bake at 350 degrees for 20 to 30 minutes, depending on the size of baking dish. Top the last 5 minutes with more grated cheese.

Mrs. Tommy Jones (Mary)
Louisville, Mississippi

BAYOU JAMBALAYA

2 5-ounce cans shrimp (or ½
   pound cooked and cleaned
   fresh shrimp)
1 10-ounce can oysters,
   undrained
6 slices bacon, cut into ¾-inch
   pieces
1 cup onion, chopped
¾ cup celery, diced
½ cup green pepper, chopped

1 cup okra, cut-up
1 clove garlic, minced
1 1-pound can tomatoes
1½ cups water
1 cup rice, uncooked
2 teaspoons salt
½ teaspoon thyme
⅛ teaspoon paprika
1 small bay leaf
2 to 3 dashes liquid hot pepper sauce

Fry bacon until crisp. Remove bacon bits from pan and drain on paper toweling. Add onion, celery, green pepper and garlic to bacon drippings; cook slowly until vegetables are tender, not brown. Add tomatoes, okra, water, rice and seasonings; mix. Cover and simmer gently 20 minutes. Add undrained oysters and bacon bits. Cover and cook 15 to 20 minutes longer until rice is tender, stirring occasionally. Mix in shrimp and heat. Makes 6 servings.

Mrs. Lonnie Shull (Hazel)
West Columbia, South Carolina

DELICIOUS SCALLOPED OYSTERS

3 dozen oysters
1 cup celery, finely cut
Rich chicken broth

Cracker crumbs
2 eggs
Butter

Cook 1 cup celery 20 minutes. Set aside. Wash oysters. Place a layer of cracker crumbs in bottom of baking dish, then a layer of oysters. Sprinkle with pepper, salt and butter. Mix in cooked celery with each layer of oysters. Repeat layers until dish is full. Cover with cracker crumbs. Pour enough rich chicken broth over this to moisten the crackers well. Allow to stand 10 to 12 minutes before baking. Bake in 400 degree oven about 20 minutes, until well set. Beat two eggs thoroughly. Pour over top and return to oven to lightly brown. Serve piping hot.

Mrs. William K. Weaver, Jr. ("B")
Mobile, Alabama

HOW TO PREPARE FRESH SHRIMP

Bring 1 quart of water to simmer in 2-quart pan. Add:

1 teaspoon salt
   Juice of one lemon

3 bay leaves

Shell and devein shrimp. Drop about 6 to 8 at a time in simmering water. Takes only 3 minutes or less, depending on size of shrimp. Take them out as they get done.

CORPUS CHRISTI FRIED SHRIMP

1 pound jumbo shrimp, shelled
with tails left on

2 egg whites
Cracker crumbs

Butterfly shrimp. Beat egg whites until stiff. Dip shrimp into egg whites, then into crumbs. Press shrimp into crumbs until well coated. Fry shrimp in deep fat until lightly browned. Serves 4.

TARTAR SAUCE

1 cup mayonnaise
1½ tablespoons onion,
minced

1½ tablespoon dill, chopped or
sweet pickle
Salt and pepper

Mix all ingredients. Chill. Makes 1¼ cups

RED SAUCE

¾ cup catsup
2 teaspoons Worcestershire sauce
2 teaspoons lemon juice

½ teaspoon prepared
horseradish
Dash Tabasco

Mix all ingredients thoroughly. Serve cold with favorite seafood.
Mrs. Vernon Elmore (Peggy)
Corpus Christi, Texas

SHRIMP-CORN CHOWDER

½ pound salt pork, diced
2 onions, chopped
½ cup celery and tops, chopped
3 tablespoons green pepper,
chopped
3 tablespoons carrots,
finely diced
½ bay leaf, crumbled
2 tablespoons flour
Salt and pepper

4 cups water
3 cups potatoes, diced
1 17-ounce can cream style corn
1 cup whole kernel corn, cooked
2 cups evaporated milk,
undiluted
1 pound shrimp, shelled, cooked
and drained
Parsley
Paprika

In large kettle cook salt pork until brown and crisp. Remove pork and pour off grease, all but 3 tablespoons. Add next 5 ingredients and cook 5 minutes. Blend in flour. Add water and potatoes and bring to a boil. Simmer, covered, 15 minutes. Add corn, milk and shrimp. Heat well. Season with salt and pepper to taste. Add pork and serve with a garnish of parsley and paprika. Makes about 2½ quarts.
Mrs. William N. Hinson (Bettye)
New Orleans, Louisiana

SHRIMP BISQUE

2 cans frozen or canned
shrimp soup
½ package garlic flavored
cheese (3-oz.)
1 4-ounce can mushrooms
⅛ teaspoon pepper

½ cup Half and Half cream
½ teaspoon salt
1 10-ounce package frozen peas,
cooked and drained
2 5-ounce cans ready to use shrimp,
drained or fresh cooked shrimp

Blend soup, cheese, cream and liquid drained from mushrooms in heavy
saucepan over low heat. Stir frequently until hot. Add seasonings, peas,
mushrooms and shrimp. Keep hot and serve on mounds of hot cooked
rice. (This is a quick after church company meal.) Serve with salad, French
bread and a dessert.
Mrs. Lee Morris (Gerry)
Oak Ridge, Tennessee

TEXAS CURRIED SHRIMP

¼ cup butter
3 tablespoons onion, diced
3 tablespoons apple, diced
3 tablespoons celery, chopped
2 tablespoons flour

2 teaspoons curry powder
1 cup milk
½ cup chicken broth
3 cups cooked, diced shrimp

Sauté onion, apple and celery in butter. Mix flour and curry and stir into
butter slowly. Add milk and broth and cook until slightly thick. Add
shrimp and serve hot over rice. Suggested condiments: chutney, chopped
salted peanuts, toasted coconut, diced bacon, chopped hard boiled eggs.
Mrs. Vernon Elmore (Peggy)
Corpus Christi, Texas

SEAFOOD SUPREME

1 cup crabmeat
1 cup shrimp, boiled and
cut up
1 cup mayonnaise
1 cup celery, chopped
3 tablespoons onion, chopped

6 tablespoons green pepper,
chopped
½ teaspoon salt
½ teaspoon pepper (or to taste)
1 teaspoon Worcestershire sauce
¾ cup potato chips, crushed

Mix first 9 ingredients together. Top with potato chips. Bake in 350 degree
oven for 30 minutes.
Mrs. James G. Stertz (Edna)
Sarasota, Florida

150

SEAFOOD CHOWDER

2 tablespoons salad oil
1 tablespoon paprika
2 large onions, sliced
1 medium green pepper, cut in strips
1 pound tomatoes, sliced
2 cloves garlic, minced
¼ cup chopped parsley
1 pound shrimp, shelled and deveined
1 cup cooked flaked lobster or 1 6½-ounce can lobster, drained
½ cup chopped stuffed olives
2 cups water
2 cups tomato juice
Salt and pepper to taste
2 dozen raw oysters, shucked

Heat salad oil; add paprika and blend. Add onions, green pepper, tomatoes, garlic and parsley. Cook over low heat until tender, stirring often. Add shrimp, lobster, olives, water, tomato juice, salt and pepper. Cover; cook over low heat for 30 minutes, stirring occasionally. Add shucked oysters, with their liquid. Mix well. Cook until the edges of the oysters curl, about 4 or 5 minutes. Serve piping hot. Makes 6 to 8 servings.
Mrs. R. Earl Allen (Joyce)
Fort Worth, Texas

SEAFOOD CASSEROLE

1 stick margarine
½ cup onion, chopped
½ cup celery, chopped
½ cup bell pepper, chopped
1 can cream of mushroom soup
1 can cream of celery soup
½ cup mayonnaise
1 dash Worcestershire sauce
1 10-ounce package frozen crabmeat (Wakefield)
1 cup boiled shrimp
1 small can tuna
3 cups cooked rice
Bread crumbs

Sauté first mixture. Drain and add to second mixture. Add seafood. Layer alternately with rice in large casserole dish. Top with bread crumbs mixed with left over margarine. Bake at 400 degrees for 30 minutes.
Mrs. Mary Ann Delk
Belvedere, South Carolina

Poultry

Rejoice, and be exceeding glad:
for great is your reward in heaven
. . . Matt. 5:12

DELICIOUS CHICKEN CASSEROLE

2½ pound fryer (2 cups cooked chicken)
½ cup mayonnaise
1 can cream of chicken soup
1 cup celery, diced

1 small onion
1 cup chicken broth
1 package Pepperidge Farm Herb-Seasoned dressing
½ cup slivered almonds

Boil chicken until done. Remove from broth and cut into small pieces. Mix together 2 cups cut-up chicken, mayonnaise, and cream of chicken soup. In small amount of chicken broth, cook together diced celery, and onion until tender. Add these plus 1 cup chicken broth to soup mixture. Pour into baking dish. Sprinkle Pepperidge Farm dressing over top and spread almonds over all. Pour more chicken broth around the sides of the casserole. Bake 30 minutes at 350 degrees. Serves 6 to 8.

Mrs. Ray K. Hodge (Joyce)
Kinston, North Carolina

CHICKEN-CHESTNUT CASSEROLE

1 cup celery, chopped
1 large onion, chopped
2 cups rice, cooked
1-3 pound cooked, boned and diced chicken

1 can cream of chicken soup
¾ cup mayonnaise or salad dressing
1 can water chestnuts, thinly sliced
½ cup butter
1 cup corn flakes, crushed

Sauté celery and onion in half of butter until clear. Mix together the chicken, rice, soup, water chestnuts and salad dressing. Melt remaining butter and mix with corn flakes. Sprinkle over top. Bake in 375 degree oven for 45 minutes or until hot and bubbly. Serves 8 to 10.

Mrs. Kenneth D. Emerson (Cleta)
Wichita, Kansas

Mrs. Fred D. Barnes (Martie)
Lenoir, North Carolina

Mrs. Charles Nanney (Rachel)
Newberry, South Carolina

CHICKEN 'N RICE

1 can cream of mushroom soup	1 cup water
1 can cream of celery soup	1 chicken, cut in pieces
1 can cream of chicken soup	Salt and pepper
1 stick butter	1 cup rice

Mix soups, butter and water together. Place on bottom of greased casserole dish. Pour half of soup, butter, water mixture over top of rice. Place chicken on top of rice with the skin up. Pour remaining soup mixture over chicken. Salt and pepper to taste. Bake at 250 degrees for 3 hours.

Mrs. Jerry DeBell (Lurline)   *Mrs. Charles Powell (Betty)*
Columbus, Ohio   *Jasper, Alabama*

JUDY'S CHICKEN

1 large or 2 small chickens, cook, bone and chop	1 cup milk
	1 soup can water
1 can cream of chicken soup	1 bag Pepperidge Farm Herb
1 can cream of mushroom soup	Dressing

Mix soups, milk and water together. Pour over chicken in baking dish. Sprinkle 1 bag of Pepperidge Farm Herb Dressing on top and bake in slow oven at 350 degrees for 30 to 40 minutes. Serves 8 to 12.

Mrs. Gerald Goss (Judy)   *Mrs. Marshall E. Sargent (Gloria)*
Hamilton, Virginia   *Stony Point, North Carolina*

CHICKEN DELIGHT

6 chicken breasts	1 bottle Russian dressing
8 ounces apricot or peach preserves	1 packet dry onion soup mix

Mix together last 3 ingredients and pour over chicken. Cook, covered, for 2 hours at 350 degrees. Serve on rice. Makes 6 servings.

Mrs. James E. Coggin (Carolyn)   *Mrs. Rufus Spraberry (Doris)*
Fort Worth, Texas   *Vernon, Texas*

INTERNATIONAL RECIPE: CHICKEN AND CASHEW NUTS

1 breast of chicken	½ cup salted cashew nuts
1 teaspoon salt	½ teaspoon sugar
¼ teaspoon powdered ginger	½ cup water
¼ teaspoon Accent powder	1 tablespoon soy sauce
3 tablespoons salad oil	2 teaspoon cornstarch
½ cup celery (cut diagonally)	1 teaspoon Brown sauce
½ cup green onions, cut 1 inch	1 clove garlic
1 small can water chestnuts	

Remove chicken breast from bone and cut into bite-size pieces. Sprinkle chicken with ginger, ½ teaspoon salt and Accent. Heat oil in heavy skillet and add chicken. Stir and toss rapidly. Do not over cook nor brown meat; cook until it loses pink color. Add 1 clove garlic, thinly sliced, celery and onions. Sprinkle with sugar and cook all together about 5 minutes. Vegetables should retain their crispness. Add water chestnuts and continue to stir together. Combine cornstarch, water, soy sauce and Brown sauce. Pour over meat and vegetables. Cook until sauce thickens slightly, about 2 minutes. Add cashew nuts and taste for further seasoning with salt or soy sauce. Serve with hot, cooked rice.

Mrs. W. A. Hinckley (Ruth)
Raton, New Mexico

CHICKEN AND WILD RICE CASSEROLE

1 cup wild rice	1½ teaspoons salt
3 cups chicken, cut up	¼ teaspoon pepper
Chicken broth	½ cup onion, chopped
1 6-ounce can sliced broiled	¼ cup flour
mushrooms	1½ cups light cream
¼ cup pimento, diced	2 tablespoons parsley
½ cup butter, melted	Slivered almonds

Cook rice according to package directions. Sauté onions in butter until just tender. In separate pan sauté drained mushrooms. Reserve liquid. Stir flour into cooled onions. Add chicken broth to mushroom liquid to make 1½ cups. Stir into flour mixture. Slowly add cream. Cook until mixture thickens, stirring constantly. Add rice, chicken, mushrooms, salt and pepper, pimento and parsley. Place in 2-quart baking dish. Spread almonds on top. Bake about 30 minutes at 350 degrees until hot through.

Mrs. Oscar McDougal (Sylvia)
Cordova, South Carolina

CHICKEN CASSEROLE

3 chicken breasts
1 can cream of chicken soup
1 can cream of mushroom soup

1 box Stove-Top stuffing mix, chicken flavor

Stew chicken breasts in saucepan. Save broth. Combine cream of mushroom soup and cream of chicken soup with about 2 cups of broth. Mix in Stove-Top stuffing mix. Tear chicken breasts in small pieces. Place one layer of soup mixture into a loaf pan, then layer of chicken pieces. Alternate layers of chicken and soup mixture. Bake at 400 degrees for about 20 minutes.
Mrs. James Kirkpatrick (Loretta)
Waynesville, North Carolina

WALNUT CHICKEN

6 large chicken half-breasts, boned and skinned
Salt
Pepper

2 egg whites
1 cup California walnuts, finely chopped
Lime sauce

Season chicken with salt and pepper. Beat egg whites lightly. Dip chicken in egg white, turning to coat. Drain well, then roll in walnuts. Place in buttered baking pan. Bake at 350 degrees for 20 to 25 minutes, just until the chicken is cooked through. Serve hot, with Lime Sauce. Makes 6 servings.

LIME SAUCE

2 tablespoons butter
2 tablespoons flour
1 cup chicken broth
¼ teaspoon salt

Dash white pepper
2 egg yolks
2 whole eggs
1 lime

Melt butter and stir in flour. Add chicken broth, salt and white pepper. Cook, stirring until mixture boils thoroughly. Beat 2 egg yolks with 2 whole eggs. Stir hot sauce into eggs. Return mixture to very low heat, and stir constantly until thickened. Remove from heat and blend in ½ teaspoon grated rind and juice from 1 lime.
Mrs. Charles H. Beal (Winona)
Sarasota, Florida

CHICKEN CONTINENTAL

3   or 4 pound chicken, cut up
⅓ cup seasoned flour
¼ cup butter
1   can cream of chicken soup
2½ tablespoons onion, grated
1   teaspoon salt

Dash pepper
1   tablespoon chopped parsley
½ teaspoon celery flakes
⅛ teaspoon thyme
1⅓ cups water
1⅓ cups Minute Rice

Roll chicken in flour and brown in butter. Remove. Stir soup, seasonings and water into drippings. Cook and stir to a boil. Spread rice in 1¾ quart casserole. Pour all but ⅓ cup soup over rice and stir to moisten. Top with chicken and remainder of soup. Bake at 375 degrees for 30 minutes. Garnish with paprika.

Mrs. Brock Watson
Fayetteville, Arkansas

PARTY CHICKEN

4   large chicken breasts, split,
    skinned and boned
8   slices bacon

1   4-ounce package chipped beef
1   can cream of mushroom soup
1   cup commercial sour cream

Wrap each chicken breast with a strip of bacon. Cover the bottom of a flat, greased 8x12x2-inch baking dish with the chipped beef. Arrange chicken breasts on chipped beef. Mix the undiluted soup and sour cream and pour over chicken. Cover and refrigerate. About 3¼ hours before serving time, heat oven to 275 degrees. Bake, uncovered, for 3 hours.

Mrs. C. S. Maynard
Little Rock, Arkansas

Mrs. Glen Waldrop (Anne)
Atlanta, Georgia

Mrs. Carl Hudson (Dottie)
Bunkie, Louisiana

Mrs. Billy T. Mobley (Mary Ellen)
Ahoskie, North Carolina

Mrs. Bob Flegal
Aloha, Oregon

Mrs. Don Watterson (Joan)
Montgomery, Alabama

CHICKEN PARMESAN ON COUNTRY HAM

½ stick butter
1 clove garlic, minced
1 cup Pepperidge Farm bread
  crumbs
1 cup Parmesan cheese

1 teaspoon salt
⅛ teaspoon pepper
6 half chicken breasts, boned
6 small slices country ham

Melt butter; add garlic and simmer. Mix crumbs, cheese, and seasonings. Dip chicken breasts in butter mixture; roll in cheese and crumbs. Place each chicken breast in foil lined pan on top of a piece of country ham. Bake at 350 degrees for ½ hour, then 300 degrees for ½ hour. This can be prepared the day before, and refrigerated until time for baking. Serves 6.
Mrs. Wendell Price (Frances)
Nashville, Tennessee

MARDI GRAS CHICKEN

3 chicken breasts, split into halves
¼ cup evaporated milk
1 cup packaged pancake mix
½ teaspoon salt
⅛ teaspoon garlic powder
1 tablespoon Mexene Chili
  Powder
1 medium green bell pepper,
  sliced into 6 thin rings

1 pimento, cut into 12 or 18 tiny
  pieces
1 medium onion, cut into thin slices
  and separated into rings
⅛ teaspoon black pepper
¼ teaspoon thyme
½ cup margarine or butter

Wash chicken; drain and pat dry. Place chicken on waxed paper and sprinkle evaporated milk on both sides. Shake dry ingredients well in paper bag; drop few pieces of chicken in at one time, shaking to coat generously. Melt margarine in electric fry pan, heated to 325 degrees. Brown fleshy side of chicken pieces first, then other sides. Reduce heat to 250 degrees and cook for 20 minutes with lid on. On top of fleshy side of chicken, arrange attractively on each piece of chicken, bell pepper ring, onion rings and then pieces of pimento placed into these rings. Replace lid and cook for 25 minutes at 275 degrees. Test for tenderness with fork. Simmer short time longer if necessary. Serve with baked beans. An easy dish to prepare for beginners. Serves 6.
Mrs. E. M. Adams (Marjorie)
Fredonia, New York

CHICKEN BREASTS HAWAIIAN

3 whole chicken breasts, split in half
5 tablespoons salad oil
½ cup dark brown sugar
½ cup vinegar
¾ teaspoon salt
⅓ teaspoon powdered ginger
1 teaspoon Soy sauce
2 tablespoons cornstarch
1 8¼-ounce can sliced pineapple, cut in chunks
1 11-ounce can mandarin orange sections, drained
½ cup halved maraschino cherries

Heat oil in skillet over medium heat. Brown chicken breasts on each side. Pour off excess oil. Combine brown sugar, vinegar, salt, ginger, and soy sauce. Pour over chicken and simmer 35 minutes, covered. Remove chicken from skillet. Blend cornstarch and 2 tablespoons pineapple syrup. Stir into skillet with remaining syrup, pineapple, orange sections, and cherries. Return chicken to skillet. Cover and simmer 5 to 10 minutes or until chicken is tender. Serve on rice.

Mrs. Kenneth Chafin (Barbara)
Houston, Texas

CHICKEN AND LOBSTER CURRY

1 pound lobster meat, cooked
1 pound white meat of chicken or capon, cooked
1 apple
1 large onion
1 stalk celery
2 bay leaves
3 ounces flour
2 ounces curry powder
1 quart chicken broth
1 cup cream
1 coconut, milk and meat

Melt butter in a very large skillet and fry the apple, cored, peeled and sliced; the onion, peeled and sliced; the celery, cut up and two bay leaves. Smooth this mixture for 15 minutes. Sprinkle flour and curry powder in the mixture; stir well and cook slowly for another 15 minutes. Add chicken broth, cream, milk and shredded meat of the coconut and again cook 15 minutes slowly. Remove from fire and strain sauce through a coarse piece of cheesecloth or a fine sieve into a large saucepan and add chicken and lobster meat. The pieces of meat and lobster should be about 1-inch square. Season to taste with salt and pepper and let the curry heat thoroughly over a very low flame.

Mrs. Edmond Walker (Lurie)
Honolulu, Hawaii

CURRIED CHICKEN AND RICE

1 stick margarine
1 cup rice
1 teaspoon onion powder
1 teaspoon salt
1 tablespoon chicken bouillon
  powder

1 teaspoon curry powder,
  or more
2¼ cups water
4 or 5 chicken breasts

Melt margarine in 9x13-inch baking pan. Add all other ingredients except chicken and stir. Place chicken on top. Add salt and pepper to chicken. Bake, uncovered, about 1 or 1¼ hours at about 350 degrees. This seems very watery, but the rice will absorb the liquid.
Mrs. Robert Post (Helen)
Tulsa, Oklahoma

CHICKEN CURRY

2 3¼ pound chickens
2 cups water
3 medium onions, chopped
2 apples, minced
8 stalks celery, minced
½ cup cooking oil

¼ cup curry powder (or to taste)
½ teaspoon ginger
½ teaspoon pepper
¼ cup flour
2 cups heavy cream
3 egg yolks, beaten

Cook and bone chickens. Combine onion, celery, and apples. Brown lightly. Add seasonings and cook 5 minutes. Add 4 cups chicken stock and cook slowly 20 minutes. Thicken with flour, stirring gently. Add chicken and let stand 3 hours. Add egg yolks and cream. Heat.
Serve over rice with choice of the following:
1. chopped boiled eggs
2. crisp bacon bits
3. raw or fried onions, chopped
4. raw or fried bananas, chopped
5. sweet pepper, chopped
6. coconut, chopped
7. peanuts, chopped
8. tomatoes, chopped
9. pineapple, chopped
Let each person add ingredients to taste. Serves 12.
Mrs. Barnwell Gibson (Lita)
Bambery, South Carolina

And they, continuing daily with one accord in the temple, and breaking bread from house to house, did eat their meat with gladness and singleness of heart. Acts 2:46

BATTER TOPPED CHICKEN PIE

1 cut up chicken	1 can cream of mushroom soup
1 small onion, diced	1 can cream of chicken soup
1 teaspoon dill weed	Salt to taste
¼ teaspoon poultry seasoning	
or sage	

Place chicken in saucepan and cover with water. Add onion, dill weed, poultry seasoning and chicken boullion cubes. Cook slowly, until tender. Remove skin from chicken. Pull chicken from bone and cut in small pieces. Add cream of mushroom soup and cream of chicken soup, undiluted. Salt to taste. Pour in baking dish and top with the following:

TOPPING

2 cups plain flour	1 tablespoon onion flakes
4 teaspoons baking powder	2 tablespoons fresh onion,
1 teaspoon salt	minced
2 tablespoons oil	Milk

Mix with enough milk to make a batter consistency half way between pancake batter and biscuits. Drop by spoonfuls on chicken mixture and bake at 425 degrees until brown. Note: Biscuit mixture can be used for dumplings. Leave chicken mixture in pot. Bring to a boil and drop dumplings in by spoonfulls. Cover and cook for 15 to 20 minutes without lifting pot lid.

Mrs. Henry Powell (Mary)   *Mrs. Tal Bonham (Faye)*
Ahoskie, North Carolina   *Yukon, Oklahoma*

GEORGIA SMOTHERED CHICKEN

1 medium fryer, cut in serving	4 tablespoons flour
pieces	Juice of ½ lemon
Salt and pepper to taste	2 tablespoons Worcestershire sauce
4 tablespoons margarine	1½ cups water

Season chicken with salt and pepper. Let stand 1 hour. Place chicken in 9x13-inch Pyrex dish; dot with margarine. Sprinkle with flour. Bake at 500 degrees until brown; reduce heat to 350 degrees. Add lemon juice, Worcestershire sauce and water. Cover tightly with foil. Continue baking 1 to 1½ hours, basting occasionally. Gravy may be thickened, if desired.

Mrs. James N. Griffith (Mimi)
Athens, Georgia

TEXAS BAR-B-CUED CHICKEN

1 3 pound chicken, cut up
¼ cup fat
1 cup celery, chopped
1 cup onion, chopped
1 cup water
¼ cup lemon juice

4 tablespoons brown sugar
3 tablespoons Worcestershire
   sauce
2 tablespoons vinegar
½ tablespoon salt
1½ teaspoon prepared mustard

Combine ingredients except chicken and fat; simmer 30 minutes. Flour chicken parts and brown in ¼ cup fat. Place in baking dish. Pour sauce over chicken. Bake 1 to 1½ hours at 350 degrees until sauce has thickened.
Mrs. A. D. Norris
Corpus Christi, Texas

EASY CHICKEN LOAF

3 cups chicken, cooked with
   celery and onion
5 cups bread crumbs
1 can mushroom soup
Chicken broth

4 eggs, beaten
Juice of 1 lemon
Salt and pepper
2 tablespoons onion
1 cup almonds, toasted

Chop chicken into small pieces. Mix bread crumbs with soup, eggs, lemon juice, salt, pepper and onion. Add enough rich broth to mix to proper consistency. Pour into a 13x9-inch pan. Sprinkle almonds on top. Bake 1 hour at 250 degrees.
Mrs. Henry A. Parker (Virginia)
Orlando, Florida

CHICKEN GOURMET

6 medium chicken breasts, cut in
   half and boned
2½-ounce can deviled ham or
   prepared herb stuffing
2 eggs, well beaten

1½ cups cracker crumbs
⅓ cup butter
1 can cream of mushroom soup
½ can water
2 tablespoons Worcestershire sauce

Remove skin and bones from breasts. Pound to flatten. Spread each with filling of deviled ham or stuffing. Roll up. Dip each roll in beaten egg; roll in cracker crumbs. Brown in skillet in butter and arrange in baking dish. Put mushroom soup, water and Worcestershire sauce in skillet where chicken was browned and stir. Pour over rolls. Cover loosely with foil. Bake in 350 degree oven 45 to 60 minutes or 300 degree oven for 1½ hours.
Mrs. Henry B. Stokes (Etta)
Buies Creek, North Carolina

CHICKEN LOAF WITH CRANBERRY TOP

1 small package cherry gelatin	1 cup hot chicken broth
¼ cup water	1 tablespoon unflavored
½ cup orange juice	gelatin
1 teaspoon lemon juice	¼ cup cold water
½ cup celery, chopped	½ cup evaporated milk
1 pound can jellied cranberry	½ teaspoon salt
sauce	2 cups cooked chicken, diced
¼ cup pecans, chopped	⅔ cup mayonnaise

Break up cranberry sauce with fork. Stir in juices and water until sauce is dissolved. Stir in gelatin. Chill until slightly set. Add celery and nuts. Pour into a 9-inch Pyrex dish and chill until firm. *SECOND LAYER:* Soften gelatin in cold water. Add hot broth and chill until partially set. Blend in mayonnaise and milk. Add chicken and salt. Spoon over cranberry layer. Chill until firm. Unmold and serve on lettuce. Serves 8 to 10.
Mrs. George McMillan (Norma)
Columbia, South Carolina

CHICKEN MYSTERY SALAD

3 cans chicken noodle soup	1½ cups whipping cream
3 cans tuna	1½ cups celery, finely chopped
3 3-ounce packages lemon	3 tablespoons green pepper,
gelatin	finely chopped
1½ cups mayonnaise	3 tablespoons onion, grated

Chill soup overnight. Remove grease from top. Rinse tuna with boiling water. Drain well. Dissolve gelatin in 1¼ cups boiling water. Add mayonnaise, unwhipped cream, celery, green pepper and onion. Stir. Add soup and tuna. Pour into 12x14-inch pan. Chill until firm.

TOPPING

1 3-ounce package strawberry	1 16-ounce package frozen
gelatin	strawberries
1 cup boiling water	

Mix gelatin in hot water. Cool. Add strawberries. Pour over the above chilled mixture. Chill until firm.
Mrs. C. E. Colton (Lois)
Dallas, Texas

CHICKEN-ASPARAGUS CASSEROLE

2 10-ounce packages frozen
   asparagus
2 cups cooked chicken, cut in
   small pieces
2 cans cream of chicken soup
1 tablespoon flour

1 cup mayonnaise
1 tablespoon lemon juice
½ cup cheese, shredded
1 small can sliced mushrooms
Toasted almonds

Cook asparagus according to package directions. Set aside. Thicken soup with 1 tablespoon flour. Stir in remaining ingredients except almonds. Spoon creamed chicken mixture over cooked asparagus in casserole. Sprinkle with almonds. Bake in 350 degree oven for 25 minutes.
Mrs. Henry B. Stokes (Etta)
Buies Creek, North Carolina

CHICKEN-BEAN CASSEROLE

1 fryer, boiled and boned
1 can of cut green beans, cooked
   and drained

1 can onion rings

SAUCE

1 can cream of chicken soup
1 can water chestnuts

¼ cup salad dressing
1½ or 2 tablespoons curry powder

In baking dish alternate layer of chicken, beans and sauce until all is used. Bake until hot through in 350 degree oven just before serving. Top with onion rings a few minutes before removing from oven. Serves 4 to 6.
Mrs. Grayson Glass (Patsy)
Galveston, Texas

CHINESE CHICKEN CASSEROLE

1 box Uncle Ben's Long-grain &
   Wild Rice
3 cups cooked, boned chicken
1 can celery soup, undiluted
1 can water chestnuts, drained
   and sliced
1 can French-style green beans,
   drained

½ cup Miracle Whip Salad
   Dressing
2 tablespoons pimentos
2 tablespoons green pepper,
   chopped
Salt and pepper to taste

Cook rice according to directions on box. Add chicken and other ingredients. Bake in a buttered casserole at 350 degrees for 30 to 35 minutes. Very good! Serves a rather large group and freezes well.
Mrs. Richard Hopper (Mary Edna)
Ardmore, Oklahoma

CHICKEN-BROCCOLI CASSEROLE

2 packages frozen broccoli, cooked
6 chicken breasts, cooked, boned and sliced
2 cans cream of chicken soup, undiluted
1 cup mayonnaise
3 teaspoons lemon juice
¾ teaspoon curry powder
½ cup sharp American cheese, shredded
Generous dash cayenne pepper
1 tablespoon margarine, melted
½ cup toasted bread crumbs
Garlic powder

Cook the broccoli and drain; arrange in greased baking dish. Place chicken on top. Sprinkle lightly with garlic powder. Mix the soup, mayonnaise, lemon juice, curry powder and pepper together and pour over chicken. Sprinkle with cheese. Combine bread crumbs with melted butter and sprinkle on top of cheese. Bake in 350 degree oven 30 minutes or until thoroughly heated.

Mrs. Carl Duck (Bonnie)
Dallas, Texas

Mrs. Page Kelly (Vernice)
Louisville, Kentucky

Mrs. R. Earl Allen (Joyce)
Fort Worth, Texas

ENGLISH PEA-CHICKEN CASSEROLE

1 3-pound fryer
1 cup spaghetti
1 cup celery, chopped
1 onion, chopped
½ stick margarine
1 can drained English peas
1 small can pimento, chopped fine
1 can cream of mushroom soup
1 cup cheese, grated
Additional cheese for topping

Boil chicken until tender and cut up. In broth cook spaghetti, celery, onion and margarine. Add cut up chicken. Stir into chicken mixture drained English peas, pimento, cream of mushroom soup and 1 cup grated cheese. Pour mixture into 12x9x2-inch pan. Sprinkle grated cheese on top and bake at 350 degrees until hot through and cheese melts. If casserole is frozen, sprinkle cheese on top just before popping in oven.

Mrs. Byron McDaniel
Center, Texas

POLYNESIAN CHICKEN

2 broiler chickens, 1½ to   Salt and pepper
   2 pounds   Butter

Have broilers split down the back; wash and dry thoroughly. Rub all over
with butter. Season with salt and pepper. Place on greased broiler and sear
one side quickly at high heat, 450 degrees. Turn and sear other side. Reduce heat to 350 degrees and cook for 15 minutes. Pour over broilers the
following sauce:

SAUCE
1 large can cling peach halves   1 tablespoon Kikoman soy sauce
1 tablespoon cornstarch   3 tablespoons vinegar

Drain peaches, reserving liquid. Into 1 cup peach syrup, stir cornstarch,
soy sauce and vinegar. Cook chicken until it is fork tender, basting frequently. Serve with broiled peach halves: Fill peach halves with chutney
and broil until bubbly and brown.
Mrs. Marvin Howard (Kitty)
Pensacola, Florida

CHICKEN ENCHILADAS

1 fryer, cooked and cut up   2 4-ounce cans roasted, peeled,
1 package corn tortillas   chopped, green chilies
Salad oil   ½ pound mild Cheddar cheese,
2 cans cream of chicken soup   grated
2 soup cans water or milk   1 large onion, grated

Fry tortillas in a small amount of oil until brown and crisp on each side.
Drain. Combine soup, water or milk, and green chilies in saucepan; bring
to a boil. Place tortillas to cover bottom of 13x9-inch pan. Layer with ½
chicken, ½ onion, ½ cheese and ½ sauce. Repeat with remaining ingredients ending with sauce. Cover pan and bake at 350 degrees for 20 minutes. Serve hot.
Mrs. B. A. Carlin (Virginia)   *Mrs. James R. Maples (Mary Jo)*
Buna, Texas   *El Paso, Texas*

Mrs. Gary Payne (Doda)   *Mrs. Buren Higdon (Polly)*
Syracuse, Missouri   *Union City, California*

Mrs. Maurice Hill
Royse City, Texas

MEXICAN CHICKEN CASSEROLE

1 3-pound chicken
1 can cream mushroom soup
1 can cream chicken soup
2 medium Jalapeno peppers,
   chopped
1 teaspoon chili powder
4 tablespoons onion, chopped

⅛ teaspoon garlic powder
¼ teaspoon black pepper
¼ teaspoon Tabasco
1 cup chicken broth
4 cups regular size Fritos
1 cup Cheddar cheese,
   grated

Cook and bone chicken. Reserve 1 cup broth. Combine soups, peppers, spices, Tabasco and chicken broth. Blend well. Preheat oven to 350 degrees. Cover bottom of 2½ or 3-quart casserole with 2 cups Fritos. Spread on half of chicken, half the sauce, then half grated cheese. Repeat, ending with grated cheese. Bake at 350 degrees for 25 to 30 minutes.
Mrs. Roy Ladd (Hazel)
Houston, Texas

CURRIED CHICKEN SPAGHETTI

1 5 pound hen
8-ounces spaghetti
2 cups onion, chopped
2 cups celery, chopped
1 cup green pepper,
   chopped
1 large can mushrooms
1 quart chicken broth

1 quart tomato juice
1 teaspoon Worcestershire sauce
1¼ teaspoons curry powder
   (optional)
Salt and pepper to taste
1 or more cups American cheese,
   grated
Sliced stuffed olives

Cook hen in water so you will have quart of well-flavored chicken broth. Have onions, celery and green pepper cut up in not too fine pieces. Sauté lightly in one stick margarine. Add sliced mushrooms and sauté along with vegetables. Cut off cooked chicken in rather large pieces. Cook and drain spaghetti which has been broken into small pieces. Mix cut-up chicken, the sauted vegetables, the cooked drained spaghetti and all of seasonings. Then add tomato juice and quart of strained broth. Cook slowly until liquid is reduced, the seasonings are well-married to each other and until thick, stirring so the mixture will not stick (handle carefully). Vital point is that it is not runny, neither is it dry. When this stage is reached, put on serving dish, sprinkle with grated cheese and decorate with sliced stuffed olives. Serves approximately 15. To serve more, you may use more spaghetti.
Mrs. Rollin Burhans (Delina)
Bowling Green, Kentucky

Main Dishes

And now abideth faith,

hope, love, these three;

but the greatest of these is love.

1 Cor. 13:13

 # Cheese & Eggs

MACARONI & CHEESE

1½ cups macaroni, cooked
1¼ cups milk
3 tablespoons butter
1 teaspoon salt
1 teaspoon onion, chopped
(optional)

1 cup soft bread crumbs
(in large bowl)
2 eggs, well beaten
3 cups Cheddar cheese, grated

Cook macaroni as suggested until tender. Add butter to milk in small pan to melt as milk scalds. Mix salt and onion to warmed milk. Pour over the bread crumbs. Add eggs and ½ the cheese. Mix all together. Place in greased baking dish. Top with rest of cheese and bake at 350 degrees for 30 to 40 minutes until lightly browned and knife inserted in casserole comes out clean. NOTE: A tasty variation is to place thick tomato slices, topped with seasoned bread crumbs on top of macaroni mixture; a few stuffed olives and pimento strips are very nice.

Mrs. John R. Riddle (Tommye)
Birmingham, Alabama

MACARONI CASSEROLE

1 small box macaroni
1 cup mayonnaise
1 can cream of mushroom soup
1 small can chopped mushrooms
1 pound cheese, grated

¼ cup onions, chopped
¼ cup bell peppers, chopped
¼ cup pimentoes, chopped
3 tablespoons butter
Pepperidge Farm Unseasoned Mix

Cook macaroni as directed. Add butter, then all ingredients. Put Pepperidge Farm Crumb Mix on top. Bake at 350 degrees for about 20 to 30 minutes. Very delicious!

Mrs. W. C. Tribble
Social Circle, Georgia

QUICHE LORRAINE

6-ounces imported Swiss
   cheese, grated
8 slices crisp bacon, crumbled
3 eggs
1 cup heavy cream

½ cup milk
½ teaspoon pepper
½ teaspoon powdered mustard
1 8-inch pie shell

Crumble bacon. Sprinkle cheese and bacon into pie shell. Beat other ingredients. Mix and pour over the cheese. Bake at 375 degrees for 45 minutes or until firm and browned.

Mrs. Barnwell Gibson (Lita)   *Mrs. Doug Watterson (Jan)*
Bamberg, South Carolina   *Dallas, Texas*

CHEESE PUDDING

9 thin slices of bread
1 stick margarine, melted
¾ pound mild Cheddar
   cheese, grated
2 cups milk

1 teaspoon salt
1 teaspoon mustard
¼ teaspoon red pepper (optional)
3 egg yolks, beaten slightly
3 egg whites

Remove bread crusts and cut bread in cubes. Pour melted margarine over bread in baking dish. Sprinkle cheese over margarine. Pour milk over ingredients. Add remaining ingredients and combine thoroughly. Beat egg whites until stiff and fold into above mixture. Must be refrigerated overnight. Bake at 350 degrees about 20 minutes or until brown. Very good with beef or pork.

Mrs. Dan Page (Elizabeth)
Greenville, South Carolina

PRESIDENT'S FAVORITE CASSEROLE

1 cup soda cracker crumbs
½ pound American cheese, grated
1 7-ounce can pimento, chopped

4 hard boiled eggs, grated
Buttered cracker crumbs
2 cups medium white sauce

In greased 8 x 8 x 2-inch baking dish, place a layer of crumbs and moisten with half of the white sauce. Next place a layer of cheese, pimento, then grated eggs. Repeat the layers; top with buttered crumbs. Bake at 350 degrees for about 25 minutes. NOTE: This dish was served to President Eisenhower at Bardstown, Kentucky, and he thought it was delicious!

Mrs. Cort R. Flint (Ilene)
Meadows of Dan, Virginia

Beef

MANICOTTI ALLA ROMANA

12 Manicotti shells

FILLING

½ stick butter
¼ cup onion, chopped
1 clove garlic, crushed
1 pound ground beef
1 10-ounce package frozen chopped spinach, thawed and drained

½ cup cottage cheese
2 eggs, slightly beaten
1 teaspoon salt

SAUCE

¼ cup butter
1½ teaspoons seasoned chicken stock base
¼ cup all-purpose flour
1½ cups milk

¼ cup chopped parsley
1 15-ounce jar spaghetti sauce with mushrooms
2 teaspoons crushed basil leaves
Parmesan cheese

Cook Manicotti according to package directions; set aside. Prepare filling. Melt butter in skillet. Add onion and garlic, Cook until onion is transparent. Add meat and brown. Remove from heat. Stir in spinach, cottage cheese, eggs and salt. Fill each Manicotti shell with about ¼-cup filling. Place in a 3-quart baking dish. Prepare sauce. In a saucepan melt butter. Blend in flour and chicken stock base. Remove from heat. Stir in milk. Heat to boiling, stirring constantly. Boil and stir 1 minute. Stir in parsley. Pour over Manicotti. Combine spaghetti sauce and basil. Pour over sauce. Sprinkle with Parmesan cheese. Bake in preheated 350 degree oven for 30 minutes. Serves 6.

Mrs. Doug Watterson (Jan)
Dallas, Texas

Whether therefore ye eat, or drink, or whatsoever ye do, do all to the glory of God.
1 Cor. 10:31

SAVORY SPAGHETTI SAUCE

2 pounds ground chuck
1½ cups onion, chopped
2 tablespoons bacon grease
3 6-ounce cans tomato sauce
2¼ cups water
⅛ teaspoon garlic powder
½ cup fresh parsley,
   chopped fine
½ cup celery, chopped

½ cup green pepper
1 tablespoon salt
1 tablespoon sugar
2 tablespoons chili powder
2 teaspoons leaf oregano
¼ teaspoon black pepper
2 bay leaves
¼ teaspoon red pepper
1 stick butter

Brown chuck in bacon grease with onions. Add all ingredients except butter. Simmer, covered, 2 to 4 hours and add butter. Serve with favorite spaghetti and French bread.
Mrs. David Wilbanks (Linda)
Excello, Missouri

BAKED ITALIAN SPAGHETTI

1 large can tomato sauce
1 6-ounce can tomato paste
1 pound lean ground beef
1 large onion, chopped
2 cloves garlic
1½ teaspoons chili powder

3 cups water
1 large bell pepper, chopped
Salt and pepper to taste
8-ounces thin spaghetti
½ pound sharp cheese,
   grated

Brown ground beef, chopped onion and chopped pepper in large skillet. Add remaining ingredients except spaghetti and cheese. Simmer slowly for 2 hours. Add more water if necessary. Cook spaghetti until tender. Rinse with water. Drain. Layer spaghetti in a large casserole alternately with sauce and grated cheese. Just as guests arrive bake at 350 degrees until cheese melts. Serves 8 to 12 people.
Mrs. Herman W. Cobb (Mary)
Cullman, Alabama

SPAGHETTI CASSEROLE

1 pound ground beef	½ teaspoon oregano
½ cup onion, chopped	1 2-ounce can sliced ripe
¾ cup spaghetti, broken into	olives, drained
1-inch pieces	2 cups cheese, grated
1 16-ounce can tomatoes	2 tablespoons parsley,
1 teaspoon garlic salt	minced

Brown beef, onion and spaghetti together, stirring, about 5 minutes. Add tomatoes, garlic salt and oregano and bring to a boil. Simmer for 10 minutes. Stir in olives and cheese and sprinkle parsley on top. Cover and heat 5 minutes.

Mrs. James W. Parker
Santa Ana, California

SPAGHETTI A LA BRUZZI

1 box Kraft Tangy Italian	1 carton cottage cheese
Spaghetti Dinner	1 pound ground beef
1 medium can mushrooms	1 6-ounce can tomato paste
1 package sliced Mozzarella	Garlic salt
cheese	

Cook spaghetti in salted water until tender. Drain. Prepare sauce according to directions on box. Sauté beef until brown. Adding mushrooms, garlic salt and sauce. Place layers of spaghetti, beef sauce, cottage cheese and Mozzarella cheese in casserole. Sprinkle with package of Parmesan cheese. Repeat layers and bake at 350 degrees for 25 minutes or until brown and bubbly.

Mrs. Gilbert E. Barrow (Barbara)
Montgomery, Alabama

POSTAVAZOOLA

1 pound ground beef	1 onion, chopped
1 can red kidney beans	1 bell pepper, chopped
1 package elbow macaroni	Wesson oil
2 cans tomato soup	Salt and pepper to taste

Sauté onion and bell pepper in oil until tender. Brown beef in skillet. Mix together beef, onion and bell pepper. Cook macaroni according to package directions. Drain, leaving a little water. Add meat mixture, beans and soup to macaroni. Season with salt and pepper. Stir and continue cooking until completely hot throughout. Recipe can be prepared ahead. At serving time, bake in 350 degree oven until hot and bubbly.

Dr. Anthony S. Kay
Crestview, Florida

JONNY MAZETTI

2 large onions, chopped
1 stalk celery, chopped
1 package wide egg noodles
2 cans spaghetti sauce
1 small can mushrooms
2 large green peppers, chopped

1½ pounds hamburger
2 cans tomato paste
1 can tomato soup
1 small bottle olives
Grated cheese

Sauté onion, pepper and celery in 2 tablespoons cooking oil. Add hamburger meat. Cook until brown. Stir in tomato paste, spaghetti sauce, tomato soup, mushrooms and olives. Pour noodles into 2 quarts boiling, salted water. Cook 12 minutes. Rinse with cold water. Drain. Add meat sauce mixture to noodles. Mix well. Pour into a greased casserole dish and top with grated cheese. Bake for 35 to 40 minutes in 350 degree oven.

Mrs. Walker Bynum (Permeillia)
Talladega, Alabama

LASAGNE

1 pound Italian sausage or
   ground beef
1 clove garlic
1 tablespoon basil
1½ teaspoons salt
2 6-ounce cans tomato paste
1 tablespoon parsley flakes
1 16-ounce can tomatoes
10-ounce Lasagne noodles

3 cups cream style cottage cheese
2 beaten eggs
2 tablespoons parsley flakes
½ cup Parmesan cheese
2 teaspoons salt
½ teaspoon pepper
1 pound Mozzarella or American
   cheese, sliced very thin

Brown meat slowly in skillet. Add next six ingredients. Simmer 45 minutes, stirring occasionally. Cook noodles in boiling, salted water until tender. Rinse in cold water. Drain. Meanwhile combine cottage cheese with beaten eggs, seasoning and Parmesan cheese. Place half the cooked noodles in a 13x9x2-inch baking dish. Layer noodles, meat, cheese and Mozzarella. Bake at 375 degrees for 30 minutes. Can be made and frozen ahead of time. For smaller families, divide ingredients and make 2 casseroles.

Mrs. John Durham (Judith)
Wake Forest, North Carolina

Mrs. John R. Bisagno (Uldine)
Houston, Texas

BEEF STROGANOFF

½ cup onion, chopped
½ cup celery, chopped
2 tablespoons oil
1 pound round steak, cut in bite size pieces
1 can sliced mushrooms
1 can cream of chicken soup
1 carton sour cream or 1 cup buttermilk
1 tablespoon Worcestershire sauce
Few drops Tabasco sauce
1 can water chestnuts, sliced (optional)
1 teaspoon Beau Monde
Salt and pepper to taste

Sauté celery, onions and mushrooms in oil. Add meat, stirring frequently. When browned, add remaining ingredients. Simmer 20 to 30 minutes. Serve over rice. Serves 6.

Mrs. Tom S. Brandon (Dolly)
Sherman, Texas

Mrs. Glenn Cox
Webbers Falls, Oklahoma

GROUND BEEF STROGANOFF

3 tablespoons margarine
1 pound ground beef
1 teaspoon garlic
1 teaspoon seasoned salt
Salt and pepper to taste
2 stalks celery, diced
1 small onion, diced
½ bell pepper, diced
1 can tomatoes
1 8-ounce package noodles
1 cup sour cream

Melt margarine in skillet. Sauté onions, pepper and celery until soft. Brown ground meat in pan. Add tomatoes and seasonings. Cook noodles as per instructions on package. Add to meat mixture and just before serving add sour cream.

Mrs. Ray W. McClung (Faye)
Little Rock, Arkansas

BAKED STEW

2 pounds lean beef, cut into pieces	1 can sliced mushrooms
2 cups onions, diced	2 teaspoons salt
2 cups potatoes, quartered	½ teaspoon pepper
2 cups carrots, cut in chunks	5 tablespoons tapioca
2 cups celery, cut large	1 teaspoon sugar
	3 cups V-8 juice

Place all ingredients in order given in roaster or Dutch oven with tight fitting lid. Bake at 250 degrees for 5 hours.
No browning necessary. When done, the gravy is thick and brown. Stew may also be cooked on top burner on low heat in a very heavy roaster.

Mrs. Charles Nanney (Rachel) *Mrs. Lonnie Shull (Hazel)*
Newberry, South Carolina *Columbia, South Carolina*

Mrs. James H. Smith (Nona) *Mrs. Earnest Cox (Debbie)*
Alexander, Tennessee *Pensacola, Florida*

Mrs. W. C. Crews, Jr. (Jo Ann)
Tualatin, Oregon

SPANISH BEEF STEW

1 chuck or arm roast, cubed	½ teaspoon thyme
1 or 2 medium onions, sliced thin	4 parsley sprigs
1 or 2 cloves garlic, crushed or whole	1½ cups stuffed olives
3 cups beef bouillon	2½ pounds potatoes, peeled and cubed
1 can tomatoes, quartered	Salt and pepper
1 bay leaf	

Brown meat in large kettle. Remove and season with salt and pepper. Cook onions in drippings and add garlic, bouillon, and ½ can of tomatoes. Add herbs and meat; bring to a boil. Cover and simmer at least 2 hours. Add olives and potatoes and cook 30 more minutes. Thicken with cornstarch. Add water, then tomatoes. Serve with homemade bread.

Mrs. Lavonn D. Brown (Norma)
Norman, Oklahoma

Jesus saith unto them, My meat is to do the will of him that sent me, and to finish his work. John 4:34

NEW ORLEANS STEW

2 pounds hamburger meat
1 can French style green beans
1 can Petit Pois English peas
1 jar stuffed olives
1 16-ounce can tomatoes
1 can tomato sauce

2 medium onions, chopped
1 package elbow or seashell
  macaroni
Salt and pepper to taste
Garlic, minced, to taste

Brown meat with onions. Drain beans and peas. Add to meat mixture. Add olives, tomatoes and tomato sauce. Cook macaroni according to directions on package. Drain. Add to other ingredients. Season with salt and pepper. Place in covered casserole. Bake one hour at 300 degrees. Serves 10 to 12.

Mrs. Frank Gunn (Sandra)
Biloxi, Mississippi

FIVE-HOUR-STEW

2½ pounds stew beef, cubed
3 large carrots, sliced medium
  thick
3 medium potatoes, cut into
  bite-size pieces
1 can garden peas, drained,
  save liquid

3 medium onions, quartered
1 bay leaf
1 teaspoon salt
Dash pepper
½ can tomato soup
½ can cream of mushroom soup
½ liquid from peas

Place first 8 ingredients in casserole. Combine tomato soup, cream of mushroom soup and liquid from peas. Pour soup mixture over casserole. Toss lightly. Cover. Bake 5 hours in 275 degree oven. Delicious and so easy!

Mrs. William Hinson (Bettye)
Fort Lauderdale, Florida

SHIP-WRECK STEW

2 tablespoons shortening	1 can Contadina tomato paste
1 cup onions, minced	2 cans water
1 pound ground beef	3 tablespoons rice
1 cup celery, chopped	1 16-ounce can whole kernel corn
½ cup bell pepper, chopped	Dash oregano, chili powder, and
4 cups white potatoes, diced	cinnamon
1 large can kidney beans	Garlic salt, salt and pepper to taste

Sauté minced onions in 2 tablespoons shortening. Add ground beef. Brown lightly. Add celery, bell pepper, potatoes, kidney beans, tomato paste and water. Sprinkle over rice. Season with oregano, chili powder, and cinnamon. Add garlic salt, salt and pepper to taste. Next add whole kernel corn. Do not stir. Simmer slowly until vegetables are cooked.

Mrs. Orvind Dangeau (Freddie Ann)
Franklin, Tennessee

CORNED BEEF SUPPER CASSEROLE

1 tablespoon cooking oil	¼ teaspoon coarse ground black
1 medium onion, diced	pepper, optional
1 12-ounce can corned beef,	4 cups cooked dry rice,
chilled and diced	long grain
1 can cream of celery or cream	2 medium tomatoes, cut in
of mushroom soup	½-inch slices
¾ cup water	½ cup fine dry bread crumbs
1 teaspoon Gravy Master or	½ cup Cheddar cheese, grated
Kitchen Bouquet	

Sauté onion in cooking oil until golden yellow. Add corned beef. Stir lightly until heated through. Combine soup, water, Gravy Master, and pepper, stirring only to blend. Spread rice in greased 13x9x2-inch baking dish. Spoon corned beef mixture over rice. Top with tomato slices. Sprinkle with bread crumbs and cheese. Bake, covered with foil, at 375 degrees, for 20 minutes. Uncover. Bake an additional 5 minutes to lightly brown tops of tomatoes. Serves 8 generously. Serve casserole with big bowl of carrot-cabbage slaw, garlic toast, beverage, and light fruit dessert. Great!!

Mrs. F. J. Rabideau (Florence)
Jacksonville, Florida

TEXAS HASH

1 onion, chopped	½ cup uncooked rice
1 green pepper, chopped fine	1 teaspoon chili powder
2 tablespoons shortening	1 teaspoon salt
1 pound hamburger meat	¼ teaspoon pepper
2 cups canned tomatoes	

Cook onion and pepper in shortening. Add hamburger meat. Brown until mixture falls apart. Stir in the tomatoes and uncooked rice. Season with chili powder, salt and pepper. Put in covered casserole. Bake at 375 degrees for 45 minutes.

Mrs. Jimmie E. Harley (Gayle)   *Mrs. Gloria Singleton*
Greenville, South Carolina   *Rankin, Texas*

SMOKED BRISKET OF BEEF
CROCK POT METHOD

2 pounds beef brisket	1 can cream of mushroom soup
4 medium white potatoes	Salt and pepper to taste
6 carrots	Liquid smoke flavoring
2 medium onions	

Line crock pot with heavy duty foil. Salt and pepper brisket of beef. Place in foil. Pour liquid smoke flavoring over meat. Pare potatoes, carrots and onions. Place on top of meat. Cover with one can cream of mushroom soup. Fold and seal the foil. Cover. Set crock pot on high for 1 to 2 hours. Turn pot on low. Continue cooking 8 to 10 hours. Thicken juice for gravy. Start beef to cooking on Saturday night and let cook until after church on Sunday for a yummy and convenient Sunday dinner.

Mrs. Carey J. Miller (Doris)
Aurora, Colorado

BARBECUE BRISKET

5 pounds beef brisket, 1½-inch
  to 2-inch thick
3 tablespoons enriched flour
1 teaspoon salt
Pepper

¼ teaspoon garlic salt
1 tablespoon brown sugar
¾ cup catsup
1½ tablespoons Worcestershire sauce
1 tablespoon vinegar

Brown brisket in 2 tablespoons oil in heavy skillet over medium heat. Mix ingredients for sauce. On heavy foil place one half of sauce. Place browned brisket on sauce. Cover top of brisket with remaining sauce. Fold over foil and seal sides and top. Place on a rack in baking pan and bake in 350 degree oven for 3½ to 4 hours. Adolphs Meat Tenderizer may be used before browning.
Mrs. Tom S. Brandon (Dolly)
Sherman, Texas

BARBECUED CHUCK ROAST

3 pounds chuck roast, 1½ to
  2-inch thick
1 teaspoon monosodium
  glutamate
⅓ cup vinegar
¼ cup catsup
2 tablespoons cooking oil,
  (optional)

2 tablespoons soy sauce
1 tablespoon Worcestershire
  sauce
1 teaspoon prepared mustard
1 teaspoon salt
¼ teaspoon pepper
¼ teaspoon garlic powder

Sprinkle both sides of roast with monosodium glutamate. Place in shallow baking dish. Thoroughly combine vinegar, catsup, cooking oil, soy sauce, Worcestershire sauce, mustard, salt, pepper and garlic powder. Pour mixture over roast and marinate for 2 to 3 hours, turning once or twice. Place roast on grill or broiler pan and broil about 6 inches from heat. Turn roast and baste with marinade every 10 to 15 minutes. Broil 35 to 45 minutes for a medium rare roast or until desired doneness. Makes 6 to 8 servings. Note: Roast is good cooked in the oven uncovered about 3 hours at 300 degrees or in crock pot for 8 hours on low.
Mrs. Bronson Wiggins (Gwen)
Reading, Ohio

BARBECUED MEATBALLS

1 pound lean hamburger meat
1 cup quick oats
½ cup milk

1 teaspoon salt
Pepper to taste

Soak oats in milk to soften. Add all ingredients. Mix well. Form into walnut size balls. Place in baking dish. Pour sauce over them. Bake in 375 degree oven for 1 hour.

BARBECUE SAUCE
½ cup catsup
½ cup water
¼ cup vinegar
1½ tablespoons Worcestershire
   sauce

1 tablespoon sugar
½ medium onion, chopped fine
¼ green pepper, chopped

Mix all ingredients. Blend well. Pour over meatballs.
Mrs. M. E. Gibson (Mary)
Wilmington, North Carolina

Mrs. Gary Cook
Salpupa, Oklahoma

MUSHROOM MEATBALLS

1 pound ground beef
1 can Cream of Mushroom Soup
½ cup fine dry bread crumbs
2 tablespoons minced onion

1 tablespoon minced parsley
   (optional)
1 egg, slightly beaten
¼ teaspoon salt

Blend 1 can mushroom soup with ½ cup water. Measure ¼ cup of the soup mixture. Combine with ground beef, bread crumbs, minced onion, minced parsley, egg and salt. Shape into meatballs about 1¼-inches in diameter. Brown in 1 tablespoon shortening in a large skillet. Add remaining soup mixture. Cover and cook over low heat about 15 minutes, stirring occasionally. Serves 4.
Mrs. Howard Golden
Phenix City, Alabama

PORCUPINE MEATBALLS

1 pound ground beef
½ cup uncooked rice
1½ teaspoons salt
½ cup sugar
⅛ teaspoon pepper

1 small onion, sliced
½ green pepper, sliced
1 tablespoon shortening
2½ cups tomato sauce
¼ teaspoon nutmeg

Combine beef, rice, salt and pepper. Form into small balls. Place in baking dish. In a skillet brown onions and green pepper in shortening. Add tomato sauce, nutmeg, salt and pepper to taste. Pour over meatballs. Cover baking dish. Bake at 350 degrees for 1 hour.
Mrs. Harry Foley
Mesa, Arizona

BARBECUED HAMBURGER

1 pound hamburger meat
2 cups onion, chopped
1 tablespoon mustard
2 tablespoons brown sugar

1 tablespoon vinegar
1 tablespoon Worcestershire
  sauce
½ cup catsup

Brown hamburger and onions in skillet. Mix remaining ingredients. Pour over meat and onions and simmer until done.
Mrs. Ronald P. Liesmann (Eunice)
Bloomington, Indiana

SKEENBURGERS

1¼ pounds hamburger meat
¼ cup Ritz crackers, crumbled
¼ cup applesauce
1¼ teaspoons Accent
¾ teaspoon Tabasco sauce

1¼ tablespoons Worcestershire
  sauce
¼ envelope Lipton onion soup mix
Salt to taste
Dash garlic

Mix all ingredients together. Form into patties. Serve on hamburger buns. Also good grilled.
Mrs. G. T. Patterson (Daisy)
Asheboro, North Carolina

DELUXE MEAT LOAF

2 medium stalks celery, chopped	¼ teaspoon pepper
1 medium onion, minced	½ teaspoon sage
1 medium carrot, minced	1 tablespoon Worcestershire
2 strips bacon, finely diced	sauce
1 medium green pepper, minced	1 cup milk
½ teaspoon celery flakes	2 eggs
½ teaspoon dry mustard	1 cup herb seasoned stuffing mix
¼ teaspoon garlic powder	1 pound lean ground beef
1 tablespoon soy sauce	1 small can mushrooms, diced
½ teaspoon salt	1 small can tomato sauce

Combine all ingredients except beef. Mix well. Let stand 30 minutes to 1 hour. Add beef. Mix thoroughly. Spoon into greased 8x5x3-inch loaf pan. Bake at 350 degrees for 1 hour and 15 minutes. Top with tomato sauce last 15 minutes of baking time, or serve hot tomato sauce separately.
Mrs. Lee Morris (Gerry)
Oak Ridge, Tennessee

FILLED MEAT LOAF

1½ pounds ground beef	½ teaspoon sage
⅓ cup onion, chopped	¼ teaspoon dry mustard
3 tablespoons celery, finely chopped	¼ teaspoon pepper
	1 tablespoon Worcestershire
1 cup corn flakes	½ cup sliced stuffed olives
½ to 1 cup milk	1 cup sour cream
2 eggs, beaten	1 cup Cheddar cheese,
2 teaspoons salt	shredded

Mix all ingredients thoroughly. Place on waxed paper about 18-inches long. Pat out meat mixture ¼-inch thick. Spread with 1 cup sour cream. Sprinkle with 1 cup shredded Cheddar cheese and ½ cup sliced stuffed olives. Roll as a jelly roll. Lift end of paper. With a spatula, gently pry the mixture from the paper, turning to form a roll. Place in greased baking pan. Bake at 350 degrees for 45 minutes to 1 hour. Serves 8.
Mrs. Bill Moore (Sue)
Houston, Texas

BARBECUED MEAT LOAF

1½ pounds lean ground beef
1 cup fresh bread crumbs
1 onion, finely chopped
1 egg
1½ teaspoons salt
¼ teaspoon pepper

2 small cans tomato sauce
½ cup water
3 tablespoons vinegar
3 tablespoons brown sugar
2 tablespoons prepared mustard
2 teaspoons Worcestershire sauce

Mix together beef, crumbs, onion, beaten egg, salt, pepper and ½ can tomato sauce. Form into loaf and put in shallow 7x10-inch pan. Combine the rest of sauce and all other ingredients. Pour over loaf. Bake in moderate oven at 350 degrees for 1 hour and 15 minutes. Baste occasionally. Serves 4 to 6.

Mrs. Robert E. Galloway (Essie)
Pineville, Louisiana

MEAT LOAF AU GRATIN

2 pounds lean ground meat
¾ cup soft bread crumbs
½ cup tomato juice
2 tablespoons parsley
1 teaspoon oregano

¼ teaspoon salt
¼ teaspoon pepper
6 to 8 slices boiled ham
¾ pound or 1½ cups Mozzarella
   cheese, grated

Mix all ingredients except ham and cheese. Roll out on waxed paper to 12x10-inch. Line with ham slices, leaving small margin on all sides. Sprinkle ham with cheese. Start from small end; roll up like a jelly roll; seal edges; place seam-side down. Place in baking dish 350 degrees for 1¼ hours. Garnish with slices of cheese on top. May be returned to oven until cheese melts.

Mrs. Don Watterson (Joan)
Montgomery, Alabama

CHEROKEE CASSEROLE

1 pound ground beef
1 tablespoon olive oil
¾ cup Bermuda onion, chopped
1 teaspoon salt
Dash pepper
⅛ teaspoon garlic powder
⅛ teaspoon ground thyme
½ small bay leaf

⅛ teaspoon oregano
1 16-ounce can tomatoes
1 can cream of mushroom soup
1 cup Minute Rice
6 stuffed olives, sliced
2 or 3 slices American cheese, cut in strips

Brown meat in olive oil. Add onion. Cook over medium heat until onion is tender. Stir in seasonings, tomatoes, soup, and rice. Add half of olive slices. Simmer 5 minutes, stirring occasionally. Spoon into baking dish. Top with cheese strips. Heat in 350 degree oven until cheese is melted. Decorate with remaining olive slices. Serves 4 to 6.

Mrs. Glenna Wheeler
Pawcatuck, Connecticut

NEAPOLITAN CASSEROLE

1 pound ground beef
½ green pepper, chopped
1 onion, chopped
½ teaspoon salt
¼ teaspoon pepper
½ teaspoon paprika
1 teaspoon Worcestershire sauce

½ package broad noodles (more if desired)
¼ cup Parmesan cheese
3 tablespoons butter
1 can tomato soup
1 cup water

Sauté green pepper and onion in butter over medium heat. Add beef. Brown. Spatula break beef into small pieces. Cook noodles in boiling water. Add salt. Drain. Combine soup, water, salt, pepper, paprika and Worcestershire sauce. Add meat mixture. Pour ½ meat mixture into 2-quart casserole. Cover with a layer of noodles. Spread the remainder of meat mixture over noodles. Sprinkle with cheese. Bake in preheated oven at 375 degrees for 30 minutes.

Mrs. Gail Gunter
Belvedere, South Carolina

Mrs. Orrin Barrett (Margaret)
Dothan, Alabama

GROUND BEEF CASSEROLE

1½ pounds lean ground beef
1 cup onions, chopped
1 12-ounce can whole kernel
  corn, drained
1 can cream of Cheddar soup
1 cup sour cream
¼ cup pimento, chopped

½ teaspoon salt
½ teaspoon pepper
3 cups noodles, cooked
1 cup cracker crumbs, crushed
½ cup Cheddar cheese, grated
3 tablespoons margarine

Brown meat. Add onions. Cook until tender. Add first 8 ingredients. Pour into greased casserole dish. Sprinkle with cracker crumbs. Spread grated cheese on top. Dot with margarine. Bake 30 minutes at 350 degrees.

Mrs. Dennis Lyle (Ressa)
Nashville, Tennessee

Mrs. John T. Davis (Georgia)
Monroe, North Carolina

Mrs. R. A. Herrington (Myrtle)
Louisville, Mississippi

Mrs. Bobby W. Barnett (Mary)
Bradford, Rhode Island

A GOOD DISH

1 number 2½ can peeled tomatoes
1 large onion, chopped
1 pound lean ground meat
1½ teaspoons salt
½ teaspoon pepper

¼ teaspoon garlic powder
2 to 3 cups cheese, shredded
1 regular size package elbow
  macaroni or noodles

Break up ground meat in skillet and cook slowly, stirring until cooked through. Add onion and cook until soft. Add tomatoes and seasonings. Simmer for about 20 minutes or until mixture cooks down and thickens. Stir frequently. Cook macaroni according to package directions. Rinse and drain thoroughly. Into deep casserole spoon layer of macaroni, then a layer of meat mixture. Top with cheese. Bake in 350 degree oven until heated through and the cheese is melted. Serves 6.

Mrs. Howard H. Ramsey (Lawonda)
Tigard, Oregon

Mrs. Henry B. Stokes (Etta)
Buies Creek, North Carolina

HAMBURGER PIE

1 pound ground beef
1 medium onion, chopped
½ small bottle catsup
½ cup Carnation milk
½ cup bread crumbs
1 teaspoon chili powder

¼ teaspoon black pepper
1 teaspoon salt
1 tablespoon Worcestershire sauce
1 cup Cheddar cheese, shredded
1 pie shell, unbaked

Brown onion and meat. Drain in colander. Return to skillet. Add remaining ingredients except cheese. Cook slowly about 15 minutes. Pour in pie shell. Bake 20 to 25 minutes in 350 degree oven. Sprinkle cheese on top the last 5 minutes of cooking time.
Mrs. John A. Grant (Lois)
Charlotte, North Carolina

BEEF CASSEROLE

2 pounds hamburger meat
1 bell pepper, chopped
1 large onion, chopped
Salt and pepper to taste
Garlic salt to taste
1 16-ounce can tomatoes

1 small can tomato sauce
1 large package macaroni
1 8-ounce package cream cheese
1 cup sour cream
Cheese, grated

Brown meat. Sauté onion and bell pepper. Add to meat. Season meat mixture to taste. Pour tomatoes and sauce over meat mixture. Simmer. Cook macaroni in salted water according to package directions. Drain. While macaroni is hot, add sour cream and cream cheese. Stir until melted. Pour over meat mixture in buttered casserole. Grate cheese and sprinkle on top. Bake at 350 degrees until cheese melts.

Mrs. Bonner C. Magness (Beth)
Liberty, Texas

Mrs. Bobby Moore (Joyce)
Memphis, Tennessee

Mrs. Forest H. Siler (Evelyn)
Lawton, Oklahoma

Mrs. John R. Riddle (Tommye)
Birmingham, Alabama

Mrs. Elbert L. Smithen, Jr. (Jo)
Midland, Texas

Mrs. James E. Carter (Ginger)
Phoenix, Arizona

All did eat the same spiritual meat;
And all did drink the same spiritual drink: for they drank of that spiritual Rock that followed them: and that Rock was Christ. 1 Cor. 10:3-4

TALLERINE
WHOLE MEAL IN ONE

1½ pound ground beef
1 medium onion, chopped
1 can cream style corn
1 can small peas
1 can tomato sauce or tomatoes
Salt and pepper to taste

1 package wide noodles
1 tablespoon ground cumin
3 tablespoons Worcestershire sauce
1 teaspoon Tabasco pepper sauce
½ teaspoon garlic (optional)
1 cup Longhorn cheese, grated

Brown ground beef in skillet. Sauté onion. Add to ground meat. Mix in Worcestershire, Tabasco, cumin, garlic and tomato sauce. Cook noodles in salted water according to package directions. Drain. Place noodles in casserole dish. Stir corn and peas into meat mixture. Pour over noodles. Mix well. Sprinkle grated cheese on top. Cover and bake 30 minutes at 350 degrees. To freeze and serve later, cover with foil. Save cheese and sprinkle on top just before baking.

Mrs. H. E. Alsup (Willie Lou)
Haysville, Kansas

Mrs. Tom Thompson (Kathy)
Pensacola, Florida

BEEF AND CORN BREAD SUPPER

1½ pounds lean ground beef
1 10-ounce can cream of
  asparagus soup
¼ cup onion, finely chopped
2 teaspoons Worcestershire sauce
¾ cup all purpose flour, sifted

½ cup corn meal
1 tablespoon baking powder
1 teaspoon salt
¼ cup shortening, melted
⅔ cup milk
Green pepper rings

Preheat oven to 425 degrees. Brown ground beef in a 10-inch cast iron skillet. Add soup, onion, and Worcestershire sauce. Simmer for about 5 minutes. Sift the flour, corn meal, baking powder and salt together in medium bowl. Add shortening and milk. Beat until smooth. Pour over ground beef mixture. Spread with narrow spatula to within 2 inches of edge. Top with green pepper rings. Bake 15 or 20 minutes. Serves 6. And do set the skillet on the table. Serve with a salad.

Mrs. J. L. Bryson (Dottie)
Mt. Airy, North Carolina

COUNTRY GARDEN CASSEROLE

2 cups raw potatoes, sliced	¼ cup green pepper, chopped
1 cup celery, diced	
1 cup carrots, sliced	1 cup canned tomatoes
1 pound ground beef	2 teaspoons salt
½ cup onions, chopped	4 tablespoons butter

Place potatoes in bottom of 1½-quart casserole dish. Sprinkle with salt and butter. Add carrots and celery. Season with salt and butter. Use 2 tablespoons butter in skillet, cooking meat until the red disappears. Arrange beef over carrots and celery. Sauté onions and pepper over medium heat. Arrange over meat mixture. Pour tomatoes over top. Dot with margarine. Cover. Bake at 400 degrees for 45 minutes.
Mrs. Joe Abram
Sylacauga, Alabama

CHILI DELICIOUS

1 to 2 pounds ground round	2 16-ounce cans tomatoes, chopped
2 tablespoons margarine	
1 cup onion, chopped	1 16-ounce can red kidney beans
1 tablespoon salt	
3 tablespoons chili powder (only 2 tablespoons if extra hot)	1 bean can water

Brown ground beef in margarine. Add onion and cook on low heat about 15 minutes. Add salt and chili powder. Cook another 15 minutes. Add chopped tomatoes. Turn heat to high. Pour in kidney beans and water. When boiling well, turn heat back to low. Simmer 30 minutes. Serve in soup bowls with crackers. Delicious! Also great served on hot dogs. Top with chopped onion and pickle relish.

Mrs. Joe Barnette (Ann)   *Mrs. Tom M. Jones (Mary)*
Charlotte, North Carolina   *Travelers Rest, South Carolina*

Mrs. Glenn Cox
Webbers Falls, Oklahoma

For I was hungered, and ye gave me meat; I was thirsty, and ye gave me drink; I was a stranger, and ye took me in. Matt. 25:35

CREAM TACOS

1½ pounds hamburger	1 can tomatoes and green chiles
1 onion, chopped	1 tall can milk
Salt and pepper to taste	1 cup Longhorn cheese, grated
1 can Enchilada sauce	6 Taco shells, uncooked

Brown hamburger with chopped onion. Add salt and pepper to taste. Add Enchilada sauce, tomatoes, green chiles, milk and grated cheese. Heat until cheese is melted. In long baking pan, put 6 Taco shells, uncooked, then ½ of mixture; layer of Taco shells and remaining mixture. Bake at 300 degrees for 30 minutes. A tossed salad and corn complete the meal.
Mrs. John Zobel
Topeka, Kansas

BEEF AND RICE ALMONDINE

1 pound ground meat	1 small onion, chopped
1 can cream of chicken soup	½ cup rice, uncooked
1 beef bouillon cube	1 teaspoon soy sauce
1 cup water	⅛ teaspoon oregano
1 cup celery, sliced	½ cup toasted almonds

Brown meat. Drain off fat. Stir in soup, bouillon cube, water, celery, onion, rice, soy sauce and oregano. Heat to boiling. Crush bouillon cube. Pour into baking dish. Cover. Bake 30 minutes at 350 degrees. Uncover. Sprinkle almonds on top. Bake 15 minutes longer or until golden brown.
Mrs. Elbert L. Smithen, Jr. (Jo)
Midland, Texas

SOMETHIN' FOR SUPPER BURGER SOUP

½ pound ground beef	1 10-ounce package frozen mixed
1 1-pound can stewed tomatoes	vegetables
1 8-ounce package tomato sauce	½ envelope dry onion soup mix
2 cups water	1 teaspoon sugar

In Dutch oven or large heavy saucepan, lightly brown beef; drain off excess fat. Stir in tomatoes, tomato sauce, water, frozen vegetables, onion soup mix and sugar. Bring to a boil. Reduce heat, cover and simmer at least 30 minutes, or longer. Excellent for crock pots. Makes 6 servings.
Mrs. James E. Carter (Ginger)
Phoenix, Arizona

HOMEMADE TAMALE PIE

2 pounds ground beef	1½ tablespoons chili powder
1½ cups corn meal	or season to taste
2 cans tomato paste	1 onion
4 cups water, boiling	

Fry ground beef slowly in heavy skillet. Add chopped onion, tomato paste and chili powder. Mix thoroughly. Prepare corn meal mush by adding the corn meal and salt to the boiling water, stirring constantly. Line pan with mush. Cover with a thick layer of beef mixture, then another of mush and another of beef. Bake slowly for 30 minutes at 350 degrees. Serve hot.

Mrs. Wallace Mitchell (Faye)
Gonzalez, Florida

ENCHILADA CASSEROLE

2 pounds ground chuck	1 can Enchilada sauce
1 large onion, chopped	½ teaspoon chili powder
½ to 1 teaspoon garlic salt	1 pound Velveeta cheese, grated
1 can cream of mushroom soup	½ pound sharp cheese, grated
1 can cream of chicken soup	12 tortillas

Cook ground meat, simmering until done. Tear tortillas in large baking dish. Layer ingredients. Bake 45 minutes at 325 degrees covered, and 15 minutes, uncovered.

Mrs. Landrum Leavell (Jo Ann)   *Mrs. Ed B. Bowles (Nell)*
New Orleans, Louisiana   *Beaumont, Texas*

Mrs. Bill Sprinkle   *Mrs. Dan Stringer (Harriet)*
Balmorhea, Texas   *Tigard, Oregon*

Mrs. Kenneth W. Nichols
Tatum, Texas

ENCHILADA PIE

1 package tortilla chips	2 medium onions, chopped
2 cans chili (no beans)	1 cup Cheddar cheese, grated

Grease two quart casserole. Layer torn tortilla pieces with canned chili, chopped onions and grated cheese. Begin with tortillas on bottom and end with the cheese and onion on top. Bake, uncovered, at 350 degrees for 45 minutes or less. Serves 4 generously.

Mrs. Robert J. Potts (Dorothy)
Columbus, Georgia

JEANETTE'S ENCHILADA CASSEROLE

1 pound hamburger	1 onion, chopped
1 dozen corn meal tortillas	½ pound Longhorn cheese, grated
1 recipe Enchilada sauce,	Salt and pepper
heated	Garlic salt (optional)

Cook hamburger in small amount of water till done. Add salt and pepper. Dip tortillas in sauce; place in 2-quart shallow Pyrex dish. Cover bottom of dish with dipped tortillas. Sprinkle ⅓ hamburger, onion and cheese over the tortillas, adding more sauce by spoonfuls before beginning the next layer. Repeat process until meat, cheese, and onion are used. Should be about 3 layers. Bake in 350 degree oven 30 minutes or can be served immediately. Serve with crackers, Fritos, or Tortos.

Mrs. Charles Casey (Jeanette)
Silver Spring, Maryland

CHILI RELLENOS CASSEROLE

1 pound ground beef	¼ cup flour
½ cup onion, chopped	½ teaspoon salt
2 4-ounce cans green chilis,	4 eggs, beaten
cut in half and seeded	1½ cups milk
1½ cups sharp natural cheddar	Pepper to taste
cheese, shredded	Dash hot sauce

Brown meat and onion; drain fat. Add salt and pepper. Place half of the chilis in 10x6x1½-inch baking dish. Sprinkle with cheese and top with meat. Arrange remaining chilis over meat. Combine remaining ingredients and beat until smooth. Pour over chili-meat mixture. Bake in 350 degree oven for 45 minutes. Serves 6.

Mrs. Cort R. Flint (Ilene)
Meadows of Dan, Virginia

MEXICAN GOULASH

3 pounds ground chuck
1 small onion
2 7-ounce cans Salsa
   (red sauce)

1 7-ounce can water
1 cup instant rice
1 can chopped green chilis,
   optional

Brown ground meat. Sauté onion and mix with meat. Add remaining ingredients and simmer until rice is done. Serves 8. To serve: Line up meat mixture, regular size Fritos, tossed green salad and grated cheese on buffet. Let guests layer these on plate as they go through the line. A hit with college students!
Mrs. Lavonn D. Brown (Norma)
Norman, Oklahoma

FIESTA

2 bags Fritos, rolled
1 large box instant rice, cooked
Chili sauce
1 pound sharp Cheddar cheese,
   grated
2 heads lettuce, torn apart
7 tomatoes, diced

3 onions, chopped
1 jar Spanish olives, chopped or
   Salad olives
10 to 12-ounces pecans, chopped
7 to 8-ounces coconut
1 bottle hot sauce
3 packages Taco flavored Doritos

Spread food buffet style. Layer ingredients in order given, except Doritos. Use Doritos as an accompaniment. Serve cake and Peppermint ice cream with peppermint candy as dessert. Serves 16 to 20.

CHILI SAUCE
4 pounds hamburger
3 onions, chopped
2 cans tomatoes
1 large can tomato sauce
2 small cans tomato puree

4 tablespoons chili powder
2-3 tablespoons powdered garlic
   or garlic salt
1 large can Ranch style beans

Cook meat and onion till brown. Add all other ingredients. Cover and simmer 1 hour, stirring as necessary. Add water if needed. May be frozen.
Mrs. Eugene A. Perry (Raneal)
Lone Grove, Oklahoma

ELDORADO CASSEROLE

1 package Doritos	1 cup cottage cheese
1 pound ground beef	1 cup sour cream
1 medium onion	2 cups Jacks cheese, grated
2 small cans tomato sauce	2 or 3 hot peppers or hot pepper
Salt and pepper to taste	sauce to taste
Garlic salt to taste	

Crumble Doritos in bottom of 9x12-inch dish. Brown ground beef and onion together. Season with salt, pepper and garlic salt. Add tomato sauce. Put ground beef mixture on top of Doritos. Mix together sour cream, cottage cheese and the chopped hot peppers. Pour over meat mixture. Top with grated cheese. Cover with foil. Bake at 350 degrees for 30 minutes.

Mrs. Billy Haggard (Wilma)
Oklahoma City, Oklahoma

ENCHILADA SAUCE

2 tablespoons shortening or oil	1 teaspoon garlic powder
	3 tablespoons chili powder
2 heaping tablespoons flour	1 teaspoon cumin powder
1 large can or 2 small cans tomato sauce	1 teaspoon salt
	1 teaspoon pepper

Heat oil in 2-quart saucepan. Stir in flour. Add tomato sauce and the same amount of water. Blend till smooth. In a small amount of water prepare remaining ingredients. Add to cooking mixture and stir well. Spices may be varied according to individual preferences.

Mrs. Charles Casey (Jeanette)
Silver Spring, Maryland

MEXICAN STEAK

4 pounds sirloin tip roast, boneless	4 fresh long green chilies, sliced or 4-ounce can green chilies
3 large onions, sliced	Salt and pepper to taste
4 large tomatoes, sliced	

Slice meat in ½-inch slices, then into 4-inch strips. Sprinkle pepper generously on both sides and press into meat. Sear each strip on both sides no longer than 1-inch. In roasting pan (or crockpot) layer onions, tomatoes, chilies and meat. Salt lightly. Repeat, ending with vegetables, as many layers as needed. Cover and cook on top of stove, simmering, for 30 minutes or if in crockpot, until *you're* ready!

Mrs. Chester C. O'Brien, Jr. (Bonnie)
Albuquerque, New Mexico

HAWAIIAN TERIYAKI

1   2 to 3 pound steak   Bananas
1   fresh pineapple

SAUCE:

½ cup Kikoman soy sauce   3   tablespoons sugar
¼ cup vinegar   3   tablespoons honey
1   teaspoon ground ginger   ½ cup water
½ teaspoon garlic powder

Combine ingredients. Pour the mixture over steak. Let marinate several hours. Broil meat quickly as desired. Cut fresh pineapple into slices, large bananas in half. Baste fruit with small amount of teriyaki sauce. Place fruit on grill when meat is almost done. If extra sauce is desired, heat left over marinade in a saucepan to spoon over meat. Serve with steamed rice and a green vegetable.

Mrs. Marvin Howard (Kitty)
Pensacola, Florida

SUKIYAKI
(Cook in Electric Skillet or Wok at the table)

1¼ pound round steak, slice   2   tablespoons butter
    diagonally very, very thin

Sauté slowly for 10 minutes. Then add the following, also cut diagonally and cook slowly for 5 minutes. (Vegetables should be crisp.)

2   onions, cut in ½-inch slices,   4 or 5 stalks celery
    then each slice cut in half   1   small head celery cabbage
12 to 16 green onions, including   ¼ cup Kikoman soy sauce
    tops   1   bouillon cube plus ¼ cup water
½ pound medium-sized   Salt to taste
    mushrooms   ⅓ bag fresh spinach

Serve over rice.

Mrs. Marvin Howard (Kitty)
Pensacola, Florida

STEAK ON TOAST

1 small box macaroni
1 medium round steak, cut in serving pieces
1 can golden mushroom soup

½ soup can water
1 pound Cheddar cheese, grated
Salt and pepper to taste
Flour for coating steak

Cook macaroni according to package directions. Set aside. Season round steak. Coat with flour. Brown steak in hot oil. Mix golden mushroom soup with one half can water. Cook until creamy. Put ½ macaroni in large baking dish. Cover with ½ steak, ½ mushroom soup and ½ cheese. Repeat process using remaining ingredients. Bake at 350 degrees until cheese is toasted.

Mrs. Kenneth Bailey (Faye)
Wake Forest, North Carolina

JAPANESE PEPPER STEAK

2 pounds steak
4 tablespoons oil
½ cup scallions or onions
2 cloves garlic, minced
5 green peppers, thinly sliced
1 cup celery, sliced

1½ cups beef broth
2 tablespoons cornstarch
¼ cup water
2 tablespoons Kikoman soy sauce
Boiled white rice

Cut meat in narrow strips. Brown steak in oil; add the scallions, garlic, green peppers and celery. Cook 5 minutes. And the broth. Cover and cook over low heat 10 minutes. Mix the cornstarch, water and soy sauce until smooth and add to the mixture, stirring steadily until it reaches the boiling point. Cook 2 minutes and serve on rice. Serves 6 to 8.

Mrs. Marvin Howard (Kitty)
Pensacola, Florida

SPAMISH CASSEROLE

1 can spam, grated or ground
½ pound sharp cheese, shredded
1 green pepper, chopped
20 saltine crackers, crumbled
3 eggs, beaten

1 small can evaporated milk
1 can cream of mushroom soup
1 onion, chopped
Dash pepper — no salt

Mix all ingredients, adding beaten eggs last. Place in 2-quart casserole. Bake at 350 degrees for 50 minutes or until firm.

Mrs. Buren Higdon (Polly)
Union City, California

BEAR BARBECUE

Cook a bear roast or bear steak in oven or pressure pan until tender. Cool and slice very thin. Alternate layers of bear and sauce, ending with sauce. Cover and bake at 325 degrees for 1 to 1½ hours until sauce has thick and dark brown appearance.

SAUCE (2 cups)

2 tablespoons honey	1 tablespoon dried minced
1 tablespoon paprika	onion
1 teaspoon salt	¼ cup vinegar
1 teaspoon dry mustard	1 cup tomato juice
¼ teaspoon chili powder	¼ cup catsup
⅛ teaspoon cayenne pepper	¼ tablespoon liquid smoke
2 tablespoons Worcestershire	½ cup water
sauce	

Mix in saucepan. Simmer until hot, then pour over meat.
Mrs. Randall Thetford (Priscilla)
Coeur D'Alene, Idaho

Pork

PORK CHOP AND POTATO CASSEROLE

6 pork chops	1 can cream of chicken soup
4 medium potatoes	Salt and pepper
1 medium onion	

Salt and pepper pork chops to taste and brown in hot fat. Place sliced potatoes in 1½-quart baking dish. Salt and pepper potatoes to taste. Arrange browned pork chops on top of potatoes. Slice onion on top of potatoes. Pour cream of chicken soup over sliced onion. Cover dish and bake in a 350 degree oven 1½ hours. Soup makes delicious gravy on potatoes as it cooks.
Mrs. Charles R. Barnes (Laura)
Severna Park, Maryland

PORK CHOP PRIDE

6 lean pork chops
Squash, thinly sliced
Tomatoes, sliced
Onions, sliced

Potatoes, sliced
Pats of butter
1 cup water

Salt and pepper 6 lean pork chops to taste. Using a deep rectangular glass pan, lay the pork chops in the pan together. Add a layer of thinly sliced squash, a layer of sliced tomatoes, a layer of sliced onions and a layer of thinly sliced potatoes. Put pats of butter on top. Pour 1 cup of water over the ingredients. Make aluminum foil tent and cover the pan. Cook at 325 degrees for 1 to 1½ hours.
Mrs. David Shofner (Myra)
Pensacola, Florida

PARTY FANCY BAKED PORK CHOPS

6 to 8 lean pork chops
1 cup rice, partly cooked
2 large tomatoes

2 large onions
2 green peppers

Lightly brown chops on each side. Place in baking dish. Put one table-spoon rice on each chop. Place a slice of onion, a slice of tomato and a green pepper ring on top of rice. Salt to taste. Bake, covered, about one to one and a half hours at 350 degrees. Add enough water while cooking to prevent scorching.
Mrs. C. Wray Ivey
Swainsboro, Georgia

Mrs. John B. Cunningham (Isobel)
Calgary, Alberta Canada

PORK CHOPS WITH AMBER RICE

6 or 8 pork chops
1⅓ cups precooked rice

1 cup orange juice
1 can chicken with rice soup

Brown pork chops. Place 1⅓ cups Minute Rice in oblong baking dish. Pour 1 cup orange juice over rice. Place in chops. Pour chicken with rice soup over rice and chops. Brown in oven at 350 degrees.
Mrs. Donald V. Wideman (Marian)
Kansas City, Missouri

GLAZED APRICOT PORK CHOPS

Salt	5 teaspoons Worcestershire sauce
6 thick pork chops	1 tablespoon cornstarch
1 5½-ounce can apricot nectar	Generous pinch of cinnamon

Sprinkle salt lightly in bottom of a large skillet. Heat until a drop of water sizzles. Add chops and brown well on both sides. Cover tightly. Cook over low heat until tender, about 30 minutes. Combine remaining ingredients. Pour over chops. Cook, uncovered, until chops are glazed and sauce is thickened. Garnish with apricot halves if desired.
Mrs. James W. Parker
Santa Ana, California

BARBECUED PORK CHOPS

4 pork chops	Juice of ½ lemon
2 tablespoons fat	2 tablespoons brown sugar
½ teaspoon salt	½ teaspoon dry mustard
2 cans Hunt's tomato sauce	⅛ teaspoon pepper
½ cup celery, finely chopped	

Brown chops in fat. Place in shallow baking dish. Combine remaining ingredients. Pour over chops. Cover dish and bake in 350 degree oven 1¼ hours, or until tender, basting occasionally. Serves 4.
Mrs. C. H. Sutherland (Aileen)
Travelers Rest, South Carolina

SKILLET PORK CHOPS

4 to 6 pork chops	1½ cups water
2 tablespoons corn oil	2 tablespoons brown sugar
¼ cup celery, sliced	1 teaspoon salt
¼ cup onion, chopped	½ teaspoon basil
2 8-ounce cans tomato sauce	1 cup regular rice, uncooked

In large skillet brown chops in hot oil. Remove chops. Cook celery and onion in hot oil until clear. Drain oil from skillet. Stir in remaining ingredients. Add chops. Simmer, covered, about 30 minutes or until chops are done.
Mrs. Wallace Henley (Irene)
Spanish Fort, Alabama

These wait all upon thee; that thou mayest give them their meat in due season.
Ps. 104:27

PORK CHOP DINNER

6 lean pork chops	3 medium onions
2 tablespoons shortening	6 carrots
Salt and pepper to taste	6 small potatoes
¼ teaspoon savory	6 cabbage wedges
1 cup tomato juice	Paprika

Lightly brown pork chops in shortening. Salt and pepper to taste. Sprinkle well with savory. Add tomato juice. Cover and simmer 45 minutes. Prepare vegetables and add to pork chops. Sprinkle with paprika and salt. Cook until vegetables are tender, about 30 minutes at 350 degrees. Add more water or tomato juice if necessary.

Mrs. Kenneth Bailey (Faye)
Wake Forest, North Carolina

HAWAIIAN PORK CHOPS

4 pork chops	3 tablespoons brown sugar
1 small can crushed pineapple	3 tablespoons Soy sauce
½ cup catsup	⅛ cup vinegar

Brown chops. Mix other ingredients and pour on chops. Cover and cook over low heat for 1 hour and 15 minutes. You may serve over rice if desired.

Mrs. Clyde Hampton (Alicia)
Hartwell, Georgia

BAR-B-Q PORK FRIED RICE

1 quart cooked cold rice	1 tablespoon soya sauce
1 egg, beaten	½ cup bar-b-que pork, diced
2 tablespoons peanut or salad oil	⅓ teaspoon salt
1 tablespoon green onion, chopped	Chinese seasoning to taste

Put oil in hot frying pan. Add egg. Stir and pour rice over, mixing together and let it fry for approximately 5 minutes. Then add diced pork and chopped green onions, salt and Chinese seasoning. Add soya sauce and mix thoroughly.

Mrs. Melba Gardner
Newcastle, California

SWEET AND SOUR SPARE RIBS

1 pound fried spareribs (or any lean pork) cut in 1-inch pieces, cooked	½ cup sugar
	Pinch of salt
	½ teaspoon soy sauce
1 small onion, cut in chunks	2 tablespoons cornstarch mixed with ½ cup water
½ green pepper, cut in chunks	
⅓ cup white vinegar	1 tablespoon salad or peanut oil
1 cup water	

Put oil in hot frying pan. Add cooked spareribs, onions and pepper. Pour vinegar, water, sugar and mix well. Cover and cook 5 minutes. Add soy sauce, salt and cornstarch mixture. Stir until thickened. Serve over hot, cooked rice.

Mrs. Melba Gardner
Newcastle, California

PORK CHOW MEIN

3 or 4 pound pork roast	2 teaspoons salt
3 or 4 tablespoons cooking oil	½ teaspoon black pepper
6 cups onions, chopped	3 cans bean sprouts
6 cups celery, chopped	½ cup water
1 cup hot water	4 tablespoons cornstarch
1 teaspoon ground ginger	2 tablespoons bead molasses
3 tablespoons soy sauce	1 teaspoon sugar

Trim all fat from pork roast and cut meat into ½-inch cubes. Cook meat in 3 or 4 tablespoons cooking oil about 10 minutes. Add onions and fry 5 more minutes. Stir in celery, 1 cup hot water, ginger, soy sauce, salt and pepper. Cover and cook 10 minutes. Add 3 cans drained and rinsed bean sprouts. When bean sprouts are heated, mix together 4 tablespoons cornstarch, 1 teaspoon sugar, 2 tablespoons bead molasses and ½ cup water. Add to first mixture. After mixture thickens, serve over fried noodles and rice. For Chop Suey, serve without noodles.

Mrs. Barnwell Gibson (Lita)
Bambery, South Carolina

. . . He set meat before them and rejoiced, believing in God with all his house.
Acts 16:34

CHINESE SWEET AND SOUR PORK (Niw Good Yuk)

½ pound pork, cut in cubes
1 large green pepper
½ cup carrots, sliced
2 rings pineapple
½ teaspoon salt
½ teaspoon dark molasses

1 tablespoon cornstarch mixed with
   1 tablespoon water
3 tablespoons cornstarch or enough
   to dredge pork
1 tablespoon water
3 cups oil

SAUCE
1 or 2 cloves garlic
¼ cup vinegar
½ cup water
Dash pepper

1½ teaspoons Kikoman soy sauce
5 tablespoons sugar
½ teaspoon monosodium glutamate

STEP I:
Roll pork cubes in cornstarch until dredged thoroughly. Add 1 tablespoon water slowly, about ½ teaspoon at a time, mixing the cubes evenly until each one is coated with a thick heavy paste. Heat deep-fat fryer, or enough oil (3 cups) to 375 degrees. Drop in cubes of pork. They will float when done. Leave a few minutes longer until golden brown. Remove and drain on paper towel.

STEP II:
Using a high flame, heat pan; add salt and sweet-and-sour mixture. When it begins to boil, add cornstarch solution and stir until gravy thickens. Next add vegetables and pineapple and stir. Add pork and molasses and stir quickly but thoroughly until gravy coats all ingredients. Serve with Oriental rice.
Mrs. Marvin Howard (Kitty)
Pensacola, Florida

HAM WITH CHERRY SAUCE

1 large canned ham
1 10-ounce jar apple or
  guava jelly
1 tablespoon prepared mustard

⅓ cup pineapple juice
1 21-ounce can cherry pie filling
½ cup light raisins

Heat ham according to time schedule on can. Half an hour before end of heating time, remove ham from oven and score fat in diamonds. Combine jelly, mustard and pineapple juice. Cook to boiling, stirring constantly. Simmer mixture 3 minutes. Pour ⅓ of glaze over ham. Return to oven for 30 minutes. Spoon glaze over ham every 10 minutes. In sauce pan, heat the cherry pie filling and ½ cup light raisins to boiling; stir occasionally. At end of heating time, transfer ham to platter. Add glaze to cherry sauce. Bring to boil. Spoon over ham. Pass remainder. Makes 3 cups sauce.
Mrs. Samuel Burnett (Donna)
Detroit, Michigan

HAM-CHEESE STRATA

8 slices bread
½ pound Old English
  Cheese Slices
4 slices boiled ham
4 eggs

2 cups milk
1 teaspoon mustard
½ teaspoon salt
1 cup cheese, grated
Dash Worcestershire

Cut crust off bread and butter. Put 4 slices of bread in bottom of greased casserole. Place cheese slices over bread and the ham on top of cheese. Place remaining 4 slices of bread over ham. Beat eggs with milk, mustard, salt and Worcestershire. Pour over top of bread. Spread grated cheese on top of this. Keep in refrigerator over night. Bake 1 hour in 350 degree oven.
Mrs. Harry Girtman
Taylors, South Carolina

HAM LOAF

1 pound cured ham, ground
1½ pounds fresh ham, ground
1 cup stuffing mix or bread
  crumbs

1 cup milk
2 eggs, beaten
Salt

Combine ingredients and shape into loaf pan. Bake in 350 degree oven 1½ to 2 hours or until done. Pour sauce over loaf every 30 minutes. Thicken sauce for gravy.

SAUCE
1 cup brown sugar
½ cup vinegar

½ cup water
1 heaping teaspoon mustard

Mrs. Tal Bonham (Faye)
Yukon, Oklahoma

HAM CASSEROLE

2 cups cooked ham, cubed
1 cup cream of mushroom soup,
  undiluted
1 cup celery, diced
1 cup rice, cooked
¾ cup mayonnaise or salad
  dressing

1 tablespoon lemon juice
3 hard cooked eggs, sliced
½ teaspoon salt
½ cup slivered almonds
1 cup crushed cornflakes

Mix all ingredients and turn into a greased casserole. Top with ½ cup slivered almonds and 1 cup crushed corn flakes. Bake for 25 minutes at 350 degrees.

Mrs. Charles H. Beal (Winona)
Sarasota, Florida

HAM EN CASSEROLE

2½ cups cooked ham, cut in ½-inch cubes
1 cup rice, uncooked
½ cup onion, chopped

2 tablespoons bacon drippings
1 cup water, boiling
1 package frozen cut green beans
1 10½-ounce can consomme

Cook rice and onion in drippings, stirring constantly until rice is lightly browned. Add ham, boiling water, frozen green beans and consomme to rice mixture. Heat until green beans are broken apart. (Canned beans may be used.) Mix well and pour into a 2-quart greased casserole. Cover tightly and bake at 350 degrees for 1¼ hours. Six servings.
Mrs. Leonard Sanderson (Anne)
Pineville, Louisiana

PINEAPPLE-HAM LOAF

1½ pounds cured ham, ground
1 pound lean ground beef
1 cup cracker crumbs
1 tablespoon dry mustard
2 eggs, beaten

1½ cups milk
3 tablespoons brown sugar
Sliced pineapple
Maraschino cherries

Mix together ham, beef, cracker crumbs, mustard, eggs and milk. Put 3 tablespoons brown sugar in bottom of 8x11-inch Pyrex loaf pan. Place slices of pineapple over bottom of pan. Press meat mixture over it so there is no air. Cook, covered, in 250 degree oven 2 hours. Remove lid about 15 minutes before it is done to let it brown slightly. Invert on a large platter. Place a drained maraschino cherry in center of each pineapple slice. Serve either hot or cold. Serves 12 to 16.
Mrs. Donald V. Wideman (Marian)
Kansas City, Missouri

SAUSAGE-RICE CASSEROLE

1   pound hot bulk sausage
3   cups regular rice, cooked
1   4-ounce can chopped
    mushrooms, drained
1   10¾-ounce can cream of
    celery soup, undiluted
1   1⅜-ounce package dry chicken
    noodle soup mix

1   onion, chopped
1½ cups water
1   green pepper, chopped
¼   cup pecans, chopped
2   small sweet pickles,
    chopped

Brown sausage in a heavy skillet or Dutch oven; drain excess grease. Stir in remaining ingredients and simmer until vegetables are tender. Spoon into a greased 2-quart casserole. Bake at 350 degrees for 20 minutes. Yield 6 to 8 servings.
Mrs. Robert Cuttino (Molly)
Lancaster, South Carolina

AUTUMN DINNER

18 little pork sausages
3   medium acorn squash

1   number 2 can apple pie filling
¼   cup brown sugar, firmly packed

Bake whole squash in 350 degree oven for 25 minutes. Place sausage links in oven on rack in shallow uncovered pan. Remove almost baked squash. Cut in half lengthwise. Combine pie filling and sugar; spoon into squash. Put sausage into apple mixture. Continue baking for 15 minutes or until tender.
Mrs. John Dunaway (Jayne)
Corbin, Kentucky

SAUSAGE DRESSING

1   onion
1   cup celery
1   cup chicken broth
1   pound hot sausage

1   large loaf bread
1   stick butter
Salt and pepper

Sauté onions and celery in butter until clear. Cook sausage in skillet, breaking into small pieces. Break bread into pieces and pour sausage, celery, onion and cup of broth over bread. Mix well and taste for salt and pepper additions. Cook 30 minutes at 375 degrees. Good for holidays.
Mrs. W. O. Vaught (Mary Frances)
Little Rock, Arkansas

SAUSAGE-BEAN CHOWDER

1 pound bulk hot pork sausage	1½ teaspoons salt
1 large can Kidney beans, undrained	½ teaspoon garlic salt
	½ teaspoon thyme
1 large can tomatoes	½ teaspoon black pepper
2 cups water	3 potatoes, peeled, raw and diced
1 large onion, chopped	½ bell pepper, chopped
2 bay leaves	

Cook sausage in skillet until brown. Pour off fat. In soup pot, combine all ingredients. Add sausage and simmer about 30 minutes or until done. Remove bay leaf.

Mrs. William A. Barclay
Lafayette, Indiana

MEAL-IN-A-DISH

In a baking dish place 3 to 4 layers sliced Irish potatoes, about 2 layers sliced onions. Salt to taste. Add 1 can of cream style corn and blobs of catsup or other tomato product. Top with sausage patties. Bake at 325 degrees for about 1½ hours or until forking to bottom shows potatoes are cooked.

Mrs. T. J. Fulk (Marilee)
Fayetteville, North Carolina

Sweets

"I was glad when they said unto me,
let us go into the house of the Lord"

Ps. 122:1

Candies

GOLDEN NUGGET FUDGE

⅔ cup Carnation milk
1⅔ cups sugar
2 cups miniature marshmallows

1½ cups butterscotch chips
1 teaspoon vanilla
2 cups nuts, chopped

Combine Carnation milk and sugar in a sauce pan. Heat to boiling; lower heat and boil 5 minutes, stirring constantly. Remove from heat. Add marshmallows, butterscotch chips, vanilla and nuts. Stir until marshmallows and chips are melted. Then drop by teaspoon on waxed paper. Cool and store.
Mrs. James B. Riley (Vera)
Gonzalez, Louisiana

FIVE MINUTE FUDGE

2 tablespoons butter
1⅔ cups sugar
2 cups miniature marshmallows
1 teaspoon vanilla

⅔ cup evaporated milk
½ teaspoon salt
1½ cups semi-sweet chocolate
½ cup nuts, chopped

Combine butter, milk, sugar and salt in saucepan over medium heat. Bring to a boil. Cook 4 to 5 minutes, stirring constantly. (Start timing when mixture starts to bubble around edges of pan.) Remove from heat. Stir in marshmallows, chocolate, vanilla and nuts. Stir vigorously for 1 minute, until marshmallows melt and blend. Pour into 8x8-inch buttered pan. Cool and cut into squares. Makes about 2 pounds.
Mrs. Richard Brogan
Clinton, Missouri

MILLIONAIRES

1 12-ounce package milk
   chocolate chips
1 14-ounce package caramels
3 to 4 tablespoons milk

2 cups pecans
¼ bar paraffin
Butter or margarine

Place caramels and milk in saucepan. Melt over low heat. Add pecans, then drop by teaspoon onto buttered waxed paper. Chill. Mix together paraffin and milk chocolate chips. Melt over low heat in heavy saucepan. Dip candy into milk chocolate and again place on waxed paper. Chill. Makes 3½ dozen.
Mrs. George McMillan (Norma)
Columbia, South Carolina

CHOCOLATE MAPLE CREAMS

⅔ cup white syrup
2 cups light brown sugar
6 tablespoons hot water
1 egg white
Few grains salt

1 teaspoon maple extract
1½ cups nuts, chopped
1 12-ounce package chocolate
   chips
4-ounces candy wax

Cook syrup, sugar and hot water over low heat; stir until sugar is dissolved. On high heat bring to 238 degrees without stirring (thread stage). Beat egg white with salt to soft peaks. Pour syrup over slowly, beating constantly. Add extract; beat until stiff. Add nuts. When you can no longer beat candy, pat it out in lightly oiled pan. Chill overnight in refrigerator. Cut in squares. In double boiler, melt wax and chocolate. Remove from heat. Dip candy and place on waxed paper.
Mrs. Bobby W. Barnett (Mary)
Bradford, Rhode Island

QUICK CHOCOLATE CANDY

2 cups sugar
6 tablespoons cocoa
¼ pound margarine
½ cup milk

1 teaspoon vanilla
1½ cups quick oats
½ cup coconut
½ cup broken nuts

Mix together sugar, cocoa, margarine and milk. Boil hard one minute. Remove from stove and quickly stir in vanilla, oats, coconut and nuts. Drop on a greased plate.
Mrs. Frank Norfleet (Virginia)
Kansas City, Missouri

Mrs. Fred D. Barnes (Martie)
Lenoir, North Carolina

BON BONS

4 tablespoons soft butter	2 cups nuts, chopped
2 cups powdered sugar	⅔ cup peanut butter
2 cups coconut	1 small bottle maraschino cherries

Mix together 4 tablespoons butter and 2 cups powdered sugar. Add coconut, chopped nuts, peanut butter and maraschino cherries. Mix well and roll into balls about the size of a small walnut, using some of the cherry juice if needed.

1 6-ounce package chocolate chips	2 tablespoons paraffin

Melt chocolate chips and paraffin in heavy saucepan. Roll balls in chocolate mixture and set on waxed paper to harden.

Mrs. Howard H. Ramsey (Lawonda)
Tigard, Oregon

Mrs. Bobby W. Barnett (Mary)
Bradford, Rhode Island

CORN FLAKE COOKY-CANDY

1 bag Nestle's semi-sweet chocolates	2 tablespoons melted paraffin
1 tablespoon peanut butter	2 cups cornflakes

Melt and mix together in top of double boiler. Drop on waxed paper.

Mrs. T. J. Fulk (Marilee)
Fayetteville, North Carolina

CHOCOLATE CHEWS

3 cups powdered sugar	2 tablespoons Buttery Flavored Wesson Oil
¾ cup powdered milk	½ cup corn syrup
2 squares unsweetened chocolate	¼ teaspoon salt
Nuts (optional)	1 teaspoon vanilla

Mix together powdered sugar and powdered milk. Set aside. In separate bowl, blend chocolate, Wesson oil, corn syrup and salt. Place mixing bowl over hot water to soften but not cook. Add 1 teaspoon vanilla. Gradually add milk and sugar mixture to chocolate mixture. Knead in dry ingredients and nuts if desired. Roll into ½-inch thick rolls. Cut in 1-inch lengths. Keep dry and cool for serving.

Mrs. Robert Hughes (Ruth)
Clovis, California

CHOCOLATE COVERED CHERRIES

1 box confectioners' sugar
¾ stick butter, melted
1 tablespoon vanilla
1 bottle maraschino cherries

Cake coloring (optional)
5 blocks Baker's Semi-sweet
   chocolate
1-inch block paraffin

Mix sugar, butter and vanilla till dry and molds together like clay. Take cherry and wrap in mixture then dip in melted chocolate and paraffin. Place on waxed paper.
NOTE: Add warm milk, teaspoon at a time to get consistency for molding sugar and butter mixture.
Mrs. Marshall E. Sargent (Gloria)
Stony Point, North Carolina

BUCKEYES

1 pound jar creamy
   peanut butter
1 box powdered sugar

½ pound margarine, melted
¾ cake paraffin
12-ounce package chocolate chips

Mix peanut butter, powdered sugar and margarine. Make into balls and refrigerate overnight. Melt paraffin and chocolate chips. Stick a tooth pick in a peanut butter ball and dip in chocolate-paraffin mixture, leaving the top plain to resemble a buckeye. Set on waxed paper to dry.
Mrs. Bill Bailey (Faye)
Elizabethtown, Kentucky

REESE CUP CANDY

1 pint jar creamy peanut
   butter
2½ sticks margarine
2 cups graham cracker
   crumbs

1½ pounds (6 cups) confectioners'
   sugar
12-ounce package chocolate bits
   (semi-sweet or milk)
¼ rectangle paraffin

Melt margarine; add peanut butter and mix well. Add crumbs and sugar and continue to stir. If mixture gets too thick, add more margarine and peanut butter. Spread in rimmed cookie sheet. Top with the following glaze: Melt together over water in top of double boiler the chocolate bits and ¼ of 1 rectangle of paraffin. Spread over the crumb-peanut butter mixture. Let candy set 15 or 20 minutes, then cut in squares.
Mrs. Ernest Walker (Hattie)
Panama City, Florida

PEANUT BUTTER BALLS

1 pound powdered sugar
1 pound peanut butter

¼ pound butter, melted
3 cups Rice Krispies

Cream together powdered sugar, peanut butter and melted butter. Add Rice Krispies. Roll into balls and dip in chocolate. Lay on waxed paper to dry.

CHOCOLATE COATING

1 large Hershey bar
6-ounce package chocolate chips

¼ pound paraffin wax

Melt in double boiler. Let cool just a minute so mixture will be a little thicker.
Mrs. Wallace E. Jones (Laura Jo)
St. Ann, Missouri

ORANGE BALLS

1 cup margarine, melted
1 small can frozen orange juice
1 box powdered sugar

1 cup pecans, finely chopped
1 box vanilla wafer crumbs
Coconut

Mix melted margarine and orange juice, then mix the powdered sugar, vanilla wafer crumbs and pecans. Stir into the orange juice, margarine mixture. Smoothly blend. Make into small balls and roll in coconut. Makes 6 dozen.
Mrs. Everett Smalts (Mary Ruth)
Duke, Oklahoma

DATE LOAF CANDY

2 cups sugar
⅔ cup milk
½ cup dates

Lump butter
1 cup nuts, chopped

Boil sugar, milk and butter. Add dates and mash. Cook until soft ball forms in water. Beat and add 1 cup chopped nuts. Pour up on damp cloth. Form into long rolls. Slice when cool.
Mrs. Kendall Hatton
Marlinton, West Virginia

COCONUT FINGERS

1½ cups flour   ½ cup butter, melted
4   tablespoons powdered sugar

Mix and spread in 8x8-inch pan. Pat down to cover bottom of pan. Bake 20 minutes in 350 degree oven.

1½ cups brown sugar   2   eggs, slightly beaten
2   level tablespoons flour   1   can coconut
¼ teaspoon salt   1   cup broken pecans
¼ teaspoon baking powder

Spread over first baked mixture and bake 20 minutes in 350 degree oven. Cut while warm.
Mrs. Kendall Hatton
Marlinton, West Virginia

YUMMIES

2   sticks margarine   1¼ cups Angel Flake coconut
2   cups dark brown sugar   2   cups pecans, chopped
1   pound box pitted dates, cut   4   cups crisp rice cereal
    in small pieces

Melt margarine and dark brown sugar. Stir in dates and coconut. Cook 6 minutes over medium heat. Stir in pecans and rice cereal. Cool. Form in finger-length rolls and roll in powdered sugar.
Mrs. Henry Powell (Mary)
Ahoskie, North Carolina

CREOLE PECAN PRALINES

2½ cups sugar   2½ cups pecans
1   small can evaporated milk   1   teaspoon vanilla
4   tablespoons butter

Cook sugar and evaporated milk together slowly in heavy saucepan until a little of the mixture dropped from spoon into a cup of cold water will form soft ball (240 degrees on candy thermometer).Remove from fire and allow to cool slightly. Add butter and vanilla and beat for a few minutes only, then add pecans. Before candy hardens, drop by spoonfuls on waxed paper.
Mrs. Wallace Mitchell (Faye)
Gonzalez, Florida

NO-FAIL DIVINITY CANDY

3 cups sugar
½ cup corn syrup
⅔ cup water
2 egg whites

⅛ teaspoon salt
1 teaspoon vanilla
1 cup nuts

Boil sugar, corn syrup and water together until it forms a hard ball when dropped in water. Beat egg whites and salt for 3 minutes in large bowl. Pour syrup slowly into beaten egg whites while beating. Continue beating until mixture passes the glossy stage. Add nuts (or fruits) and vanilla. Continue beating until mixture forms a peak when beater is raised. Pour on buttered platter or drop on waxed paper.
VARIATIONS IN FLAVORINGS: Peppermint, Almond, Orange, Lemon.
ADDITIONS: Candied lemon or orange peel, candied fruits, coconut.
Mrs. Justus L. Garrett (Janis)
Monroe, Georgia

FRUIT NUGGETS

8-ounces diced Liberty pineapple
   (natural, red and green)
4-ounces each (red and green)
   diced cherries
4-ounces pitted dates, chopped

1 cup pecans, chopped
½ cup all-purpose flour
3 egg whites
½ cup sugar

In a mixing bowl, mix fruits and pecans with flour. Beat egg whites until stiff. Gradually add sugar, continuing to beat until very stiff. Fold into fruit mixture. Drop by rounded teaspoon 1-inch apart on greased baking sheet. Bake at 300 degrees for 30 minutes. Remove immediately to wire rack to cool. Store airtight. Makes about 3 dozen.
Mrs. Wyatt M. Gilbert (Irene)
Clarksville, Georgia

PARTY STRAWBERRIES

1 large package
   strawberry-flavored gelatin
1 cup ground coconut or cookie
   coconut

1 cup pecans, ground
¾ cup Eagle Brand Condensed milk
1 teaspoon vanilla

Mix, chill and shape into strawberries. Roll in red sugar crystals. Use slivered almonds dyed green with food coloring for stems. Serves about 50.
Mrs. John A. Moore (Julia)
Greenville, North Carolina

SPICED CANDIED NUTS

1 cup white sugar
½ teaspoon cinnamon (scant)
¼ cup Carnation milk

2 teaspoons water
1½ cups whole nuts
½ teaspoon vanilla

Mix sugar and cinnamon together in saucepan. Stir in Carnation milk diluted with 2 teaspoons water. Boil until a few drops form a soft ball in cold water. Remove from heat. Add nuts and vanilla. Stir until mixture can no longer be stirred. Turn out on waxed paper and separate nuts quickly.
Mrs. James B. Riley (Vera)
Gonzales, Louisiana

ORANGE FLAVORED NUTS

1½ cups pecans, walnuts or
  peanuts
1 cup sugar
⅓ cup evaporated milk
1 tablespoon white corn syrup

Pinch of salt
½ teaspoon vanilla
1 teaspoon orange rind, grated
½ teaspoon cinnamon

Mix sugar, milk, corn syrup and cinnamon. Cook until soft ball stage. Remove from fire. Add orange rind, salt and vanilla. Add nuts. Stir until hard enough to pour on waxed paper. Spread well before coating hardens. Break apart when cool.
Mrs. Tommy M. Jones (Mary)
Travelers Rest, South Carolina

PEANUT BRITTLE

2 cups white sugar
1 cup white corn syrup
½ cup cold water
2 teaspoons soda

1 teaspoon vanilla
¼ stick margarine
1 pound raw spanish peanuts

Mix sugar, water and syrup. Boil until syrup becomes thready, stirring often. Add peanuts and stir until peanuts are slightly brown. Remove from heat. Add butter, flavoring and soda. Mix well. Pour into long shallow, buttered cookie sheet. Cool. Break into pieces.
Mrs. Kendall Hatton
Marlinton, West Virginia

Brownies

CHOCOLATE CHIP BROWNIES

1   white cake mix
2   eggs
1   large package chocolate chips
½ cup vegetable oil

½ cup pecans, chopped
2   tablespoons water
1   teaspoon vanilla

Mix beaten eggs, water and oil into cake mix. Stir in pecans and chocolate chips. Spread thinly on a lightly greased 12x18-inch cookie sheet that has sides. Bake 25 to 30 minutes at 300 degrees. Let cool a few minutes and slice into desired shape.
Mrs. Travis S. Berry (Bernice)
Plano, Texas

PEANUT BUTTER BROWNIES

½ cup peanut butter
⅓ cup butter or margarine
1   cup white sugar
¼ cup brown sugar, packed
2   eggs
1   cup all-purpose flour

1   teaspoon baking powder
¼ teaspoon salt
1   6-ounce package semi-sweet
    chocolate chips
½ teaspoon vanilla

Beat first 2 ingredients until blended. Gradually add sugars and beat until fluffy. Add eggs, one at the time; then add flour, baking powder and salt, beating well. Stir in chocolate chips and add vanilla. Spread in buttered 9-inch square pan. Bake in moderate oven at 350 degrees for 30 to 35 minutes. Cool in pan, then cut in 2½-inch squares. Makes 16 squares.
Mrs. C. S. Maynard
Little Rock, Arkansas

OUT OF THIS WORLD BROWNIES

⅔ cup flour
¼ teaspoon salt
½ teaspoon baking powder

2 eggs
⅓ cup butter
2 squares bitter chocolate

Thoroughly cream butter and sugar; add eggs and beat well. Blend in melted chocolate, vanilla and flour. Add nuts to batter. Bake in greased 8x8x2-inch pan for 35 minutes at 325 degrees. Be careful not to overcook.

TOPPING

1 or more very large Hershey
   bars

Marshmallows

Remove brownies from oven while still hot, cover with marshmallows. Spread shaved Hershey bar on top to completely cover. Return to oven and let melt on retain heat. Delicious!
Mrs. John McMillan (Arrie)
Orangeburg, South Carolina

FAVORITE BROWNIES

2 cups sugar
1½ cups flour
4 eggs
1 cup butter or margarine

4 tablespoons cocoa
1 cup nuts
2 teaspoons vanilla

Melt butter with cocoa. Beat eggs and add sugar. Add butter and cocoa to mixture, then add flour, small portions at a time. Pour into greased and floured pan. Bake at 350 degrees for approximately 30 minutes. Remove from oven while still soft. Cut into squares while still hot.

ICING

¾ box confectioners' sugar
½ stick margarine
Dash salt

1 teaspoon vanilla
Canned evaporated milk

Mix dry ingredients. Stir in margarine and vanilla. Add canned milk until creamy.
Mrs. Gilbert E. Barrow (Barbara)
Montgomery, Alabama

BUTTERSCOTCH BROWNIES

⅔ cup butter or margarine (1½ sticks)
2 cups light brown sugar
3 eggs
2¾ cups all-purpose flour

2 teaspoons baking powder
1 teaspoon vanilla
1 6-ounce package chocolate chips
½ cup nuts

Melt butter over low heat. Add sugar, eggs, flour, nuts and chocolate chips. Bake 30 minutes in 350 degree oven. Cool in pan and cut into squares.
Mrs. Bill Bailey (Faye)
Elizabethtown, Kentucky

 # Cookies

BUTTERSCOTCH REFRIGERATOR COOKIES

1 stick butter, soft
1 cup dark brown sugar, packed
1 egg
½ teaspoon vanilla

2 cups all-purpose flour
½ teaspoon cream of tartar
½ teaspoon soda
½ cup broken pecans

In electric mixer, blend butter and brown sugar until creamy. Beat in egg and add vanilla. Mix well. Sift together flour, cream of tartar and soda. Add to first mixture. Add nuts. Put on waxed paper with enough flour to handle. Make into 1 or 2 rolls, depending upon the size cookies you want. Roll in waxed paper, then in aluminum foil and refrigerate until needed. Slice thinly and place on ungreased cookie sheet. Bake at 350 degrees watching carefully not to let brown too much. NOTE: A ½ pecan on each cookie is decorative. Nuts may be omitted and coconut or raisins used.
Mrs. Howard E. Spell
Clinton, Mississippi

CHOW MEIN NOODLE COOKIES

2 6-ounce packages butterscotch morsels
1 5½-ounce can chow mein noodles
1 6½-ounce can peanuts

Melt morsels in pan over hot water. Add noodles and peanuts, stirring well. Drop by teaspoonfuls onto waxed paper and refrigerate about 10 minutes until hardened.
Mrs. Richard Brogan
Clinton, Missouri

POTATO CHIP COOKIES

1 cup margarine
1 cup sugar
1 cup brown sugar
2 eggs
1 teaspoon vanilla
2 cups potato chips, coarsely crushed
1 6-ounce package butterscotch chips
2½ cups all-purpose flour
1 teaspoon baking soda

Cream margarine and sugars. Add eggs and vanilla; beat well. Add crushed potato chips and butterscotch chips. Sift flour and soda; stir into creamed mixture. Drop by teaspoon on greased cookie sheet. Bake 10 to 20 minutes at 375 degrees.
Mrs. Elbert L. Smithen (Jo)
Midland, Texas

COCOA KRISPIES

1 bottle white Karo syrup
1 stick butter or margarine
1 box light brown sugar
1 box Cocoa Krispies
1 cup peanut butter

Place Karo syrup, butter and brown sugar in large saucepan and bring to a full boil. Take off burner. Add Cocoa Krispies and peanut butter. Stir well and put in buttered oblong pan or dish. When cool, cut into squares.
Mrs. Billy J. Dickerson (Vesta)   *Mrs. B. W. Dougharty (Margaret)*
Mango, Florida   *Santa Fe, New Mexico*

BANANA NUGGET COOKIES

1½ cups all-purpose flour
1 cup sugar
½ teaspoon soda
¾ teaspoon cinnamon
½ teaspoon salt
¾ cup shortening

1 egg, well beaten
1 cup ripe bananas, mashed
1¾ cup quick oats
1 cup nuts, chopped (optional)
1 16-ounce package chocolate
   morsels

Combine dry ingredients; cut in shortening. Add egg, banana, oats, nuts and chocolate morsels. Beat until thoroughly blended. Drop by teaspoonfuls onto a greased cookie sheet. Bake at 375 degrees for 10 minutes or until cookies are done. Yield 4 dozen.
Mrs. Gary Payne (Doda)
Syracuse, Missouri

CHOCOLATE CRINKLE

½ cup shortening
4 squares unsweetened chocolate
2 cups sugar
2 teaspoons vanilla
4 eggs

2 cups flour
2 teaspoons baking powder
⅛ teaspoon salt
½ cup nuts, chopped (or coconut)
Powdered sugar

Melt shortening and chocolate. Add sugar and vanilla and mix well. Add eggs, one at a time, beating after each addition. Sift dry ingredients. Add chocolate mixture with nuts and mix well. Chill dough several hours. Form into small balls. Roll in powdered sugar. Bake at 350 degrees for 12 to 15 minutes. Makes 5 to 6 dozen.
Mrs. C. E. Colton (Lois)
Dallas, Texas

FORGOTTEN COOKIES

2 egg whites
¾ cup sugar

½ cup nuts
6-ounces chocolate chips

Beat egg whites to soft peaks. Blend in sugar and continue to beat until very stiff. Fold in nuts and chocolate chips. Drop by scant teaspoons onto a large, greased cookie sheet. Place in hot 375 degree oven. Turn off the heat to the oven. Leave overnight or until oven is room temperature. Easy — but good!
Mrs. Jimmie E. Harley (Gayle)
Greenville, South Carolina

CHOCOLATE CHEESE COOKIES

Mix in order:

1½ cups shortening or 3 sticks margarine
3½ cups sugar
4 eggs
4 teaspoons vanilla
1 pint cottage cheese, beaten until smooth in blender

5½ cups all-purpose flour
1 cup cocoa
2 teaspoons baking powder
1 teaspoon soda
½ teaspoon salt

Chill dough overnight. Drop from teaspoon into powdered sugar and roll into ball. Place on lightly greased cookie sheet. Bake 12 minutes only at 350 degrees. Makes 12 dozen. Mix with electric mixer until too stiff, then use spoon or hand. Mix thoroughly.

Mrs. Howard H. Ramsey (Lawonda)
Tigard, Oregon

CATHEDRAL COOKIES

Melt:
12-ounce package chocolate chips   4 tablespoons margarine
Remove from heat.

Beat:
2 eggs and gradually add to chocolate mixture.

Add:
1 cup nuts, chopped
1 small package colored miniature marshmallows

Form into long roll. Roll in powdered sugar. Refrigerate. Slice and serve.

Mrs. Ray W. McClung (Faye)   *Mrs. Dwayne Francis (Glenda)*
Little Rock, Arkansas   *Malden, Missouri*

Mrs. Dwain R. Laramore (Dawn)
Flint, Michigan

BAPTIST CHEWS

1 box brown sugar	1 teaspoon vanilla
4 eggs, beaten	1 cup nuts, chopped
2 cups all-purpose flour	½ cup coconut

Mix brown sugar, eggs and flour together. Add vanilla, nuts and coconut. Bake at 350 degrees for 15 minutes in a 15x18-inch greased, floured pan.

ICING
1 box powdered sugar	Milk
½ cup margarine	

Cream powdered sugar and margarine. Add enough milk to spread.
Mrs. Roy D. Moody, Jr. (Sharon)
Tulsa, Oklahoma

CHINESE CHEWS

1 cup all-purpose flour	½ cup butter
2 tablespoons sugar	½ teaspoon salt

Mix well. Press in oblong pan and bake at 300 degrees for approximately 15 minutes or until light brown.

1½ cups brown sugar	½ cup coconut
2 eggs	1 cup nuts, chopped

Mix ingredients and pour over baked crust. Bake in a slow oven at 325 degrees for 45 minutes.

Mrs. C. E. Colton	*Mrs. Roy D. Moody, Jr. (Sharon)*
Dallas, Texas	*Tulsa, Oklahoma*

ORANGE CHEWS

1 cup all-purpose flour	½ cup granulated sugar
½ teaspoon baking powder	½ cup margarine
½ teaspoon soda	1 teaspoon vanilla
⅛ teaspoon salt	1 cup oatmeal
1 egg	1 cup diced orange slices
½ cup light brown sugar	1 cup nuts, broken

Sift together first four ingredients. Combine next four ingredients and beat until creamy, then add to dry ingredients. Stir in vanilla, oatmeal, orange slices and nuts. Drop by teaspoon on a greased baking sheet. Bake about 12 minutes at 350 degrees.

Mrs. T. T. Crabtree (Bennie)
Springfield, Missouri

DATE FINGERS

In saucepan combine:

1 stick margarine	2 egg yolks
¾ cup sugar	½ cup dates, chopped

Cook 5 to 7 minutes. Mixture will thicken. Remove from heat and add:

1 teaspoon vanilla	1 cup Rice Krispies
1 cup nuts	

Shape into "fingers" about 2-inches long and roll in coconut.

Mrs. Omer E. Hyde (Neva)
Eugene, Oregon

FIG PINWHEEL COOKIES

Grind together:	Blend in:
1 pint fig preserves	1 egg
1 cup nuts	1 teaspoon vanilla
Cream:	Sift together and add:
½ cup margarine	2 cups all-purpose flour
½ cup brown sugar	½ teaspoon soda
½ cup sugar	½ teaspoon salt

Chill dough. Divide into 2 parts for ease in handling. Roll out dough very thin on waxed paper. Spread with fig and nut mixture. Roll dough jelly roll fashion and chill again. Slice cookies and bake 10 to 12 minutes at 325 degrees.

Mrs. Elbert L. Smithen (Jo)
Midland, Texas

FRUIT CAKE BALLS

1 cup brown sugar	1 pound dates, cut up
1 cup butter	1 teaspoon baking soda
3 eggs	1 heaping teaspoon cinnamon
3 cups all-purpose flour	1 pound candied pineapple,
7 cups pecans, broken	cut up

Mix all ingredients by hand in large pan. Do not flour fruit. Roll into small balls. Bake 20 or 30 minutes at 300 degrees.
Mrs. Charles H. Beal (Winona)
Sarasota, Florida

MOTHER'S FRUITCAKE COOKIES

7 cups pecans	1 cup butter or Crisco
1 cup black walnuts	3 eggs
6 slices candied green pineapple, diced	1 cup brown sugar
	3 cups all-purpose flour
2 cups red candied cherries, diced	1 teaspoon cinnamon
	1 teaspoon nutmeg
2 cups dates, chopped	½ cup milk
1 box white raisins	1 teaspoon soda

Cut up fruits and nuts finely and set aside. Cream butter and sugar. Add eggs; then add flour, soda, cinnamon and nutmeg mixture alternately with milk. Add flavoring, nuts and fruits. Mix well. Drop on cookie sheet and bake 20 minutes at 300 degrees.
Mrs. J. L. Bryson, Jr. (Dottie)
Mt. Airy, North Carolina

GINGER SNAPS

¾ cup shortening	2 teaspoons soda
1 cup sugar	¼ teaspoon salt
¼ cup molasses	1 teaspoon cloves
1 egg, beaten	1 teaspoon cinnamon
2 cups all-purpose flour, sifted	1 teaspoon ginger

Cream shortening and sugar. Add molasses and beaten egg. Beat well. Sift flour and measure. Add spices to flour and sift together. Add dry ingredients to creamed mixture and mix well. Roll in small balls; slip in sugar and place on greased sheet. Bake at 375 degrees for 12-15 minutes.
Mrs. Russell Dilday (Betty)
Atlanta, Georgia

LEMON BALLS

1 10-ounce box vanilla wafers
1 stick margarine, melted
1 box powdered sugar
1 can frozen lemon juice
   concentrate
1 cup pecans

Mix all ingredients thoroughly. Form into small balls and roll in coconut.
Mrs. C. David Matthews (Sue)
Waco, Texas

CORN FLAKE MACAROONS

Mix in a 1½ quart saucepan:
2 tablespoons butter or
   margarine
⅓ cup evaporated milk
¾ cup sugar

Cook and stir to a full, all-over boil. Continue to boil and stir over medium heat for 2 minutes. Take off heat.

Stir in:
½ teaspoon vanilla
1½ cups cornflakes
1 cup coconut
½ cup broken nuts (optional)

With 2 teaspoons, drop quickly on waxed paper. Let stand until set. Makes 24.
Mrs. Wallace E. Jones (Laura Jo)
St. Ann, Missouri

OATMEAL COOKIES

1½ cups flour
1 teaspoon baking powder
1 teaspoon soda
½ teaspoon salt
1 cup shortening
1½ cups light brown sugar
½ cup white sugar
2 eggs
1 teaspoon vanilla
3 cups quick cooking oats
1 cup nuts
Powdered sugar

Sift together flour, baking powder, soda and salt. Cream shortening, sugar, eggs and vanilla. Add to first mixture. Stir in 3 cups quick cooking oats and nuts. Form balls and shake in a bag of powdered sugar to coat. Place on greased cookie sheet. Press with fork. Bake at 350 degrees for 12 to 15 minutes or until light brown.
Mrs. Bobby L. Eklund (Janis)
Hurst, Texas

INSTANT CHOCOLATE OATMEAL COOKIES

2 cups sugar	2½ cups One Minute oats
½ cup milk	½ cup peanut butter
¼ cup cocoa	1 teaspoon vanilla
½ stick butter or	Nuts or coconut
margarine	M & M's (optional)

Boil sugar, milk, cocoa and butter mixture one minute to full boil. Stir in oats, peanut butter and vanilla. Add nuts or coconut. Drop on waxed paper. Decorate with plain M & M's for color, if desired, or use pecan or walnut halves.

Mrs. C. R. Trammell (Beth) *Mrs. Odell Bell (Opal)*
Little Rock, Arkansas *Petersburg, Illinois*

RANCHEROS

2 cups flour	1 teaspoon vanilla
½ teaspoon salt	¾ cup coconut
1 teaspoon soda	2 cups quick oats
½ teaspoon baking powder	1 6-ounce package chocolate chips
1 cup shortening	¾ cup peanuts, shelled
1¼ cups brown sugar	
2 eggs	

Sift first 4 ingredients. Set aside. Cream sugar and shortening until light and fluffy. Beat in eggs, vanilla and coconut. Add sifted dry ingredients, oats, chips and peanuts. Drop by teaspoonfuls onto ungreased baking sheet. Bake at 375 degrees for 8 to 10 minutes.

Mrs. Keith Hamm
El Dorado, Kansas

PREACHER COOKIES

2 cups sugar	½ cup cocoa
1 stick margarine	½ cup coconut
½ cup milk	1 teaspoon vanilla
2 cups quick oatmeal	

Combine sugar, margarine and milk in saucepan. Place on medium heat. Boil about 3 minutes. Add remaining ingredients which have been measured, to hot mixture. Stir quickly and drop by teaspoons onto waxed paper. Makes about 3 dozen.

Mrs. Ross Terry (Roxie)
Mulberry, Indiana

OATMEAL WHEAT GERM COOKIE

¾ cup butter
¾ cup honey
2 eggs
2 teaspoons vanilla
2 cups all-purpose flour

¾ teaspoon salt
½ teaspoon soda
½ cup oats
⅓ cup wheat germ
½ cup coconut

Cream butter, honey, eggs and vanilla. Stir dry ingredients into creamed mixture. Add wheat germ, nuts, coconut and oatmeal.
Mrs. Lynn P. Clayton (Brenda)
Wichita, Kansas

WHEAT GERM COOKIES

¾ cup butter
¾ cup honey
2 eggs
¾ teaspoon salt
½ teaspoon soda

1 teaspoon vanilla
2 cups whole wheat flour
1 cup wheat germ
¾ cup walnuts, chopped

Cream together butter, honey, eggs and vanilla. Stir dry ingredients in mixture. Add wheat germ and walnuts. Grease cookie sheet if not teflon. Bake in a 350 degree oven about 10 minutes or until light brown. Makes 5 dozen dry bread type. For moist cookies, put mix in refrigerator overnight.
Mrs. Lynn P. Clayton (Brenda)
Wichita, Kansas

PEANUT BUTTER COOKIES

1 cup shortening
1 cup granulated sugar
1 cup brown sugar
2 eggs

1 teaspoon vanilla
1 cup peanut butter
3 cups self-rising flour

Thoroughly cream shortening, sugars, eggs, and vanilla. Sift dry ingredients into creamed mixture. Drop by rounded teaspoons onto ungreased cookie sheet. Press with back of fork dipped into water. Bake in 350 degree oven for about 10 minutes. Yield: 5 dozen.
Mrs. Dean Smith (Glenda)
Gate City, Virginia

NO-BAKE PEANUT BUTTER COOKIES

1 cup peanut butter	1 12-ounce package semisweet
1 cup powdered sugar	chocolate chips
2 tablespoons butter	¼ pound parafin wax
1½ cups Rice Krispies	

Combine peanut butter, powdered sugar and butter. Mix well. Stir in Rice Krispies. Shape into balls and slightly flatten with fork. Melt chocolate chips and parafin wax in double boiler. Use a toothpick to dip balls into melted chocolate. Cool on waxed paper.
Mrs. Wallace Mitchell (Faye)
Gonzalez, Florida

PECAN-RAISIN COOKIES

1 stick margarine	1¼ cups brown sugar
2 eggs, beaten	2 cups all-purpose flour
1 teaspoon soda, dissolved in	4 cups pecans
1 tablespoon boiling water	2 cups raisins

Mix ingredients in order and bake at 200 degrees for 1 hour. Cool thoroughly and wrap in a dry cloth and place in an air tight container. These are like fruit cake; they do not get stale. Makes 200 cookies.
Mrs. Thomas J. Ayo
Baton Rouge, Louisiana

CRISP SUGAR COOKIES

1 cup granulated sugar	2 teaspoons vanilla
1 cup powdered sugar	1 teaspoons cream of tartar
2 eggs, well beaten	1 teaspoon soda
1 cup margarine	4¼ cups flour
1 cup cooking oil	

Thoroughly cream together sugar, margarine and eggs. Stir in oil and vanilla. Sift together dry ingredients. Add to creamed mixture and blend well. Refrigerate until dough is firm. Form into small round balls and place on cookie sheet. Press with fork and sprinkle with sugar. Bake at 350 degrees until lightly brown.
Mrs. W. A. Burkey (Enid)
Fairfield, California

BROWN SUGAR SPRITZ

1   cup margarine
¾ cup light brown sugar, firmly
     packed
1   egg yolk

½ teaspoon vanilla extract
¼ teaspoon salt
2   cups flour, unsifted

Cream margarine and brown sugar together until light and fluffy. Beat in egg yolk, vanilla and salt. Blend in flour. Knead several times until dough is soft and pliable. Press dough through cookie press onto greased baking sheets. Decorate if desired. Bake in 300 degree oven about 8 minutes or until lightly brown. Remove from baking sheets and cool on wire racks.
Mrs. Bill Hicken (Billie)
Jacksonville, Florida

GUM DROP COOKIES

4   eggs, well beaten
2   cups brown sugar
½ teaspoon salt
2   cups all purpose flour

1   cup nut meats, cut up
½ pound gum drops, cut in small
     pieces

Mix in order given. Spread in 9x13-inch pan. Bake 25 to 30 minutes at 350 degrees. Cut and remove from pan while warm.
Mrs. E. Halliburton
Willoughby, Ohio

MY FAVORITE COOKIE

2   sticks margarine
1   cup granulated sugar
1   cup brown sugar
2   eggs, well beaten
1   teaspoon soda

1   teaspoon salt
1   teaspoon vanilla
2   cups broken nuts
4   cups all-purpose flour, sifted

Let margarine soften in mixing bowl. Mix with granulated sugar and brown sugar. Add well beaten eggs, soda, salt and vanilla. Add broken nuts and mix well. Stir in flour. Mix thoroughly. Tear off 6 pieces of waxed paper about 18-inches long. Divide dough into 6 parts. Shape each part into a long roll on a sheet of the waxed paper. Store in refrigerator until ready to bake. Slice in thin slices and cook on the same waxed paper sheet. Bake at 350 degrees for about 8 minutes.
Mrs. James W. Parker
Santa Ana, California

THUMBPRINT COOKIES

¼ cup butter
¼ cup soft shortening
¼ cup brown sugar, packed
1 egg yolk
½ teaspoon vanilla

1 cup flour, sifted
¼ teaspoon salt
¾ cup nuts, finely chopped
1 egg white

Prepare finely chopped nuts. Thoroughly mix together the first 5 ingredients. Sift together the flour and salt. Add to shortening mixture. Roll in balls the size of a small walnut. Beat 1 egg white slightly with fork. Dip balls in egg white. Roll in finely chopped nuts. Place 1-inch apart on greased baking sheet. Bake 5 minutes in 375 degree oven. Remove from oven and immediately press thumb gently in top of each cookie. Return to oven and bake 8 minutes longer. After cool, fill with icing, either pale green, orange, or yellow. Makes 2 dozen.

Mrs. C. E. Colton (Lois)
Dallas, Texas

SNICKERDOODLES

1 cup margarine
1½ cups sugar
2 eggs
2¾ cups all-purpose flour, sifted
2 teaspoons cream of tartar

1 teaspoon soda
¼ teaspoon salt
2 tablespoons cinnamon
2 tablespoons sugar

Heat oven to 400 degrees. Mix shortening, sugar and eggs thoroughly. Sift together flour, cream of tartar, soda and salt. Stir into above mixture. Form dough into balls about the size of walnuts. Roll in mixture of sugar and cinnamon. Place about 2-inches apart on an ungreased baking sheet. Bake 8 to 10 minutes.

Mrs. H. T. Karn (Deborah)
Clanton, Alabama

AUNT GERTIE'S SAND TARTS

1 pound sugar (2¼ cups)
¾ pound butter or margarine
   (1½ cups)
2 eggs, beaten

3 cups flour, sifted
1 teaspoon salt
1 teaspoon vanilla

Cream sugar and butter. Add eggs and beat. Add flour, salt and vanilla. Mix well. Drop by small teaspoon on ungreased cookie sheet. Press pecan or walnut half in center and bake at 325 degrees until brown around edges. They should be thin and crisp.

Mrs. Ted Cotten (Dorothy)
Longview, Washington

WEDDING COOKIES

1 cup butter or margarine
¾ cup confectioners' sugar
2 cups all-purpose flour

1 teaspoon vanilla
1 cup pecans, chopped

Sift flour and sugar. Cut in butter. Add vanilla and pecans. Roll into small balls, with fingers moistened in water. Bake at 325 degrees for 30 minutes or until done. Cool slightly, then roll in confectioners' sugar.
Mrs. Rhett Padgett (Doris)
Pensacola, Florida

SOUTHERN TEA CAKES

2¼ cups all-purpose flour, sifted
¼ teaspoon salt
2 teaspoons baking powder
½ cup butter

1 cup sugar
2 eggs, beaten
½ teaspoon vanilla
1 tablespoon milk

Sift flour, salt and baking powder together. Cream butter, sugar and eggs. Add vanilla, milk and dry ingredients. Blend well. Place dough on a lightly floured board. Sprinkle a little flour over dough and roll to about ½-inch thick. Cut with cookie cutter and place on cookie sheet. Bake 12 to 15 minutes at 350 degrees or until lightly browned on top.
Mrs. William E. Stiles
Marietta, Georgia

VANILLA DROP COOKIES

2½ cups all-purpose flour, sifted
½ teaspoon baking soda
½ teaspoon salt
½ cup shortening

1 cup sugar
2 eggs, well beaten
½ cup buttermilk
1 teaspoon vanilla

Measure and sift dry ingredients. Set aside. Cream shortening. Add sugar gradually, beating after each addition. Add beaten eggs. Stir in dry ingredients alternately with buttermilk and vanilla mixture. Drop by teaspoonfuls on ungreased baking sheet. Bake in hot oven, 425 degrees for 10 minutes or until brown. Makes about 3 dozen cookies.
Mrs. Hugh L. Smith (Virginia)
Henderson, Texas

YUM COOKIES

1 cup brown sugar
¾ cup white sugar
1 egg
½ teaspoon vanilla

¾ cup Crisco
1⅓ cups all-purpose flour
½ teaspoon soda

Cream sugars, egg, vanilla and Crisco together in mixing bowl. Mix flour and soda. Add to creamed mixture and blend well. Spoon out on cookie sheet. Bake 10 to 12 minutes at 350 degrees. NOTE: Add ¾ cup peanut butter if desired.
Mrs. Joe Howard
Wynnewood, Oklahoma

HOLLY COOKIES

1 stick margarine
34 large marshmallows
1 teaspoon vanilla
1¼ teaspoon green food coloring

4½ cups cornflakes
Red Hots

Place margarine, marshmallows, vanilla and food coloring in double boiler and let melt. Add cornflakes and mix well. Drop by teaspoonfuls onto plate and add Red Hots to each for decoration.
Mrs. Everett Lemay
Mt. Vernon, Illinois

HEALTH

1 cup margarine
1 cup brown sugar
1 cup white sugar
2 eggs, beaten
1 teapsoon vanilla
1 cup walnuts, peanuts, or coconut

1 teaspoon baking powder
1 teaspoon salt
1 cup whole wheat flour
2 cups Rice Krispies
2 cups oatmeal

Cream margarine; add sugar, beaten eggs and vanilla. Beat well. Add remaining ingredients, in order given. Drop on greased cookie sheet. Bake at 375 degrees for 10 to 12 minutes. Let cool slightly before removing from sheet. Makes 90 cookies.
Mrs. Keith Hamm
El Dorado, Kansas

CANADIAN BARS

½ cup butter, melted
5 tablespoons sugar
5 tablespoons cocoa
1 teaspoons vanilla
1 egg

2 cups graham crackers, crushed
½ cup coconut
½ cup nuts, chopped

Combine all ingredients. Press firmly into a 9 inch square pan.

FROSTING
4 tablespoons butter
2 tablespoons milk
2 cups confectioners' sugar

2 tablespoons instant vanilla pudding

Combine all ingredients. Spread over crumb mixture. Refrigerate 1 hour.

TOPPING
1 cup chocolate pieces
1 tablespoon butter

1 tablespoon hot milk

Melt chocolate. Add butter and milk and blend well. Spread over all.
Mrs. Willard M. Milleson (Catherine)
Hibbing, Minnesota

CHOCOLATE SCOTCHAROOS

1 cup sugar
1 cup light corn syrup
1 cup peanut butter
6 cups Rice Krispies

1 6-ounce package chocolate chips
1 6-ounce package butterscotch chips

Combine sugar and corn syrup in 3-quart saucepan. Cook until it boils. Remove from heat. Stir in peanut butter. Mix in Rice Krispies. Pat in 13x9-inch buttered pan. Let harden. Melt over hot water chocolate chips and butterscotch chips. Spread over Krispie mixture. Chill about 5 minutes.
Mrs. John R. Walker (Peggy)
Clarksville, Tennessee

CHRISTMAS CRESCENT COOKIES

½ pound butter or margarine
2 cups pecans, chopped
2 teaspoons vanilla
½ teaspoon salt

2 cups all-purpose flour
5 tablespoons sugar
1 tablespoon water

Cream butter and sugar. Sift together flour and salt. Add to butter and sugar mixture. Stir in water, vanilla and nuts. Shape into cresents. Bake in slow 325 degree oven about 20 minutes. While warm, roll in powdered sugar.

Mrs. Bill Bailey (Faye)
Elizabethtown, Kentucky

CHOCOLATE MINT BARS

1 cup butter
2-ounces unsweetened chocolate
4 eggs
2 cups sugar

1½ teaspoons peppermint
  flavoring
1 cup all-purpose flour, sifted
2 cups nuts, chopped

Melt butter and chocolate; cool. Beat eggs until light and fluffy. Add sugar gradually. Add chocolate and flavoring. Stir in flour and nuts. Mix thoroughly. Spread in greased, 10x15-inch jelly roll pan. Bake at 350 degrees for 25 minutes. Cool.

TOPPING

¼ cup butter
3 cups powdered sugar, sifted
2 to 4 tablespoons cream
⅛ teaspoon salt

1 teaspoon peppermint flavoring
2-ounces unsweetened chocolate
2 teaspoons butter

Cream butter and ½ of sugar. Add 2 tablespoons cream, salt, flavoring and remaining sugar. Beat until smooth. Add remaining cream until mixture is of spreading consistency. Spread on first part. Melt chocolate and butter. Cool. Dribble on frosting and then gently swirl over all. Place in refrigerator until chocolate topping is firm. About 5 minutes. Cut into bars.

Mrs. John J. Wolf (Elizabeth)
Houston, Texas

CONGO BARS

2⅔ cups all-purpose flour
2½ teaspoons baking powder
½ teaspoon salt
⅔ cup margarine, melted
2¼ cups brown sugar

3 eggs
1 cup pecans
1 package semi-sweet chocolate
chips

Sift together flour, baking powder and salt. Set aside. Melt margarine in large saucepan. Stir in brown sugar and allow to cool slightly. Add eggs, one at a time, beating well. Add flour mixture, nuts and chocolate chips. Pour into a greased 15x10x1-inch pan. Bake at 350 degrees for 30 minutes. Cut into squares. Yield: 50 to 60 squares

Mrs. D. H. Jones (Jo)
Pensacola, Florida

FUDGE NUT BARS

1 cup butter
2 cups light brown sugar, packed
2 eggs
2 teaspoons vanilla, divided

2½ cups all-purpose flour, sifted
1 teaspoon baking soda
1 teaspoon salt, divided
3 cups quick-cooking rolled oats

Cream butter; gradually add sugar. Add eggs, one at a time, beating well after each addition. Add vanilla. Combine flour, soda and 1 teaspoon salt; stir into creamed mixture. Stir in oats. Spread about ⅔ of oat mixture in bottom of 9x12x2-inch pan. Set aside.

FILLING

1 12-ounce package semi-sweet chocolate bits
1 cup sweetened condensed milk

½ teaspoon salt
2 tablespoons butter
1 cup nuts, chopped
2 teaspoons vanilla

In saucepan combine chocolate bits, milk, butter and salt. Cook over low heat, stirring, until mixture is smooth. Remove from heat; add nuts and vanilla. Spread over layer in pan. Dot with remaining oat mixture, spreading as evenly as possible. Bake in 350 degree preheated oven for 25 to 30 minutes, or until lightly browned. Cool and cut into bars.

Mrs. Wade H. Robertson (Alice)
Window Rock, Arizona

DATE BARS

¾ cup all-purpose flour, sifted
1 cup sugar
⅛ teaspoon salt
¼ teaspoon baking powder
½ cup cooking oil

2 eggs, unbeaten
½ teaspoon vanilla
1 cup dates, chopped
1 cup nuts, chopped

Sift together flour, sugar, salt and baking powder. Make a well in flour mixture and add in order oil, eggs and vanilla. Beat until smooth. Add dates and nuts. Mix well. Pour into well greased 11x7x1½-inch pan. Bake at 350 degrees for 35 to 40 minutes. Cut while warm. Dust with powdered sugar.
Mrs. Everett M. Lemay
Mt. Vernon, Illinois

FRUIT BAR COOKIES

1 cup raisins
1 cup sugar
1 cup water
½ cup shortening or margarine
½ teaspoon cinnamon
¼ teaspoon nutmeg

⅛ teaspoon cloves
2 cups all-purpose flour
½ teaspoon salt
1 teaspoon soda
1 cup nuts
½ cup dates, cut-up

Mix first 4 ingredients together and bring to a boil. Add cinnamon, nutmeg and cloves. Let this mixture cool to lukewarm and add flour, salt and soda which has been sifted together. Stir in nuts and dates. Spread on cookie sheet with sides and bake at 350 degrees for about 30 minutes. Cover with frosting shortly after taking from oven.

FROSTING
1½ cups powdered sugar
2 teaspoons water, boiling (more if needed)

1 teaspoon vanilla
1 teaspoon butter or margarine

Mix ingredients and blend well. Cut bars into squares or oblongs.
Mrs. Bill Bailey (Faye)
Elizabethtown, Kentucky

FILLED BAR COOKIES

¾ cup shortening (part butter)   1¾ cup self-rising flour, sifted
1 cup brown sugar, packed   1¼ cups rolled oats

Mix thoroughly. Place ½ of this crumb mixture in greased and floured oblong 13x9½x2-inch pan. Press and flatten with hands to cover bottom of pan.

FILLING
3 cups cut-up dates   1½ cups water
½ cup sugar

Mix together in saucepan. Cook over low heat, stirring constantly, until thickened (about 10 minutes). Cool. Spread filling over crumb mixture. Cover with remaining crumb mixture, patting lightly. Bake at 400 degrees 25 or 30 minutes until lightly browned. Cut into bars and remove from pan while still warm. Makes about 2½ dozen bars.
Mrs. Howard Golden
Phenix City, Alabama

HELLO DOLLY COOKIES

1 stick soft margarine   1 cup graham cracker crumbs

Press in bottom of a 9x9x2-inch Pyrex dish.

1 cup flaked coconut   1 can sweetened condensed milk
1 cup semi-sweet chocolate bits   1 cup pecans, broken
1 cup (6-ounce package)
   butterscotch bits

Add first three ingredients in layers. Pour condensed milk over all. Sprinkle pecans over top. Bake 25 or 30 minutes at 350 degrees. Cool in dish. Cut into small squares.
Mrs. Bernard Jenkins (Pauline)
Pensacola, Florida

LEBKUCHEN (German Christmas Cookies)

6-ounces honey
2 tablespoons sugar, well heaped
Pinch salt
2 tablespoons cooking oil
2 tablespoons water
1 egg yolk
1 teaspoon cocoa, heaped
6 drops lemon flavoring
Large pinch ground allspice
1 teaspoon cinnamon

9-ounces all purpose flour
1 teaspoon baking powder
2½-ounces ground almonds
2½-ounces ground hazelnuts
    or pecans
1¾-ounces candied lemon peel,
    diced
2½-ounces dried apricots,
    cut small

Warm and mix together the first 5 ingredients. Transfer to a mixing bowl and cool. Add the egg yolk, cocoa, flavoring, spices and ⅔ of the flour, which has been sifted with the baking powder. Knead in the rest of the flour, nuts, lemon peel and apricots. Roll out the pastry ¼-inch thick and cut out round shapes or oblongs. Bake on a greased cookie sheet in a moderately hot oven, 375 to 400 degrees for 15 to 20 minutes.

ICING
4½-ounces powdered sugar   1 egg white, beaten

Blend powdered sugar and egg white. If too thick to spread, add a few drops of water. Ice the cookies thinly and sprinkle with colored sugar.NOTE: Cocoa may be added to a portion of the icing for chocolate variety.
Mrs. Robert Fling
Munich, West Germany

LEMON BARS

1 cup all-purpose flour, sifted   ¼ cup powdered sugar
½ cup melted butter

Mix and press into greased pan. Bake at 350 degrees for 20 minutes.

BATTER
1 cup granulated sugar
½ teaspoon baking powder
2 eggs

2 tablespoons flour
3 tablespoons lemon juice

Mix batter and pour over first mixture when taken from oven. Bake at 350 degrees for 25 minutes. Remove from oven. Cut into bars while warm. Cool and sprinkle with powdered sugar.
Mrs. Carol McCurley
Bellevue, Texas

TWO-LAYER COOKIES

¾ cup brown sugar
¾ cup margarine, melted

1½ cups all-purpose flour

Mix and spread in 9x13-inch pan. Bake at 350 degrees about 10 minutes or until slightly brown. Let cool while mixing second part.

1½ cups brown sugar
3 tablespoons flour
2¼ teaspoons baking powder

3 eggs, slightly beaten
1 cup coconut
1 cup nuts, broken

Mix first 3 ingredients. Add slightly beaten eggs, then coconut and nuts. Spread on first part and bake at 350 degrees about 30 minutes until light brown.
Mrs. Omer E. Hyde (Neva)
Eugene, Oregon

SPECIAL K BARS

6 cups Special K cereal
1 cup coconut
1 cup sugar

1 cup Karo syrup
1 cup peanut butter

Mix Special K cereal and coconut in large bowl. Heat sugar and Karo syrup until just boiling ¼-inch around edge of pan. Add 1 cup peanut butter and stir well. Pour over Special K mixture and mix well. Pat down in greased 9x13-inch pan. When cool add topping.

TOPPING
1 cup semi-sweet chocolate chips
1 cup Butterscotch chips

1 cup pecans, chopped

Melt over low heat in double boiler. Stir well. Add chopped nuts.
Mrs. Everett Lemay
Mt. Vernon, Illinois

SOUR CREAM APPLE SQUARES

2 cups all-purpose flour
2 cups brown sugar
½ cup margarine, softened
1 cup nuts, chopped
2 teaspoons cinnamon
1 teaspoon soda

½ teaspoon salt
1 cup dairy sour cream
1 teaspoon vanilla
1 egg
2 cups apples, finely chopped

Combine first 3 ingredients in large bowl. Blend at low speed until crumbly. Stir in nuts. Press 2¾ cups crumb mixture into ungreased 13x9-inch pan. To remaining mixture, add cinnamon, soda, salt, sour cream, vanilla and slightly beaten egg; blend well. Stir in apples. Spoon evenly over base. Bake in 360 degree oven for 25 to 30 minutes or until toothpick comes out clean. Cut into squares. Serve with whipped cream, if desired. Makes 12 to 15 squares.
Mrs. Dan Stringer, Jr. (Harriet)
Tigard, Oregon

GELATIN SQUARES

CRUST
¾ cup butter
⅓ cup brown sugar

1½ cups flour

Mix together and spread in 10½x15½-inch greased pan. Bake 15 minutes in 350 degree oven.

TOPPING
3 cups sugar
¾ cup water
3 envelopes gelatin
¾ cup cold water

2 drops red food coloring
½ cup nuts, finely chopped
1 teaspoon mint flavoring

Mix together sugar and ¾ cup water. Bring to a boil and boil 3 minutes. Add gelatin to ¾ cup cold water. Add to hot syrup gradually. Beat at high speed 15 minutes. Add 2 drops red food coloring, ½ cup finely chopped nuts and 1 teaspoon mint flavoring. Chill. Cut in small squares and roll in fine powdered coconut. Keep in freezer at least one day before serving.
Mrs. O. R. Harris
Lynnwood, Washington

PECAN SQUARES

1 cup butter
1 cup brown sugar
1 egg yolk
1 egg white

2 cups all-purpose flour
1 teaspoon vanilla
2 cups pecans, chopped

Cream butter and sugar; add egg yolk, then flour and flavoring. Mix with hand. Pat dough out thin in a greased cookie sheet. Dip hands in water to prevent sticking. Sprinkle nuts over dough and mash in. Beat white of 1 egg just a little; spread over dough with hands. Cook in middle of oven 20 minutes at 250 degrees. Take out of oven and cut in small squares. Return to oven and cook 15 or 20 minutes, or until cookies are nice and brown.
Mrs. Walker Bynum (Parmeillia)
Talladega, Alabama

LAVON'S PUMPKIN SQUARES

24 single graham crackers, crushed (about 1¾ cups)
⅓ cup sugar
½ cup butter or margarine, melted
2 eggs
¾ cup sugar
1 8-ounce package cream cheese, softened
1 16-ounce can pumpkin (about 2 cups)
3 egg yolks

½ cup sugar
½ cup milk
½ teaspoon salt
2 teaspoons cinnamon
1 envelope unflavored gelatin
¼ cup cold water
3 egg whites
¼ cup sugar
1 cup whipping cream, chilled or Cool Whip
1 tablespoon sugar
1 teaspoon vanilla

Heat oven to 350 degrees. Mix graham cracker crumbs and ⅓ cup sugar. Stir in melted butter; pat in buttered baking dish. 13x9x2-inches. Beat 2 eggs, ¾ cup sugar and cream cheese until light and fluffy. Pour over graham cracker crust. Bake 20 minutes. Beat pumpkin, egg yolks, ½ cup sugar, the milk, salt and cinnamon in top of double boiler. Cook over boiling water, stirring frequently until thick, about 5 minutes. Sprinkle gelatin on water in small saucepan. Stir over low heat just until dissolved; stir into pumpkin mixture. Cool. Beat egg whites until foamy. Gradually beat in ¼ cup sugar; beat until stiff and glossy. Gently fold beaten egg whites into pumpkin mixture. Pour over baked mixture; refrigerate. Just before serving, beat whipping cream and 1 tablespoon sugar in chilled bowl until stiff. During last minute of beating, add vanilla. Cut dessert into squares and garnish with whipped cream.
Mrs. William Riley (Doris)
Pensacola, Florida

FROSTY STRAWBERRY SQUARES

1 cup all-purpose flour, sifted	1 cup white sugar
¼ cup brown sugar	2 cups fresh strawberries or
½ cup walnuts, chopped	10 ounce package frozen
½ cup butter, melted	strawberrries
2 egg whites	

If using frozen berries, thaw and reduce the amount of sugar to ⅔ cup. Combine flour, brown sugar, nuts and butter. Bake in shallow pan in 350 degree oven 20 minutes, stirring occasionally. Sprinkle ⅔ cup of the baked crumbs in 13x9x2-inch pan. Combine egg whites, granulated sugar, berries and lemon juice. Using mixer, beat at high speed about 10 minutes. Fold whipped cream into strawberry mixture. Spoon over crumb mixture in pan. Top with remaining mixture. Freeze at least 6 hours.
Mrs. O. R. Harris
Lynnwood, Washington

 # Desserts

BLACKBERRY ROLL

2 cups drained blackberries	1 cup Crisco
¾ cup sugar	2 tablespoons sugar
2 teaspoons lemon juice	Water enough to mix well (have
2 cups all-purpose flour	dough stiff)
½ teaspoon salt	

Blend blackberries, sugar and lemon juice. Combine flour, salt, Crisco, sugar and water to make dough. Roll dough smoothly. Spread with blackberries. Roll up the dough into a nice roll. Bake in moderate 325 degree oven 25 to 30 minutes. Spread with hard sauce while hot.

HARD SAUCE

2 egg yolks	1 pound butter
1½ cups sugar	

Cream mixture well until smooth. Refrigerate until hard. Spread over hot blackberry roll.
Mrs. Henry B. Stokes (Etta)
Buies Creek, North Carolina

ANGEL DELIGHT

1 angel food cake, broken in bits	2 3-ounce packages strawberry
½ pint whipped cream or Cool Whip	gelatin

Prepare gelatin as package directs but using 3 cups boiling water. Cool. Fold in whipped cream. Pour mixture over cake bits. Mix well and place in refrigerator. Slice or serve in wedges.
Mrs. H. G. Edwards
Moberly, Missouri

BLUEBERRY DELIGHT

1 cup all-purpose flour	⅓ cup brown sugar
1 stick margarine	½ cup pecans, chopped

Put margarine in flour with pastry cutter. Combine all ingredients. Press into pan. Bake 15 minutes at 325 degrees or until slightly brown. Cool and crumble finely and press into pan again.

1 8-ounce package cream cheese	⅓ cup lemon juice
1 can Eagle Brand milk	1 can Blueberry pie filling

Whip together cream cheese, Eagle Brand milk and lemon juice until thick. Spread over crumbs. Pour blueberry pie filling over cheese. Place in refrigerator until ready to serve.
Mrs. Harold D. Scarbrough (Gloria)
Abilene, Texas

CHERRY TORTE

1 cup self-rising flour	1 stick margarine
¼ cup brown sugar	¾ cup pecans, chopped

Mix and press into an 8x13-inch baking dish. Bake at 350 degrees for 10 to 15 minutes. Cool and chill for 2 hours.

FILLING

1 large Cool Whip	¾ cup sugar
1 8-ounce package cream cheese	1 teaspoon vanilla

Mix ½ of Cool Whip with other ingredients. Spread on cooled crust.

TOPPING

1 can cherry pie filling

Spread over Cool Whip mixture. NOTE: Blueberries or strawberries, freshly capped, may be used for a variation in flavor.
Mrs. Howard Knight (Joyce)
Morehead City, North Carolina

CHERRY-BERRIES ON A CLOUD

6 egg whites
½ teaspoon cream of tartar
¼ teaspoon salt
1¾ cups sugar
2 cups chilled whipping cream

2 3-ounce packages cream cheese
1 cup sugar
1 teaspoon vanilla
2 cups miniature marshmallows

Heat oven to 275 degrees. Butter a 13x9x2-inch baking pan. In a large mixing bowl beat egg whites, cream of tartar and salt. Beat in 1¾ cups sugar a little at a time and continue beating until stiff and glossy. Do not underbeat. Spread in buttered pan. Bake 1 hour. Turn off oven and leave meringue in oven with door closed 12 hours or longer. In a chilled bowl, beat whipping cream until stiff. Blend cream cheese, 1 cup sugar and the vanilla. Gently fold the whipping cream and marshmallows into cream cheese mixture. Spread over the meringue. Chill 12 to 24 hours. Cut into serving pieces and top with cherry berry topping.

TOPPING

1 can cherry pie filling
1 teaspoon lemon juice

2 cups sliced fresh strawberries
or 16-ounce thawed frozen berries

Combine ingredients.
Mrs. Silas New
Somerset, Kentucky

COOKIE DELIGHT

1 package chocolate chip cookies
1 package coconut macaroon cookies

Cool Whip
Milk

Dip cookies in milk and alternate in a casserole dish. Use a flat dish. Spread the Cool Whip over the cookies and repeat with the cookies again dipped in milk. Cover over with the Cool Whip. You may make as many layers as needed. Crush 2 or 3 cookies very fine and sprinkle over the top of Cool Whip. Delicious! Refrigerate at least 12 hours before serving.
Mrs. Mollie B. Martin
Florence, South Carolina

CRÊPES WITH FRUIT CREME

1 cup self-rising flour	1½ cups milk
1 tablespoon sugar	Butter or oil
3 eggs, beaten	Creme filling
3 tablespoons butter, melted	2 cans blueberries, drained

Stir together flour and sugar. Blend eggs, 3 tablespoons butter and milk. Add to flour mixture, beating until smooth. Preheat well greased 6-inch skillet or crêpe pan. Pour 2 tablespoons of batter into pan and rotate quickly so batter covers bottom. Cook on medium heat 1 to 2 minutes on each side. Spread with cream filling. Add drained blueberries across center of crêpe and roll up.
NOTE: Fresh sliced strawberries may be substituted for blueberries. Makes 24.

CREAM FILLING

¾ cup confectioners' sugar	4 12-ounce packages cream cheese, softened

Cream ingredients together.
Mrs. Barry Landrum (Charlotte)
Greenville, Mississippi

BAKED CARAMEL CUSTARD

2 eggs	½ teaspoon vanilla
4 tablespoons sugar	Pinch salt
1½ cups milk, scalded	

Melt sugar in a heavy skillet being careful not to scorch. When melted, add to scalded milk gradually and boil until sugar is all dissolved. Let cool; flavor with vanilla and a dash of salt. Beat eggs slightly and add to cooled milk. Bake in custard cups which are placed in a pan of hot water. Bake at 325 degrees for 45 to 60 minutes. Test by inserting knife blade in custard. Blade should come out clean when custard is done.
Mrs. Robert S. Scales (Ann)
Oklahoma City, Oklahoma

SWISS CHOCOLATE CRUNCH

1 package Swiss Chocolate
Deluxe cake mix
1 small package chocolate
instant pudding mix

½ cup nuts, chopped, or
½ cup flaked coconut
1 stick butter or margarine,
melted

Preheat oven to 350 degrees. Prepare chocolate pudding and spread pudding in bottom of a 9-inch square pan. Combine dry cake mix, nuts or coconut and melted butter. Mixture will be crumbly. Sprinkle over pudding. Bake at 350 degrees for 40 to 50 minutes until center of crunch springs back when touched. Serve with ice cream, whipped cream or serve warm with coffee cream.
Mrs. Raymond Sanders (Jan)
West Texas Baptist Area

DATE NUT LOAF

½ pound graham crackers,
crushed fine
½ pound chopped dates

½ pound miniature marshmallows
1 cup nuts, chopped
½ pint whipping cream, whipped

Mix all ingredients together and shape into long loaf, about 2½-inches in diameter on waxed paper. Roll paper around loaf. Refrigerate over night or until very firm. Slice and serve.
Mrs. Nat McKinney
Carthage, Tennessee

DRESSED-UP JELLO

1 13-ounce can evaporated milk,
very cold
1 cup water, boiling

1 small package gelatin, any flavor
½ cup sugar
¼ cup lemon juice

Mix boiling water with gelatin and sugar. Let this mixture set until cool. Add lemon juice. Combine mixture with evaporated milk and whip. Pour into sherbet glasses. Chill for 2 hours.
Mrs. Paul L. Bard (Rosa)
Olean, New York

And Elijah said unto her, Fear not; go and do as thou hast said: But make me thereof a little cake first, and bring it to me, and after make for thee and for thy son. 1 Kings 17:13

DESSERT MOLD FOR CHRISTMAS

1 small package orange-flavored gelatin
1 small package lemon-flavored gelatin
1 small package cherry-flavored gelatin
1 small package lime-flavored gelatin
¼ cup sugar
1 cup pineapple juice
2 cups whipped cream or Dream Whip
1 cup graham cracker crumbs
¼ cup butter, melted

Dissolve each package gelatin except the lemon in 1 cup boiling water plus ½ cup cold water. Pour each one into ice tray or shallow pan and place in refrigerator to congeal. Dissolve lemon-flavored gelatin and ¼ cup sugar in 1 cup pineapple juice, heating and stirring until just dissolved. Chill until syrupy. Now take 2 cups whipped cream and fold into the lemon gelatin mixture. Cut congealed gelatin into cubes. Add all together. Combine 1 cup graham cracker crumbs and ¼ cup melted butter. Line bottom of pan or mold. Pour in gelatin mixture. Chill at least 8 hours or overnight.

Mrs. James W. Parker
Santa Ana, California

Mrs. R. A. McKinney (Ruby)
North Greenville, South Carolina

FROZEN FRUIT SUPREME

1 3-ounce package gelatin, any flavor
1 can fruit cocktail
Additional canned fruit as desired
1 carton Cool Whip

Prepare gelatin as package directs. When gelatin becomes syrupy, fold in fruits and Cool Whip. Pour in oblong dish. Place in freezer until firm enough to cut. Place warm, wet towel on bottom of dish after you have taken sharp knife and cut around edges. Slice as you would ice cream. Delicious! Serves 10 to 12.

Mrs. Fred King (Elaine)
Oregon City, Oregon

EASY AND ELEGANT ECLAIRS

½ cup butter
1 cup water, boiling
1 cup all-purpose flour
½ teaspoon salt

4 eggs
Vanilla pudding
Chocolate cream frosting

Add ½ pound butter to 1 cup boiling water. Stir to melt butter. Add 1 cup flour and ½ teaspoon salt all at once. Cook, stirring vigorously, until mixture is smooth and forms a soft ball that does not separate. Cool mixture slightly. Add 4 eggs, one at a time. Beat vigorously after each egg is added. Beat until mixture is smooth. Drop batter onto greased cookie sheet, or put through a pastry bag 1-inch wide and 3-inches long. Bake in very hot oven at 450 degrees for 15 minutes, then in a slow oven at 325 degrees for 25 minutes. Fill with vanilla pudding and frost with chocolate cream frosting.

CHOCOLATE CREAM FROSTING

1½ cups sugar
6 tablespoons butter or margarine

6 tablespoons canned milk
½ cup chocolate chips

Mix margarine, sugar and canned milk together. Boil one minute at a rolling boil and then add chocolate chips. Beat until it begins to thicken. Frost cooled eclairs.

Mrs. James E. Carter (Ginger)
Phoenix, Arizona

FRUIT BOWL

2 envelopes unflavored gelatin
½ cup cold water
1½ cups water, boiling
1 cup sugar
¼ teaspoon salt
2 cups fruit juice
2 tablespoons lemon juice

2 teaspoons grated lemon rind
2 cups strawberries, sliced
2 cups orange sections
1 cup pineapple tidbits
1 cup bananas
2 cups grapes, melon balls or peaches

Soften gelatin in cold water and dilute in hot water. Mix together sugar, salt, fruit juice, lemon juice and grated lemon rind. Add gelatin to this mixture. Have fruit ready and stir in first mixture. You may double recipe and serve from a punch bowl over slices of chiffon or angel food cake. Set a bowl of whipped cream or Cool Whip near by so guests can help themselves. A delightful dessert for Sunday School class meetings. Serves 36 to 40.

Mrs. Rollin Burhans (Delma)
Bowling Green, Kentucky

HEAVENLY HALO MOLD

1 large can crushed pineapple
2 3-ounce packages lemon gelatin
3 cups miniature marshmallows
2½ cups water, boiling
1 cup Dream Whip or whipped
cream
1 loaf Angel food cake, cut in
½-inch cubes

Drain pineapple, reserving 1 cup syrup. Dissolve gelatin and marshmallows in boiling water. Add syrup and chill until almost thickened, then whip. Fold in pineapple, cream and cake. Pour into 10-inch tube pan. Chill until firm. Unmold on serving plate. Garnish with frosted grapes and grated orange rind. Serves 12 to 14.
Mrs. Jack Bilbo (Mary)
Pensacola, Florida

HEATH BAR DESSERT

1 10-ounce package Lorna Doone
cookies, crushed
1 stick margarine, melted

Mix crushed cookies and margarine together. Pat into 9x13-inch pan and bake 15 minutes at 350 degrees. Cool.

2 cups milk
2 small packages instant vanilla
pudding
1 quart soft vanilla ice cream

Mix together milk and instant vanilla pudding. Add soft vanilla ice cream. Pour mixture into cool crust and chill.

2 cups Cool Whip
4 Heath bars, crushed

Spread Cool Whip over top, then sprinkle crushed Heath bars over topping. Cut in squares.
Mrs. Howard H. Ramsey (Lawonda)
Tigard, Oregon

HOT FRUIT DESSERT

1 can peaches
1 can apricots
1 can pitted black cherries
½ glass orange juice
½ glass lemon juice
4 tablespoons brown sugar
Grated lemon and orange rind

Drain juice from fruit and place in baking dish. Bake at 350 degrees for 1 hour. Add remaining ingredients and return to oven for five minutes. This is also a good dish to accompany the meat course.
Mrs. Carl Bates (Myra)
Charlotte, North Carolina

JELLO DESSERT

1 stick butter	2 eggs, separated
1 cup sugar	1 cup crushed pineapple, drained
1 cup pecans, chopped	2 packages cherry gelatin
1 box graham crackers	

Add to gelatin 2 cups water and 2 cups pineapple juice. Chill for about 1 hour. Cream butter and sugar till fluffy. Add egg yolks, one at a time. Beat egg whites till stiff. Fold into butter mixture. Add nuts and pineapple. Put 1 layer of graham crackers in bottom of pan. Spread filling evenly over graham crackers. Top with another layer of graham crackers. Pour partly chilled gelatin over top of last layer of graham crackers. Chill 4 hours before serving. Serves 15.

Mrs. A. L. McGee
Castle Hayne, North Carolina

LEMON FLUFF

1 large can Pet milk	¼ cup lemon juice
1 3-ounce package lemon gelatin	1 cup sugar
1¾ cups hot water	2½ cups vanilla wafer crumbs

Chill unopened can of milk until ice cold, 3 to 4 hours. Dissolve gelatin in hot water. Chill till practically set. Whip till light and fluffy. Add lemon juice and sugar. Whip chilled milk and fold into gelatin mixture. Line bottom of 9x13-inch pan with crumbs. Pour gelatin over crumbs. Top with remaining crumbs. Chill till firm. Cut into squares. Garnish with maraschino cherries. Makes 12 squares.

Mrs. Bill Wilson (Marie)
Mobile, Alabama

LEMON JELLO-ICE CREAM DESSERT

2 3-ounce packages lemon gelatin	1 large can crushed pineapple, well drained
2 cups water, boiling	1 cup miniature marshmallows
2 pints softened vanilla ice cream	½ cup chopped pecans
	1 angel food cake

Dissolve gelatin in boiling water. When cool, mix in softened vanilla ice cream. Stir until melted then chill until partially set. Fold in well drained crushed pineapple, marshmallows and pecans. Line bottom of pan with slices of angel food cake. Spoon in ½ remaining gelatin mixture on top. Keep refrigerated. NOTE: Can frost with 1 cup powdered sugar mixed with juice of 1 lemon if desired.

Mrs. John Bisagno (Uldine)
Houston, Texas

LEMON LUSH

½ cup pecans, chopped   1 stick margarine, melted
1 cup flour

Mix and pat in 9x13-inch pan. Bake at 350 degrees for 15 minutes or until lightly browned. Cool.

1 8-ounce package cream   1 cup powdered sugar
  cheese, soft   1 cup Cool Whip

Mix and spread over crust. Let set.

3 packages instant lemon   3 cups milk
  pudding mix   Chopped nuts

Mix together and spread on other layers. Let set. Spread remainder of large size Cool Whip on top. Sprinkle with chopped nuts.
Mrs. Donald V. Wideman (Marian)
Kansas City, Missouri

MARSHMALLOW LOAF

4 egg whites   Green food coloring
1 tablespoon unflavored gelatin   Vanilla
½ cup water, boiling   Lemon extract
½ cup cold water   Powdered sugar
1 cup sugar   Chopped pecans or walnuts
Almond extract   Whipped cream
Red food coloring

Beat egg whites until stiff. Stir 1 tablespoon of gelatin into ½ cup boiling water until dissolved. Add ½ cup cold water and 1 cup sugar to gelatin mixture. Stir gelatin-sugar mixture into egg whites. Beat well and divide into 3 parts.
1. Flavor with almond extract and color pink with 3 drops red food coloring.
2. Leave white and flavor with vanilla
3. Flavor with lemon extract and color green with food coloring.
Let stand until you are sure the colors will not run together, stirring now and then. Dust loaf pan with powdered sugar after lining with waxed paper. Put in pink layer. Sprinkle with chopped pecans or walnuts. Next layer white mixture, then more nuts, then layer green mixture. Let stand in refrigerator several hours or overnight. Serve in slices with whipped cream. Very unusual and good! You can vary flavors (for example, cocoa mix can be used) and colors to suit any color scheme.
Mrs. Abner V. McCall
Waco, Texas

ORANGE DELIGHT

2 cups orange juice
1 pound marshmallows
1 pint whipping cream

1 medium angel food cake, broken into bits

Dissolve marshmallows in 2 cups orange juice over medium heat, stirring constantly. Cool. Whip 1 pint whipping cream and fold into cooled orange juice mixture. Pour over broken bits of angel food cake and let stand at least 4 hours before serving. Overnight is better. Cut into squares. Serve with whipped cream and maraschino cherries. Makes 15 large or 20 small servings.

Mrs. Charles H. Beal (Winona)
Sarasota, Florida

OREO ICE CREAM DESSERT

20 Oreo chocolate cookies
⅓ cup margarine, melted

½ gallon vanilla or coffee ice cream

Roll Oreo cookies with rolling pin to make crumbs. Add ⅓ cup melted margarine. Stir well and pack firmly into bottom of 13x8x½-inch Pyrex dish. Place in freezer and allow to become very firm. Spread vanilla ice cream over this then return to freezer till firm.

CHOCOLATE SAUCE TOPPING:

2 squares bitter chocolate
½ cup sugar
1 tablespoon margarine

1 small can Carnation milk
Chopped pecans (optional)

Melt 2 squares chocolate in double boiler with ½ cup sugar, 1 tablespoon margarine and canned milk. Cook over hot water, stirring until thick. Cool, then pour over ice cream. Sprinkle chopped pecans on top. Return to freezer.

Mrs. J. R. White (Nell)
Montgomery, Alabama

PINEAPPLE DELIGHT

¾ pound vanilla wafers
1½ cups sugar
1 cup pecans, chopped
½ cup pineapple juice

½ pound butter or margarine
1 3-ounce package lemon gelatin
1 cup crushed pineapple, drained
4 eggs

Heat pineapple juice to boiling. Add gelatin and stir until dissolved. Set aside to cool. Cream sugar and butter. Add well beaten egg yolks, pineapple, gelatin and nuts. Beat egg whites until stiff and fold into mixture. Roll vanilla wafers on dough board with rolling pin to make crumbs. Place one half of vanilla wafer crumbs in bottom of loaf pan and pour mixture on top. Then put ½ of crumbs on top and pat down a little. Place in refrigerator 24 hours before serving. Delicious!
Mrs. H. E. Alsup (Willie Lou)
Haysville, Kansas

IOWA COOL

1 package instant pistachio pudding
1 large can crushed pineapple

1 cup miniature marshmallows
1 small carton Cool Whip

Place dry pudding in bowl. Add pineapple and juice. Stir in marshmallows. Mix well. Fold in Cool Whip. Chill and serve.
Mrs. Cecil Finfrock (Hope)
Valdosta, Georgia

PINEAPPLE PARADISE

1 pound vanilla wafers
1 box powdered sugar
1 pint Cool Whip
1 number 2 can crushed pineapple

4 eggs
1 cup pecans, chopped
½ cup margarine

Grease pan with butter and mix ingredients as follows and place in pan in layers. Roll ½ of vanilla wafers and place crumbs in bottom of pan. Cream butter. Add sugar, then eggs, one at a time. Beat 2 minutes. Add drained pineapple to Cool Whip, then nuts. Spread smoothly over mixture. Roll other ½ of vanilla wafers and sprinkle on top. Chill 20 hours before serving.
Mrs. Hugh L. Smith (Virginia)
Belvedere, South Carolina

"COMPANY'S COMING DESSERT"

3 egg whites
1 teaspoon vanilla
18 soda crackers, crushed
6-ounces pineapple preserves
1 small can coconut

1 cup sugar
½ pint whipping cream
1 teaspoon cream of tartar
½ cup nuts

Beat egg whites till foamy. Add cream of tartar and sugar. Beat until stiff. Fold in crackers, nuts and vanilla. Bake in a well-greased pan for 35 minutes at 325 degrees. Whip cream. Fold in pineapple preserves. Spread on cooled mixture. Sprinkle coconut over top. Chill overnight.
Mrs. Richard Hopper (Mary Edna)
Ardmore, Oklahoma

TWO TONE DESSERT

1 cup all-purpose flour
½ cup butter

½ cup nuts, chopped

Mix well and pat down in 9x13-inch pan. Bake at 350 degrees for 10 minutes. Let cool.

1 8-ounce package cream cheese, softened
1 cup powdered sugar

1 large carton Cool Whip

Mix softened cream cheese with powdered sugar. Add Cool Whip. Spread over cooled crust.

2 3-ounce packages pistachio instant pudding mix

2½ cups milk
1 small carton Cool Whip

Mix pistachio pudding mix with 2½ cups milk. Spread on cheese mixture. Refrigerate, then spread 1 small carton Cool Whip on top. Return to refrigerator.
Mrs. Lloyd Elder
Texas Baptist Convention

RICE KRISPIES-ICE CREAM DESSERT

2½ cups Rice Krispies
1 cup pecans, chopped
1 cup Angel Flake coconut

1 stick margarine
¾ cup brown sugar
Vanilla ice cream

Melt margarine in cookie tray. Stir in Rice Krispies, pecans and coconut. Toast 30 minutes in 250-300 degree oven stirring often to keep from burning. Remove from oven and add ¾ cup brown sugar while hot. Put layer in bottom of pan. Add layer of vanilla ice cream then add layer of Rice Krispies topping. Place in freezer.
Mrs. J. R. White (Nell)
Montgomery, Alabama

RICHELIEU MOLD

1 16-ounce can pitted dark sweet cherries
1 3-ounce package cherry gelatin
1 cup water, boiling

2 tablespoons orange juice
¾ cup orange sections, diced
1 cup whipped topping
¼ cup toasted almonds, chopped

Drain cherries, reserving ¾ cup syrup. Dissolve gelatin in boiling water. Add reserved syrup and orange juice. Fold in cherries and oranges. Pour into 4 cup mold or individual molds. Chill until firm. Unmold and serve with whipped topping combined with almonds. Makes 6 servings.
Mrs. Robert Cuttino (Molly)
Lancaster, South Carolina

ROCKY ROAD DESSERT

1 pound angel food cake, broken into bits
2 6-ounce packages chocolate chips, melted
4 egg yolks

2 tablespoons sugar
1 tablespoon water
4 egg whites
1 pint whipping cream

Beat egg yolks and blend in melted chocolate, sugar and water. Beat egg whites and fold into chocolate mixture. Beat whipping cream and fold in. Pour mixture over broken bits of angel food cake. Mix and chill for several hours.
Mrs. Charles H. Beal (Winona)
Sarasota, Florida

STRAWBERRY DESSERT

1 pound box vanilla wafers, rolled fine	3 egg whites
3 egg yolks	¾ cup nuts
½ cup butter	½ pint whipping cream
1 cup powdered sugar	2 cups strawberries, freshly sliced

Layer crumbs in bottom of greased 10x12 inch-pan. Reserve 1 cup crumbs for top. Beat egg yolks slightly. Cream egg yolks with butter and powdered sugar till light. Add stiffly beaten egg whites and fold together gently. Spread over crumbs. Sprinkle nuts over this. Place sliced strawberries on top of nuts. Spread whipped cream on top of strawberries. Cover with reserved crumbs.

Mrs. Vernon H. Mitchell (Ruth)   *Mrs. Arthur M. Allen*
Pueblo West, Colorado   *Buford, Georgia*

STRAWBERRY YUM-YUM

1 stick margarine	1 cup sugar
2 cups graham cracker crumbs	1 cup cold milk
2 packages Dream Whip	2 cups strawberries
1 8-ounce package cream cheese	

Melt margarine and stir in crumbs. Place half of mixture in bottom of baking dish. Whip 2 packages Dream Whip and cream cheese with 1 cup sugar and 1 cup cold milk. Pur ½ of the Dream Whip mixture on crumbs. Spread 2 cups strawberries on creamed mixture. Spread remainder of creamed mixture on top of strawberries. Sprinkle remainder of crumbs on top. Chill 3 hours or longer.

Mrs. Ray K. Hodge (Joyce)
Kinston, North Carolina

 # Puddings

AUTUMN PUDDING

1 egg	1¼ teaspoons baking powder
¾ cup sugar	¼ teaspoon salt
1 teaspoon vanilla	1 cup apples, peeled and chopped
¼ cup all-purpose flour	½ cup nuts, chopped

Beat egg, sugar and vanilla until fluffy. Sift together dry ingredients. Add to first mixture, blending by hand. Fold in apples and nuts. Pour into well-greased 9-inch square pan. Bake at 350 degrees for 25 minutes.
Mrs. James W. Parker
Santa Ana, California

MOIST BREAD PUDDING

1 15-ounce can Eagle Brand milk	3 tablespoons margarine, melted
3 cups water, boiling	3 eggs, slightly beaten
3 cups diced or broken bread crumbs (stale bread, biscuits, rolls, etc.)	½ teaspoon salt
	2 teaspoons vanilla extract
	Cinnamon to taste
	Raisins, optional

Combine condensed milk and water. Add margarine and let it melt. Pour over bread crumbs to soften. Stir in remaining ingredients. Pour into 1½-quart casserole or baking dish. Set dish in a shallow pan of hot water to bake. Bake at 325 degrees about 1 hour or until knife blade inserted near center comes out clean. Very nourishing to take to the sick.
Mrs. Don Moore (Shirley)
Ft. Smith, Arkansas

MISSIONARIES' BRAZILIAN PUDDING

1 can Eagle Brand condensed milk
1 can homogenized milk
4 eggs
1 teaspoon vanilla

Beat eggs slightly. Add can of condensed milk. Add same can full of homogenized milk and 1 teaspoon vanilla. Pour into custard cups or baking dish. Set in pan of water and cook in a slow oven at 300 degrees until firm. A knife blade run into the center will come out clean. Good to take to a sick friend.
Mrs. Thomas E. Halsell (Elizabeth)
Indianapolis, Indiana

GINGER'S CHOCOLATE GRAHAM CRACKER PUDDING

12 whole graham crackers, rolled fine
3 egg whites, beaten stiff
½ pound marshmallows, cut into pieces
¾ cup nut meats, chopped
½ cup butter
1 cup powdered sugar
3 egg yolks
1 can chocolate syrup

Place ½ of the crackers in 9½x13-inch baking dish. Combine beaten egg whites with marshmallows and nuts. Pour over cracker crumbs that are in dish. In a small mixer bowl combine egg yolks with butter and powdered sugar. Mix briefly. Add chocolate syrup and beat until stiff. Pour over nuts and marshmallow mixture. Cover with remaining crumbs. Let set 6 to 8 hours. Best when left for 24 hours.
Mrs. James E. Carter (Ginger)
Phoenix, Arizona

DATE PUDDING

1½ cups brown sugar   2 tablespoons butter
2 cups hot water

Cook slowly into a syrup while mixing batter.

BATTER
1 cup all-purpose flour   ½ cup brown sugar
1 teaspoon cinnamon   ½ cup milk
2 teaspoons baking powder   ½ cup chopped dates
1 teaspoon cooking oil   ½ cup nut meats

Pour syrup into 9x12-inch pan. Add batter by teaspoons, distributing evenly on top of syrup. Bake for 30 minutes at 325 degrees. When serving turn each piece upside down. Top with whipped cream.
Mrs. Harry Foley
Mesa, Arizona

BAKED PEACH PUDDING

2 cups fresh peaches, sliced   ½ teaspoon salt
¾ cup sugar   1 teaspoon baking powder
½ cup milk   1 cup all-purpose flour
4 tablespoons butter or margarine

TOPPING
1 cup sugar   ¼ teaspoon salt
1 tablespoon cornstarch   1 cup water, boiling

Arrange peaches in bottom of a greased 8x8x2-inch pan. Cream butter with ¾ cup sugar. Sift together flour, ½ teaspoon salt and baking powder. Add to creamed mixture alternately with milk, in 4 or 5 additions. Beat until smooth. Spread batter over fruit. Mix 1 cup sugar with cornstarch and ¼ teaspoon salt. Sift over the batter. Pour the boiling water over all. Bake at 325 degrees for 1 hour. Serve warm with cream. This makes a pudding with a cake top and a thick syrup at the bottom. Serves 6.
Mrs. John Dunaway (Jayne)
Corbin, Kentucky

Ice Cream & Toppings

FRUIT PUNCH SHERBET

6 ripe bananas, mashed
2⅔ cups sugar
1 number 2 can apricots, cut up
1 large can crushed pineapple

1 large or 2 small cans frozen
   orange juice, diluted as directed
Juice from apricots
Juice of 2 lemons

Mix and freeze. Serve with ginger ale. FANTASTIC!
Mrs. Adrian Rogers (Joyce)
Memphis, Tennessee

ORANGE-PINEAPPLE SHERBET

6 12-ounce cans Orange Crush
1 can condensed milk

1 20-ounce can crushed pineapple
   with juice

Mix well and place in ice cream freezer.
Mrs. Robert K. Davis (Pat)
Elba, Alabama

LIME SHERBET

2 3-ounce packages lime
   flavored gelatin
2 cups water, boiling
2 cups sugar

2 large cans cream
2 quarts milk
6 lemons

Combine gelatin, sugar and boiling water. Stir until dissolved. Add milk, cream and juice of lemons. This mixture will be curdled but will be smooth and creamy when frozen. You can decrease the amount of lemon juice to taste.
Mrs. Jaroy Weber (Tippy)
Lubbock, Texas

GREAT POPSICLES

1 3-ounce package
   orange-flavored gelatin
1 ⅝-ounce package grape
   Kool-Aid

1 cup sugar
2 cups water, boiling
1¾ cups cold water

Dissolve gelatin, Kool-Aid and sugar in boiling water. Stir in cold water. Freeze in popsicle holders, ice trays or small paper cups.
Mrs. Jerry Kennedy
Franklinton, Louisiana

BUTTER PECAN ICE CREAM

6 eggs
1 cup sugar
1 teaspoon vanilla
1½ teaspoons butter
   flavoring
1 can evaporated milk

1 can Eagle Brand Condensed milk
1 pint coffee rich, frozen
Enough milk to fill freezer
1½ cups toasted buttered
   pecans, salted

Beat eggs and sugar together. Add vanilla and butter flavoring. Stir in remaining ingredients. Mix well, adding enough milk to fill freezer. Freeze.
Mrs. Landrum Leavell (Jo Ann)
New Orleans, Louisiana

NO-COOK VANILLA ICE CREAM

4 eggs
2¼ cups sugar
4 cups whipping cream

4½ teaspoons vanilla
½ teaspoon salt
5 cups milk or enough to fill freezer

Beat together eggs and sugar. Add and mix in whipping cream, vanilla, salt and milk. Pour in freezer and freeze.
Mrs. Roger Roberto
Parma, Ohio

QUICK HOME MADE ICE CREAM

1 small box instant vanilla pudding mix	6 eggs, well beaten
1 cup sugar	1 can Eagle Brand Condensed milk
Pinch salt	1 tablespoon vanilla flavoring
	Sweet milk

Mix together instant vanilla pudding mix, sugar, salt and well beaten eggs. Add Eagle Brand milk and vanilla. Finish filling 1 gallon-size freezer with sweet milk.

Mrs. Everett Smalts (Mary Ruth)
Duke, Oklahoma

VANILLA ICE CREAM

(For 1 ½ gallon electric churn or manual)

5 egg yolks	1 quart whipping cream
2½ cups sugar	2 quarts homogenized milk
¾ cup water, boiling	1 tablespoon vanilla

Beat egg yolks until light. Add sugar and beat. Add boiling water very slowly and stir well. (If this is lumpy, strain it, but it will be smooth if boiling water is poured in slowly enough!) Add cream, milk and vanilla. Pour into freezer. Beat 5 egg whites until stiff, stir into mixture in freezer and freeze. If fruit is desired, blend fruit in blender and decrease amount of milk.

Mrs. Conrad Willard (Lena Mae)
Miami, Florida

ICE CREAM BALLS WITH CHOCOLATE SAUCE

1 gallon vanilla ice cream	1½ cups toasted pecans, chopped
1 pound salted peanuts, chopped	Hot Fudge Sauce

Allow ice cream to soften. Form into balls and roll in chopped nuts. Cover well and put in freezer. When serving, top with Hot Fudge Sauce.

HOT FUDGE SAUCE

½ cup cocoa	⅓ cup light corn syrup
¾ cup sugar	⅓ cup margarine
⅔ cup evaporated milk	1 teaspoon vanilla

Combine cocoa and sugar in saucepan. Blend in evaporated milk and light corn syrup. Cook, stirring constantly, until boiling point. Boil and stir 1 minute. Add margarine and vanilla. Serve hot.

Mrs. James Richardson (Cissa)
Leland, Mississippi

GERMAN CHOCOLATE SAUCE

1-ounce Baker's German Sweet
   Chocolate
1-ounce Baker's Bitter Chocolate

1 number 2 can Pet milk
1 scant cup sugar
1 tablespoon butter

Place all ingredients into a large saucepan and cook until the mixture thickens. Stir sauce constantly while cooking. Remove from heat. Add butter and beat until smooth. Serve hot over vanilla ice cream. Keeps well in refrigerator and can be reheated.
Mrs. James Landes (Irene)
Dallas, Texas

PEANUT BUTTER CHOCOLATE SAUCE

1 cup light Karo syrup
1 cup crunchy peanut butter

1 cup Hershey's Chocolate syrup

Mix and serve over vanilla ice cream.
Mrs. Gary Cook
Sapulpa, Oklahoma

SUPERB CHOCOLATE SAUCE

½ cup butter
2¼ cups confectioners' sugar
⅔ cup evaporated milk

2 squares bitter chocolate
Vanilla

Place first 4 ingredients in double boiler. Do not stir. Cook 30 minutes, then beat and add vanilla. Cool. Store in jar in refrigerator. Use as topping for ice cream or cake. May be used as a dip for pineapple chunks, small squares of angel food cake, cherries, etc. when used as hot sauce in fondue dish.
Mrs. Tom S. Brandon (Dolly)
Sherman, Texas

Mrs. Rollin Burhans
Bowling Green, Kentucky

STRAWBERRY DELIGHT

4 cups blended fresh strawberries   1 bottle Certo
   (Measure after blending)   ¼ cup lemon juice
7 cups sugar

Mix thoroughly; put into covered freezer containers and let stand overnight at room temperature, then put in freezer. Keep stored in freezer
indefinitely. May be used as topping for ice cream or a spread. When used
for a meal, return unused portion to freezer.
Mrs. Conrad Willard (Lena Mae)
Miami, Florida

Cakes

CARAMEL TOPPED APPLE CAKE

1¼ cups salad oil   3 cups cake flour
2 cups sugar   1 teaspoon salt
3 eggs   1 teaspoon soda
1 teaspoon vanilla   1 cup nuts, chopped
3 cups raw apples, chopped

Do not use mixer. Beat eggs; add sugar, oil and vanilla. Stir in 3 cups
apples. Sift and measure 3 cups flour with salt and soda. Mix nuts in flour.
Add apple batter to flour and nut mixture. Mix well. Bake in tube pan or
sheet pan at 325 degrees for about 1 hour.

TOPPING (½ is enough)
1 stick margarine or butter   2 cups light brown sugar
½ cup evaporated milk

Combine above and bring to a boil. For a thicker filling cook longer and
whip until thick and creamy. Cool and spread on cake.
Mrs. Frank F. Norfleet (Virginia)   *Mrs. Branson Wiggins (Gwen)*
Kansas City, Missouri   *Reading, Ohio*

Mrs. Bruce H. Price (Eva)
Kingsport, Tennessee

APPLE SAUCE CAKE

1 cup butter	3 cups all-purpose flour
2 cups sugar	1 teaspoon nutmeg
2 cups applesauce	1 teaspoon cinnamon
1 cup broken pecans or walnuts	1 teaspoon vanilla
1 cup raisins	1¾ teaspoons soda

Cream sugar and butter until light and fluffy; add applesauce and raisins and nuts which have been dredged in ¼ cup of the measured flour. Sift all dry ingredients together and add to the mixture. Pour into loaf or tube pan and bake 2 hours in a slow oven at 325 degrees. Ice with caramel icing. Cake keeps indefinitely and gets better all the time.
Mrs. Jerry DeBell (Lurline)
Columbus, Ohio

APRICOT CRUMBLE CAKE

1 8-ounce package Philadelphia cream cheese	2 cups cake flour, sifted
½ cup Parkay margarine	1 teaspoon baking powder
1¼ cups sugar	½ teaspoon baking soda
2 eggs	¼ teaspoon salt
¼ cup milk	1 10-ounce jar Kraft apricot or peach preserves
1 teaspoon vanilla	

Blend cream cheese, margarine and sugar thoroughly. Add eggs, milk and vanilla. Sift together flour, baking powder, baking soda and salt. Blend well with batter. Pour ½ of batter into greased and floured 13x9-inch pan. Cover with preserves and top with remaining batter. Bake at 350 degrees for 35 to 40 minutes.

TOPPING

2 cups shredded coconut	1 teaspoon cinnamon
⅔ cup brown sugar	⅓ cup margarine, melted

Spread on cake and broil until golden brown.
Mrs. A. F. Tuck
Champaign, Illinois

APRICOT NECTAR CAKE

1 box yellow cake mix
⅔ cup Wesson oil
⅔ cup apricot nectar

1 small package orange gelatin
4 eggs
Grated peel of 1 orange

Place all ingredients in large mixing bowl. Mix well. Pour into greased and floured bundt pan. Bake at 350 degrees for 55 minutes.

GLAZE
⅓ cup apricot nectar

1½ cups powdered sugar

Mix together and pour over hot cake.
Mrs. James W. Parker
Santa Ana, California

BANANA CAKE

1½ cups sugar
½ cup shortening
2 eggs
2 to 3 large bananas
⅔ cup buttermilk

2 cups flour
1 teaspoon soda
1 teaspoon baking powder
1 teaspoon vanilla
½ teaspoon salt

Cream together sugar and shortening. Add eggs, bananas and milk. Mix well and add dry ingredients. Bake at 350 degrees for 25 to 30 minutes in 2 8-inch square pans.

CREAM CHEESE ICING
½ stick margarine
3-ounces cream cheese

1 teaspoon vanilla
Powdered sugar

Mix cheese and butter until soft with mixer. Add vanilla and mix well. Add sugar until it is a good frosting consistency. Double all ingredients for a large amount of frosting. Use 8-ounces cream cheese.
Mrs. Sam Friend (Donna)
Bothell, Washington

Mrs. Everett Smalts (Ruth)
Duke, Oklahoma

BLACK BANANA CAKE

2½ teaspoons cinnamon
1 teaspoon allspice
1 teaspoon nutmeg
1 teaspoon cloves
3 cups all-purpose flour
½ pound raisins
½ cup chopped dates
1 cup pecans, chopped
2 cups sugar

1 cup butter or margarine
4 eggs
5 tablespoons buttermilk
2 teaspoons soda
¾ cup strawberry jam
1 cup blackberry jam
2 large bananas, mashed
1 small jar maraschino cherries, drained

Sift together first 5 ingredients. Dredge with small amount of flour, raisins, dates and pecans. Set aside. Cream together sugar and butter. Add eggs, one at a time, beating well after each addition. Stir in buttermilk, soda, jam and bananas. Add flour mixture, blending well. Add the fruit mixture along with maraschino cherries. Line a 10-inch tube pan with greased brown paper. Bake at 275 degrees about 2 hours. This cake keeps well and is better than most fruit cakes.

Mrs. Glen Ferguson
Irvine, Kentucky

DELICIOUS AND EASY BLUEBERRY CAKE
(You'll Love This One!)

1 Duncan Hines Butter Cake Mix

Mix cake and cook according to package directions. Let cool on cake rack.

BLUEBERRY FILLING

1 pint blueberries (or use 1 can blueberry pie filling)

⅔ cup sugar
3 tablespoons cornstarch

Mix sugar and cornstarch. Add blueberries and blend well. Cook over medium heat until thick. Cover with waxed paper and let cool.

FROSTING

½ pint sour cream
13-ounces Cool Whip

½ teaspoon vanilla

Blend Cool Whip with sour cream. Add vanilla. Spread on cooled cake. Spoon blueberry filling between layers and on top of cake. Allow filling to dribble down sides of cake.

Mrs. Joseph P. DuBose, Jr. (Sybil)
Graceville, Florida

BUTTER CAKE

2 sticks butter or margarine
2 cups sugar

5 eggs
2 cups all-purpose flour

Cream butter. Add sugar and beat well. Add eggs, one at a time, beating well after each addition. Blend in flour and mix well. Bake in tube or bundt pan at 350 degrees for 1 hour.
Mrs. Robert E. Galloway (Essie)
Pineville, Louisiana

BUTTERNUT CAKE

1 cup Crisco
2 cups sugar
4 eggs
1 cup milk

2½ cups all-purpose flour, sifted
½ cup self-rising flour
1 tablespoon butter flavoring

Cream Crisco, sugar and eggs at high speed for 10 minutes. Add 1 cup flour, beat one minute on 3rd speed. Add rest of flour and milk. Beat 1 minute on low speed. Add flavoring. Mix well. Bake in 3 layer pans, approximately 30 minutes at 350 degrees.

FROSTING

1 stick margarine
1 box confectioners' sugar
1 8-ounce package cream cheese

1 tablespoon butter flavoring
1 cup nuts, chopped

Mix above and spread on cake.
Mrs. O. R. Harris
Lynnwood, Washington

CARROT CAKE

2 cups sugar	2 teaspoons cinnamon
4 eggs	Dash of salt
1 cup oil	3 cups carrots, grated
2¼ cups all-purpose flour	1 cup nuts, chopped
2 teaspoons soda	1 teaspoon vanilla
2 teaspoons baking powder	

Cream sugar, eggs and oil. Sift together flour, soda, baking powder, cinnamon and salt. Add to creamed mixture. Beat well. Add carrots, nuts and vanilla. Bake in 3 9-inch pans at 350 degrees for 25 to 30 minutes. Cool and frost.

FROSTING

1 stick butter or margarine	1 teaspoon vanilla
2 8-ounce packages cream cheese	¾ cup nuts, chopped
1 box powdered sugar	

Blend well and spread on cake layers.

Mrs. R. William Dodson (Janelle)   *Mrs. Bobby W. Barnett (Mary)*
Martin, Tennessee   *Bradford, Rhode Island*

Mrs. Rufus Spraberry (Doris)
Vernon, Texas

CHERRY ANGEL WHIP CAKE

1   package Angel Food Cake mix

Bake as directed. Cool.

1 cup sugar	1 package cherry flavored
½ cup water	gelatin
1 8¾-ounce can crushed	2 cups whipping cream
pineapple	

Blend sugar, water, pineapple and gelatin in medium saucepan. Bring to boil and simmer for 10 minutes (no less), stirring occasionally. Chill until very stiff. Whip 2 cups of cream till thick. Fold in the gelatin mixture. Slice cake through center to make two layers. Put cream mixture between layers and frost sides and top of cake. Chill about 4 hours or overnight. Very good!

Mrs. Shelden H. Russell (Roberta)
San Jose, California

CHOCOLATE CAKE

1 package Duncan Hines Yellow cake mix	½ cup Wesson Oil
1 package instant chocolate pudding	1 tablespoon vanilla
	4 eggs
1 cup sour cream	1 cup milk chocolate chips
	1 cup nuts, chopped (optional)

Mix first 6 ingredients well. Add chips and nuts. Bake in greased tube or Bundt pan at 350 degrees for 50 minutes. Cake will be moist. Do not overbake.

Mrs. Elaine Horton
Pensacola, Florida

CHOCOLATE BAR SWIRL CAKE

1 cup butter or margarine	1½ cups sour cream
2 cups sugar	¼ cup honey or light corn syrup
1 teaspoon vanilla	¾ cup pecans, chopped
5 eggs	1 8-ounce milk chocolate bar
2½ cups all-purpose flour	½ cup (5½-ounce can)
¾ teaspoon baking soda	chocolate-flavored syrup
¼ teaspoon salt	

Cream butter, sugar and vanilla until light and fluffy. Add eggs; beat well. Combine flour, baking soda and salt; add alternately with sour cream to creamed mixture. Stir honey and pecans into 2 cups batter; set aside. Melt chocolate syrup over warm water; blend into remaining batter. Pour into greased and floured 10-inch tube pan. Spoon honey batter evenly over chocolate batter. Bake on lowest rack of oven at 350 degrees for 45 minutes. Decrease temperature to 325 degrees without opening oven door and continue to bake 50 to 55 minutes until done. Cool cake in pan 1 hour; remove from pan and cool completely. Frost with cocoa honey frosting.

COCOA HONEY FROSTING

⅓ cup margarine or butter	2 tablespoons honey
⅓ cup unsweetened cocoa	1 teaspoon vanilla
2 to 3 tablespoons milk	2 cups confectioners' sugar

Combine butter, cocoa, milk, honey and vanilla in small mixer bowl. Add sugar; beat until smooth. Use to fill and frost 8 or 9-inch layer cake or 10-inch tube cake. . Yield: 1½ cups.

Mrs. A. Douglas Watterson (Jan)
Dallas, Texas

MILKY WAY CAKE

8 Milky Way bars	1 stick margarine

Melt in double boiler; set aside.

2 cups sugar	1 cup buttermilk
1 stick margarine	½ teaspoon soda
4 eggs	2 teaspoons vanilla
2½ cups flour	½ cup nuts, chopped

Cream sugar and margarine. Add eggs, one at a time, beating after each addition. Add flour, buttermilk and soda. Stir in candy bar mix, vanilla and nuts. Bake in tube pan for about 1 hour at 350 degrees.

FROSTING

3 Milky Way bars	2 cups powdered sugar
1 stick margarine	Milk if necessary
1 teaspoon vanilla	

Melt Milky Way bars and margarine in double boiler. Add vanilla and powdered sugar. (Sometimes takes more, add gradually.)

Mrs. V. Allen Gaines (Leila)
Newport News, Virginia

Mrs. Hershel Blair
Poteau, Oklahoma

CHOCOLATE MARSHMALLOW CAKE

2 sticks margarine	4 eggs
2 tablespoons cocoa	1 cup nuts, chopped
2 cups sugar	1 7-ounce jar Marshmallow Cream
1½ cups all-purpose flour	

Mix above ingredients together and pour into a greased loaf pan, 9x12x2-inch. Bake at 350 degrees for 20 to 25 minutes or until done. Cover with marshmallow cream while cake is still hot. Spread icing on top of marshmallow cream and swirl it in.

ICING

2 tablespoons cocoa	1 box powdered sugar
1 stick margarine	6 tablespoons milk or cream

Mix all together. Beat until smooth.

Mrs. T. T. Crabtree (Bennie)
Springfield, Missouri

Mrs. Billy D. Allen (Elray)
Springfield, Illinois

Mrs. Damon Vaughn (Carolyn)
Bossier City, Louisiana

$100.00 CAKE

½ cup margarine
3 eggs, divided
2 cups all-purpose Pillsbury flour
1¼ cups sweet milk
2 teaspoons baking powder
2 cups sugar

1 teaspoon salt
1 cup nuts
1 teaspoon vanilla
2 squares unsweetened chocolate, melted

Cream margarine and sugar. Add egg yolks, one at a time, then chocolate mixture. Sift dry ingredients. Add alternately with milk. Fold in beaten egg whites. Bake at 350 degrees for 30 minutes. Makes two 8-inch layers.

FROSTING

1 box powdered sugar
1 egg, beaten
Juice of 1 lemon
1½ squares chocolate, melted

1 stick margarine
1 teaspoon vanilla
1 cup nuts

Mix all together in mixing bowl. Beat with electric mixer until creamy and ready to spread.
Mrs. Albert Moore (Lorraine)
Whiting, Indiana

CHOCOLATE CHIP AND CREAM CHEESE CAKE

1 stick butter or margarine, soft
1 large package cream cheese
1¼ cups sugar
2 eggs, beaten
1 teaspoon vanilla
¼ cup milk

2 cups cake flour
¼ teaspoon soda
1 teaspoon baking powder
¼ teaspoon salt
1 6-ounce package chocolate chips

Cream together butter, cream cheese and sugar. Add eggs and vanilla. Mix together dry ingredients. Add alternately dry ingredients and milk to butter mixture. Stir in chocolate chips. Pour into greased tube pan. Top with cinnamon and sugar. Decorate with pecan halves. Cook at 350 degrees for about 50 minutes.
Mrs. Page Kelley (Vernice)
Louisville, Kentucky

BASIC CREAM CHEESE CAKE

3 sticks margarine	1½ teaspoons vanilla
1 8-ounce package cream cheese	1½ teaspoons butter flavoring
3 cups sugar	3 cups all-purpose flour
Dash of salt	6 eggs

Beat together margarine, cream cheese and sugar until creamy. Add remaining ingredients in order listed, eggs being added one at a time. Mix with electric mixer. Pour into tube pan and bake at 350 degrees for 1½ hours. Or bake a 3 layer cake at 300 degrees for 25 to 30 minutes.

COCONUT AND NUT ICING FOR THREE LAYER CAKE

1 cup coconut, toasted	1 box confectioners' sugar
1 cup pecans, toasted chopped	1 teaspoon vanilla
1 stick margarine	1 teaspoon butter flavoring
1 8-ounce package cream cheese	

Toast and stir coconut and pecans until golden brown. Cream margarine, sugar, cream cheese and flavoring. Add cooled coconut and pecans. Spread on cooled cake.

Mrs. Ted Callahan
Jackson, South Carolina

NO BAKE CHERRY CHEESE CAKE

2 cups graham cracker crumbs	2 packages Dream Whip
1 stick margarine	1 8-ounce package cream cheese
½ cup sugar (may be omitted)	1 can cherry pie filling

Pour cracker crumbs and melted margarine in a 8x12-inch Pyrex baking dish. Add ¼ cup sugar; pat in bottom of dish. Beat Dream Whip as directed on box. Add cream cheese which has been warmed to room temperature. Add remaining sugar; beat well. Spread over cracker crumbs. Add pie filling; chill. Do not freeze. Yield: 10 servings.

Mrs. A. W. Robbins (Irma)   *Mrs. W. E. Pettit*
Franklinton, Louisiana   *Winston-Salem, North Carolina*

INDIVIDUAL CHEESE CAKES

28 to 30 vanilla wafers
1¼ pounds cream cheese (2 large and 1 small package)
¾ cup sugar
1½ tablespoons all purpose flour

¼ teaspoon orange rind, grated
¼ teaspoon lemon rind, grated
¼ teaspoon vanilla
3 medium eggs
1 can cherry pie filling

Line muffin tins with baking cups. Beat cream cheese till fluffy. Mix sugar, rinds, flour and vanilla in large bowl. Blend in cheese and eggs one at a time. Mix well after each addition. Place 1 vanilla wafer in each baking cup. Spoon mixture over wafers. Bake at 325 degrees for 15 to 20 minutes or until centers are set. Cool to room temperature. Spoon 1 tablespoon cherry pie filling on top. Chill until serving.
Mrs. Roland Miljevich (Cecelia)
Wakefield, Michigan

GREAT NO BAKE CHEESE CAKE

1 package graham crackers, crushed

1 stick margarine

Mix and place in 2 pyrex dishes as a liner. Save ¼ cup for top.

1 large package Philadelphia cream cheese
1 cup sugar
1 small package lemon gelatin

1 cup water, boiling
Juice of 1 large lemon
1 large can Carnation milk

Chill Carnation milk in freezer about 1 hour. Beat together cream cheese and sugar. Mix gelatin and boiling water and let cool but not jell. Add to cream cheese and sugar mixture. Stir in juice of lemon. Set aside. Whip Carnation milk, then add to abouve mixture. Pour into oblong pyrex dishes lined with cracker crumbs. Sprinkle ¼ cup cracker crumbs on top. Refrigerate for several hours.

Mrs. C. E. Harvey (Ethelene)
Shreveport, Louisiana

Mrs. Dale Allen (Anne)
St. Louis, Missouri

Mrs. Carl Duck (Bonnie)
Dallas, Texas

CAKE AND CHEESE CAKE

1 cup all-purpose flour	¾ cup sugar
1 teaspoon baking powder	2 eggs
¼ teaspoon salt	1 tablespoon milk
½ cup butter	1 teaspoon vanilla

Sift together flour, baking powder and salt. In bowl, cream well butter and sugar. Add eggs, beating well after each addition. Stir in milk and vanilla. Add to dry ingredients. Mix well. Pour in tall spring-form pan. Cover with the following cream cheese mixture.

1 8-ounce package cream cheese	1 teaspoon vanilla
⅔ cup sugar	2 eggs
½ cup sour cream	

Mix cream cheese with sugar. Add sour cream and vanilla. Blend in eggs, one at a time. Mix well. Bake at 325 degrees for 40 to 45 minutes.

TOPPING

1 cup sour cream	1 teaspoon vanilla
2 tablespoons sugar	

Cover cake with topping. Bake 5 minutes more. Cool at least 5 hours.
Mrs. Forest H. Siler (Evelyn)
Lawton, Oklahoma

COCONUT CAKE

1 box Deluxe Yellow Cake mix

Mix and bake as directed.

ICING

2 cups powdered sugar	2 14-ounce packages of frozen
2 cups sour cream	coconut

Make 3 layer cake, if preferred. Outer edge of cake need not be iced. Cover with Saran Wrap. Make at least a day ahead. Store in refrigerator.
Mrs. T. L. Cashwell, Jr. (Helen)   *Mrs. Warren Armour*
Raleigh, North Carolina   *Paris, Tennessee*

Mrs. C. E. Hall
Hickman, Tennessee

COCONUT AND ORANGE CAKE

1 Duncan Hines Butter cake mix
6 oranges

1 can Angel Flake coconut or fresh coconut

Mix cake according to package directions. Bake 3 layers. While cake is baking, squeeze juice from oranges. When layers are cool, place first layer on plate; soak with ⅓ of the orange juice. Spread 7-Minute Frosting on top and sprinkle with Angel Flake coconut or fresh coconut. Repeat with other two layers.

7-MINUTE FROSTING

2 egg whites
1½ cups sugar
½ teaspoons salt

¼ cup water
1 teaspoon vanilla

Mix all except flavoring in double boiler. Cook on medium heat. Beat on high speed while frosting is cooking. Remove from heat in 5 to 7 minutes. Add flavoring. Cool.

Mrs. L. A. Jennings (Lola)
Eastman, Georgia

NO-BAKE COCONUT CAKE

1 envelope plain gelatin
½ cup cold water
4 eggs, separated
2 tablespoons flour
¼ teaspoon salt
2 cups milk

1 cup frozen coconut or Angel Flake
1 10-inch angel or chiffon cake
1 cup whipping cream
2 tablespoons sugar

Combine gelatin with ½ cup cold water and let stand until needed. Beat egg yolks with flour until smooth. Gradually add milk. Cook over low heat stirring constantly, until custard coats the spoon. Stir gelatin mixture into hot custard. Refrigerate for an hour. Beat egg whites until stiff and fold into the cooled custard. Whip cream; add 2 tablespoons sugar. Line a 13x9x2-inch pan with cake slices. Pour ½ custard over these. Sprinkle ½ coconut over the custard. Make a second layer like the first. Top with the whipped cream. Refrigerate. This keeps well.

Mrs. Wallace P. Mitchell (Faye)
Gonzalez, Florida

SOUR CREAM COCONUT CAKE

1 package Duncan Hines cake mix
1 package Dream Whip (right from the envelope)
4 eggs
1 cup cold water
½ cup Wesson oil

Combine cake mix, Dream Whip, eggs, water and oil in large bowl. Blend until moistened. Beat 4 minutes at medium speed. Pour batter into 3 9-inch greased and floured pans. Bake at 350 degrees for 30 minutes. Frost with Sour Cream Frosting.

SOUR CREAM FROSTING
1½ or 2 cups powdered sugar
1 large carton sour cream
1 package frozen or flaked coconut

Mix sugar and cream. Spread on cake layers. Sprinkle with coconut.
Mrs. R. A. Herrington (Myrtle)
Louisville, Mississippi

BOHEMIAN COFFEE CAKE

2½ cups all-purpose flour
1 cup brown sugar
1 cup white sugar
1 teaspoon soda
1 teaspoon cinnamon
1 teaspoon nutmeg
1 teaspoon salt
1½ cups coconut
1 cup nuts, chopped
1 cup Wesson Oil
1 cup buttermilk
2 eggs
2 teaspoons vanilla

Mix oil and sugar. Add eggs. Sift dry ingredients together. Add alternately with buttermilk and vanilla to oil mixture. Stir in coconut and nuts. Mix with spoon. Grease and flour cake pans or a tube pan. Bake 45 minutes to one hour at 350 degrees. Frost cool cake with the following.

FROSTING
1 8-ounce package cream cheese
½ stick margarine
1 pound powdered sugar
1 cup nuts, chopped

Mix ingredients together. (May need to be thinned with a little cream).
Mrs. Melba Gardner
Newcastle, California

JEWISH APPLE COFFEE CAKE

3 cups all-purpose flour
2½ cups sugar
3 teaspoons baking powder
1½ teaspoons salt
4 medium apples

2 teaspoons cinnamon
5 tablespoons sugar
4 eggs, beaten
1 cup corn oil
2 oranges, juiced

Sift together 3 cups flour, 2½ cups sugar, 3 teaspoons baking powder and 1½ teaspoons salt. Slice thin 4 apples and set aside. Mix together 2 teaspoons cinnamon and 5 tablespoons sugar and set aside. Place 4 eggs, 1 cup corn oil and juice of 2 oranges in mixing bowl. Add flour mixture to make batter. Grease and flour angel food pan. Layer into pan batter, apples, cinnamon and sugar; then nuts, making 3 layers. Bake at 350 degrees for 1 hour and 30 minutes or until toothpick comes out clean. Serves 12.

Mrs. Roy D. Moody (Sharon)
Tulsa, Oklahoma

ENGLISH COFFEE CAKE
(No egg)

3 cups all-purpose flour
2 cups sugar
1½ sticks margarine (¾ cup)
½ teaspoon cloves
1 teaspoon cinnamon

1 teaspoon nutmeg
2 cups buttermilk
2 teaspoons soda
½ cup chopped dates or raisins
½ cup nuts, chopped

Mix first 6 ingredients until crumbly. (Use pastry blender). Reserve ½ cup of this mixture. Mix soda with buttermilk and add to flour mixture. Stir in dates or raisins and nuts. Pour into greased 13x9-inch pan or 2 round pans. Sprinkle reserved ½ cup topping over cake. Bake at 350 degrees for 40 to 45 minutes. Serves 12 to 15. A very good last minute dessert.

Mrs. A. B. Coyle (Joan)
Memphis, Tennessee

DOUGHNUT BALLS

2 cups all-purpose flour	1 teaspoon nutmeg
¼ cup sugar	¼ cup oil
3 teaspoons baking powder	¾ cup milk
1 teaspoon salt	1 egg, beaten

Mix together dry ingredients. Add oil, milk and beaten egg. Stir with a fork until thoroughly mixed. Drop from teaspoon into deep, hot oil (375 degrees). Fry until brown, about 3 minutes. Drain on paper towels, then roll in a mixture of cinnamon and sugar. Makes 2½ dozen.
Mrs. Howard H. Ramsey (Lawonda)
Tigard, Oregon

FRENCH MARKET DOUGHNUTS

3½ cups all-purpose flour, sifted	1 cup milk
1 package active dry or cake yeast	¼ cup sugar
2 tablespoons lukewarm water	½ teaspoon nutmeg
1 egg	¾ teaspoon salt
2 tablespoons salad oil	Confectioners' sugar, sifted

Scald milk; add granulated sugar salt and nutmeg. Cool until lukewarm. Dissolve yeast in lukewarm water. Add oil and egg, then yeast to lukewarm milk mixture. Gradually add flour, beating well. Place in a greased bowl. Cover with waxed paper and then clean towel. Let rise in warm place until double in bulk (85 degrees). Turn dough out onto well-floured surface. Dough will be soft. Knead gently. Roll into 18x12-inch rectangle. Cut into 3x2-inch rectangle. Cover with clean towel and let rise ½ hour. Makes 36. Fry doughnuts, a few at a time at 375 degrees in deep fat. Let get golden brown. Drain on paper towels, crumpled. Drop doughnuts in brown paper bag. Sprinkle with confectioners' sugar. Shake well until thoroughly coated. Serve hot.
Mrs. John Coker (Marilyn)
New Orleans, Louisiana

DATE CAKE

1 package seedless dates	1 egg
1 cup water, boiling	1½ cups all-purpose flour
1 teaspoon soda	¼ teaspoon salt
¼ cup shortening or butter	1 cup walnuts
1 cup sugar	1 teaspoon vanilla

Cut dates in small pieces and place in bowl. Add soda; pour in boiling water. Cream shortening. Add sugar and egg. Beat well and add to date mixture. Blend flour, salt and vanilla. Add to first mixture. Stir in walnuts. Bake at 375 degrees for 35 minutes. Do not overcook. Serve with whipped cream.

Mrs. Glenn Cox
Webbers Falls, Oklahoma

BLACKBERRY FRUIT CAKE

1⅔ cup sugar	1½ cups dark raisins
3 eggs, reserve 2 whites for filling	1 cup buttermilk
1 cup shortening	1 teaspoon allspice
1 cup black walnuts	1 teaspoon cinnamon
1 cup pecans	1 teaspoon vanilla
1 cup sweetened blackberries or	1 teaspoon lemon flavoring
blackberry jam or preserves	¾ cup self-rising flour

Cream shortening and sugar until light and fluffy. Add eggs, one at a time, beating well after each. Alternately stir in spices, flour and buttermilk. Add flavorings. Lightly dust berries, nuts and raisins with flour and fold into mixture, or add jam (if used) and beat well. Pour into 3 greased and floured 9-inch layer pans. Bake at 325 degrees for about 35 minutes or until done.

FILLING

2½ cups sugar	1 grated coconut
Milk from 1 coconut	2 egg whites

Place sugar, milk and egg whites in double boiler. Cook over hot water, beating constantly until fluffy. Spread on cake. Add coconut.

Mrs. William E. Stiles
Marietta, Georgia

CHRISTMAS CAKE
or WHITE FRUIT CAKE°

1 pound butter
2 cups sugar
4 cups all-purpose flour
½ pound candied pineapple
3 cups pecans

6 eggs, beaten
1 tablespoon baking powder
2 teaspoons vanilla
½ pound candied cherries

Cream butter and sugar. Reserve one cup flour; sift other dry ingredients together and add alternately to batter with beaten eggs. Add remaining flour to chopped fruit and nuts. Stir well until each piece of fruit is covered. Add to batter and pour into well greased and floured tube pan. Bake at 300 degrees for 2 hours. Cake freezes well.

Mrs. Herman W. Cobb (Mary)
Cullman, Alabama

Mrs. Sam Friend (Donna)
Bothell, Washington

Mrs. Sidney M. Maddox (Dorothy)
Hopkinsville, Kentucky

FAST FIXIN' FRUIT "N" CAKE

1 package Betty Crocker sour
   cream yellow cake mix
¼ cup oil
2 eggs

½ cup water
1 20-23 ounce cherry pie filling
   (other flavors are good, too)

Preheat oven to 350 degrees. Pour oil into 13x9x2-inch pan; tilt pan to cover bottom. Put cake mix, eggs and water into separate bowl and blend with fork. Spread batter evenly in pan. Spoon pie filling onto batter; use fork to fold into batter to create marble effect. Bake at 350 degrees for 35 to 40 minutes, checking center with toothpick. Cooled cake may be sprinkled with confectioners' sugar. Delicious topped with Cool Whip or ice cream.

Mrs. V. Allen Gaines (Leila)
Newport News, Virginia

ICE BOX FRUIT CAKE

1 quart pecans, chopped
1 box graham crackers, crushed
1 large can condensed milk
1 can coconut

1 cup maraschino cherries, drained
1 package miniature marshmallows
1 box raisins

Mix all ingredients in large bowl. If not moist enough, add ½ cherry juice. Line large cake tin with foil and press mixture into the tin. Refrigerate 24 hours. Keep refrigerated.

Mrs. Cheryl Stacey
Holt, Florida

GRAHAM CRACKER CAKE

12-ounces graham crackers, finely crushed
6 eggs
2 cups sugar

2 sticks margarine
1 cup nuts
¾ cup milk
7-ounces Angel Flake coconut

Cream sugar and margarine. Beat eggs one at a time and add to first mixture. Add graham crackers and milk alternately. Stir in nuts and coconut. Pour into tube pan, greased and floured. Bake 1 to 1½ hours at 350 degrees. Cool at least 10 minutes before removing from pan.
Mrs. Howard Golden
Phenix City, Alabama

OUR FAVORITE FRUIT CAKE

¾ pound candied cherries
4 cups nut meats
½ pound pitted dates
½ pound candied pineapple
¼ pound candied citron
½ pound seeded raisins
¼ cup flour
1 cup butter
½ cup sugar

½ cup honey
5 eggs, well beaten
1 teaspoon salt
1 teaspoon baking powder
1 teaspoon allspice
½ teaspoon nutmeg
¼ cup orange or grapefruit juice
1½ cups all-purpose flour

Halve cherries, nuts and dates; cut pineapple and citron. Dredge fruits in ¼ cup flour. Cream butter and sugar; add honey and eggs. Beat well. Add flour sifted with dry ingredients alternately with fruit juice. Beat thoroughly. Pour batter over floured fruit and mix well. Line tube pan or loaf pans with waxed paper, allowing the paper to extend a little above all sides of pan. Pour batter into pans. Bake slowly at 250 degrees for 3 to 4 hours. Place pan containing 2 cups water on bottom shelf of oven while baking. This gives cake a greater volume and a more moist texture. Decorate cake with nuts and fruit while baking.
Mrs. John A. Moore (Julia)
Greenville, North Carolina

FRUIT COCKTAIL CAKE

1½ cups sugar
2 eggs, beaten
2 cups cake flour
2 teaspoons baking soda
1 teaspoon salt

1 can fruit cocktail and juice
1 cup brown sugar
1 can coconut
1 cup nuts, chopped

Combine sugar, eggs, flour, soda, salt, fruit cocktail and juice. Mix well and pour into greased 9x13-inch pan. Make mixture of brown sugar, coconut and nuts. Sprinkle on top of batter. Bake 45 minutes at 325 degrees.

ICING

1 stick margarine, melted
1 cup sugar

1 teaspoon vanilla
½ cup evaporated milk

Combine all ingredients. Bring to a boil. Boil 1½ minutes. Spoon over warm cake.

Mrs. Robert K. Davis, Jr. (Pat)
Elba, Alabama

Mrs. Victor Bollinger (Fern)
Toledo, Ohio

Mrs. Ross Terry (Roxie)
Mulberry, Indiana

Mrs. Bennie Oliver (Dorothy)
Hamilton, Alabama

Mrs. Joe Abram
Sylacauga, Alabama

Mrs. William M. Halliburton
Willoughby, Ohio

ICE BOX CAKE

1 cup real butter
3 egg yolks
1 cup nuts, chopped
1 large can crushed pineapple

1 pound vanilla wafers
2 cups sugar
1 teaspoon salt
Whipped cream

Cream butter; add sugar gradually. Beat until light and fluffy. Add un-beaten egg yolks, one at a time. Add pineapple and juice, salt and vanilla. Mix well. Add nuts. Roll wafers fine and place ½ in bottom of 9x9x2-inch Pyrex dish. Cover with butter mixture and pack down. Place in refrigerator overnight and serve with whipped cream. Serves 16. A WINNER!

Mrs. Adrian Rogers (Joyce)
Memphis, Tennessee

Mrs. Wendell Price (Frances)
Nashville, Tennessee

HEAVENLY HASH CAKE

1 12-ounce package chocolate
   chips
2 eggs, separated
2 tablespoons sugar
1 cup walnuts

1 teaspoon vanilla
1 cup cream, whipped or
   2 cups Cool Whip
1 angel food cake

Melt chocolate chips in a double boiler. Stir in the beaten egg yolks, sugar and vanilla. When cool, fold in the cream that has been whipped, then fold in the stiffly beaten egg whites. Break the cake into serving size pieces in a 13x9-inch greased cake pan and pour the suace over this. Add walnuts. Refrigerate overnight before serving. Freezes well.

Mrs. Archie E. Brown (Louise)
Vandalia, Illinois

Mrs. H. Perry Cox (Carol)
Houston, Texas

OLD FASHIONED JAM CAKE
(This was my grandmother's recipe and I use to make
this cake every Saturday when I was a girl.)

1 cup Crisco
2 cups sugar
3 egg yolks, well beaten
1 cup blackberry jam
3 cups all purpose flour
½ teaspoon salt

1 teaspoon soda
1 teaspoon cinnamon
1 cup buttermilk
3 egg whites, stiffly beaten
2 tablespoons cocoa dissolved in a
   little hot water

Thoroughly cream shortening and sugar. Add egg yolks and jam. Blend well. Add sifted dry ingredients, then buttermilk and cocoa. Fold in egg whites. Bake in 350 degree oven 40 to 45 minutes.

Mrs. Henry B. Stokes (Etta)
Buies Creek, North Carolina

NANCY'S JAM LAYER CAKE

1 cup butter or margarine, softened
2 cups sugar
5 eggs
1 2-ounce package pre-melted baking chocolate or 1 square chocolate, melted
1 cup seedless blackberry jam

3 cups all-purpose flour, sifted
1 teaspoon soda
½ teaspoon salt
½ teaspoon each ground cloves and allspice
½ teaspoon each cinnamon and nutmeg
1 cup buttermilk

Cream butter and sugar until light and fluffy. Add eggs one at a time, beating well after each addition. Add jam and beat well; add chocolate and beat well again. Add sifted flour, soda, salt and spices alternately with buttermilk, beating until smooth, beginning and ending with flour mixture. Pour into 3 greased and floured 9-inch layer pans. Bake in preheated slow oven at 325 degrees for about 35 minutes or until cake begins to pull from side of pans. Do not overbake.

MINUTE FUDGE FROSTING

2 cups sugar
¼ cup light corn syrup
½ cup milk
1 stick margarine
1 square unsweetened chocolate, cut up or 1 2-ounce package pre-melted chocolate

¼ teaspoon salt
1 teaspoon vanilla

Mix all ingredients except vanilla in saucepan. Stir over low heat until chocolate and margarine melt. Bring to a full rolling boil, stirring constantly. Boil 1 minute at 220 degrees. Remove from heat. Beat until luke warm. Add vanilla and continue beating until a smooth spreading consistency.

Mrs. Thomas Williams (Nancy)
Falmouth, Kentucky

And they gave him a piece of a cake of figs, and two clusters of raisins: and when he had eaten, his spirit came again to him . . . . 1 Sam. 30:12

LEMON ANGEL FOOD CAKE

1 box Angel Food Cake Mix
¼ cup lemon juice

Several drops yellow food coloring

Mix cake according to package directions substituting, ¼ cup lemon juice for water in cake batter. Add food coloring.

FROSTING

1 can Eagle Brand milk
½ cup lemon juice

½ pint whipped cream
Several drops yellow food coloring

Mix lemon juice with Eagle Brand milk. Fold in whipped cream and food coloring. Freezes well.
Mrs. Elbert L. Smithen (Jo)
Midland, Texas

MINCEMEAT CAKE

2 cups sugar
1 stick margarine
4 eggs
1 teaspoon vanilla
1 teaspoon lemon flavoring

3 cups self-rising flour, sifted
1 cup milk
1 pound jar mincemeat
1 pound box raisins
1 pound nuts, chopped

Cream together sugar and margarine. Add beaten eggs, one at a time, and beat until smooth. Add flavorings. Alternately stir in flour and milk followed by mincemeat. Lightly dust nuts and raisins with flour and fold into mixture. Pour into greased and floured tube pan. Line pan with paper which is also greased. Bake at 325 degrees for approximately 1 hour and 30 minutes or until done.
Mrs. Frank H. Crumpler (Glenda)
Mechanicsville, Virginia

LEMON CUPS

1 cup sugar	Grated rind of 1 lemon
4 tablespoons all-purpose flour	3 egg yolks, well beaten
⅛ teaspoon salt	1½ cups milk
2 tablespoons butter, melted	3 egg whites, stiffly beaten
5 tablespoons lemon juice	

Combine sugar, flour, salt and butter. Add lemon juice and rind; Mix egg yolks and milk. Add to first mixture; mix well. Fold in beaten egg whites. Pour into greased custard cups. Set in pan of hot water and make in moderate 325 degree oven for 45 minutes. When baked, each dessert will have custard on bottom and sponge cake on top.

Mrs. T. J. Fulk (Marilee)
Fayetteville, North Carolina

LAZY DAISY OATMEAL CAKE

1¼ cups water, boiling	2 eggs
1 cup oats	1½ cups all-purpose flour,
½ cup butter (softened)	sifted
1 cup granulated sugar	1 teaspoon soda
1 cup brown sugar,	½ teaspoon salt
firmly packed	¾ teaspoon cinnamon
1 teaspoon vanilla	¼ teaspoon nutmeg

Pour boiling water over oats and let stand 20 minutes. Beat butter until creamy; gradually add sugar and beat until fluffy. Blend in vanilla and eggs. Add oats mixture; mix well. Sift flour, soda, salt, cinnamon and nutmeg. Add to creamed mixture. Pour batter into a 9-inch square pan. Bake in a preheated 350 degree oven for 50 minutes.

TOPPING

1 cup brown sugar	½ cup nuts, chopped
1 cup coconut	4 tablespoons butter
½ cup cream	

Pour over cake and broil for few minutes.

Mrs. Ross Terry (Roxie)   *Mrs. Tom M. Jones (Dian)*
Mulberry, Indiana   *Travelers Rest, South Carolina*

Mrs. B. C. McGohon (Barbara)   *Mrs. J. O. Wade (Linda)*
Birmingham, Alabama   *Plant City, Florida*

MAGIC HOLIDAY CAKE

1 cup sugar	1 teaspoon almond flavoring
4 eggs	2 pounds dates, chopped
1 cup all-purpose flour	4 cups pecans, coarsely chopped
2 teaspoons baking powder	1 small bottle maraschino cherries
1 teaspoon vanilla	and juice

Combine ingredients as listed, in large mixing bowl. Pour into 2 small greased and floured loaf pans. Bake at 325 degrees for 25 minutes. Reduce heat to 300 degrees and bake for 1 hour or until done.
Mrs. Charles M. Becton (Janie)
McAlester, Oklahoma

MISSISSIPPI MUD CAKE

2 sticks margarine	1 teaspoon vanilla
½ cup cocoa	Pinch of salt
2 cups sugar	1½ cups all-purpose flour
4 eggs	

Melt margarine, cocoa and sugar in saucepan. Mix well. Add eggs, vanilla and salt. Beat together. Add 1½ cups flour. Mix well again. Pour into greased 9x13-inch pan. Bake at 350 degrees for 25 to 35 minutes. Sprinkle miniature marshmallows on hot cake. Frost immediately.

FROSTING

1 pound box powdered sugar	⅓ cup cocoa
½ cup milk	½ stick margarine

Mix all ingredients together about 10 minutes before cake is done. Pour over hot cake.

Mrs. Cornelius Davis (Barbara)   *Mrs. Gladys McKee*
Lakeland, Florida   *Ringgold, Georgia*

Mrs. Roy L. Head (Vonceil)
Belvedere, South Carolina

ORANGE-DATE NUT CAKE

2 sticks margarine
2 cups sugar
4 cups all-purpose flour
Dash of salt
1 teaspoon soda

4 eggs
1⅓ cups buttermilk
2 cups nuts
2 packages dates
1 pound orange slice candy

Cream the butter and sugar. Add eggs, then add 1 cup of buttermilk. Mix soda with the ⅓ cup of milk. Sift flour and salt, then mix chopped nuts, dates and candy with flour. Add this to the creamed mixture. Cook in a tubed pan 2½ hours at 275 degrees.

ICING

2 cups brown sugar

1 small can orange juice, undiluted

Mix sugar and undiluted orange juice and pour over cake while hot.
Mrs. Branson Wiggins (Gwen)
Reading, Ohio

ORANGE SLICE CAKE

3 cups all-purpose flour
½ teaspoon salt
1 pound diced orange, sliced
1 8-ounce package diced dates
2 cups pecans
1 small can Angel Flake coconut

1 cup margarine
2 cups sugar
4 eggs
1 teaspoon soda
½ cup buttermilk

Sift together flour and salt. Sprinkle ½ of this flour over the orange slices, dates, pecans and coconut. Cream margarine and sugar. Add eggs. Beat well. Add 1 teaspoon soda dissolved in ½ cup buttermilk. Add flour and fruit mixture. Pour into greased and floured tube pan. Bake 1 hour and 45 minutes at 300 degrees.

ICING

1 cup orange juice

2 cups powdered sugar

Pour over cake while hot and let stand in pan overnight in refrigerator. HINT: To help release cake from pan, set pan in hot water for a few minutes. This cake is a good substitute for those who don't care for citrus in fruit cakes. A good holiday cake!
Mrs. Bill Haggard (Wilma)
Oklahoma City, Oklahoma

Mrs. R. A. Herrington (Myrtle)
Louisville, Mississippi

Mrs. Franklin Hall (Joanne)
Newport News, Virginia

ORANGE-PINEAPPLE CAKE

1 Duncan Hines Butter cake mix	1 stick margarine
4 eggs	1 can Mandarin oranges and juice

Mix above ingredients together and bake as directed on box. Make 4 thin layers or 3 regular size layers. Cool.

TOPPING

1 large Cool Whip	1 box instant vanilla pudding
1 large can crushed pineapple, drained	

Mix ingredients together. Blend well. Drizzle pineapple juice over each layer. Frost with topping. FANTASTIC!!!!

Mrs. Bryant M. Cummings
(Margaret Ann)
Clinton, Mississippi

Mrs. Ray G. Ming (Ray)
Cantonment, Florida

Mrs. Tilman Burks (Quinnie)
Pensacola, Florida

Mrs. John T. Davis (Georgia)
Monroe, North Carolina

Mrs. T. J. Fulk (Marilee)
Fayetteville, North Carolina

Mrs. Henry Chiles
Pierre, South Dakota

Mrs. Clyde Hampton (Alicia)
Hartwell, Georgia

GUESS WHAT'S IN IT CAKE

56 Ritz crackers, crushed	1 teaspoon baking powder
1½ cups nuts, chopped	1 teaspoon vanilla
6 egg whites, beaten medium fluffy	2 envelopes dessert topping mix
	1 8-ounce package cream cheese
2 cups sugar	2 cups crushed pineapple

Mix crushed crackers and nuts. Add sugar slowly with baking powder and vanilla to beaten egg whites. Combine with first mixture. Pour into a 9x13-inch buttered pan. Bake 30 minutes at 350 degrees. Make dessert topping mix according to directions given. Beat softened cream cheese until smooth. Add to topping mix and beat until smoothly blended. Add drained pineapple. Spread on cooled cake.

Mrs. Victor N. Bollinger (Fern)
Toledo, Ohio

GLORIA'S PINEAPPLE CAKE

2 cups all-purpose flour
2 eggs
1 number 2 can crushed
  pineapple and juice

2 cups sugar
2 teaspoons soda

Grease and flour 13x9x2-inch pan. Mix all together by hand, using pineapple and juice. Pour into greased and floured pan. Bake at 350 degrees for 30 minutes.

FROSTING
½ stick margarine, melted
8-ounces soft cream cheese

¾ box powdered sugar
1 teaspoon vanilla

Mix together. Spread on cake while cake is still hot.
Mrs. Gloria Singleton
Rankin, Texas

Mrs. Keith Hamm
El Dorado, Kansas

PINEAPPLE-CARROT CAKE

1¾ cups sugar
1¼ cups Wesson oil
4 eggs, unbeaten
2 cups all purpose flour
2 teaspoons baking powder

2 teaspoons soda
1 teaspoon salt
2 teaspoons cinnamon
3 cups carrots, grated
½ cup nuts, chopped

Cream sugar and Wesson oil. Add eggs. Sift flour, baking powder, soda, salt and cinnamon; add to first mixture. Fold in grated carrots and nuts. Pour into 3 greased and floured 9-inch cake pans. Bake at 350 degrees for 25 to 30 minutes.

FROSTING AND FILLING
1 large can crushed pineapple
½ stick margarine
1 8-ounce package cream cheese

2 teaspoons vanilla
1 box confectioners' sugar

Drain crushed pineapple, reserving several tablespoons of liquid for frosting. Cream together margarine, cream cheese, vanilla and confectioners' sugar. Add enough pineapple juice to make mixture spread. Place small amount of frosting along with drained pineapple between each layer. Spread remaining frosting on cake.
Mrs. George S. Munro (Eva)
Fort Thomas, Kentucky

PINEAPPLE-ZUCCHINI CAKE

3 eggs
2 cups sugar
2 teaspoons vanilla
1 cup cooking oil
2 cups zucchini, peeled and
   grated
1 teaspoon baking powder

1 teaspoon salt
1 teaspoon soda
1 cup crushed pineapple
½ cup raisins, cooked and drained
1 cup nuts
3 cups all-purpose flour

Beat eggs, sugar, vanilla and oil until fluffy. Add zucchini, flour, baking powder, soda and salt. Stir in pineapple, raisins and nuts. Pour into greased and floured sheet pan. Bake at 325 degrees until brown and spongy.

ICING

¼ cup butter, softened
½ cup cream

6-ounces butterscotch bits, melted
1 box powdered sugar

Mix and spread over cooled cake.
Mrs. Harry Foley
Mesa, Arizona

PEACH CAKE

2 cups sugar
1 cup Wesson oil
2 eggs
4 cups all-purpose flour
2 teaspoons soda
1 teaspoon each nutmeg and salt

1 teaspoon each cloves and
   cinnamon
1 teaspoon allspice
1 29-ounce can peaches and juice
1 cup nuts

Place all ingredients in a bowl and mix till peaches are chopped. Pour in a greased and floured tube pan. Bake at 350 degrees for 1 hour and 20 minutes. Check after 1 hour.
Mrs. Eugene A. Perry (Raneal)
Lone Grove, Oklahoma

PEACH PRESERVE CAKE

3 eggs
¾ cup oil
½ teaspoon salt
1 cup buttermilk
2 cups sugar
2 cups flour

1 teaspoon vanilla
1 teaspoon cinnamon
1 teaspoon nutmeg
1 teaspoon soda
1 cup peach preserves
¾ cup black walnuts

Place oil in mixer. Add sugar and beat until fluffy. Add eggs one at a time. Sift together dry ingredients. Add alternately with buttermilk and vanilla. Beat well. Fold in peach preserves and black walnuts. Pour into greased and floured tube pan. Bake at 300 degrees for 2 hours.
Mrs. W. E. Darby (Mary)
Jefferson City, Tennessee

PLANTATION CAKE

½ cup butter
1 cup sugar
1 egg
1⅔ cups all-purpose flour, sifted
1½ cups nuts, chopped
½ teaspoon salt

1 teaspoon soda
1 teaspoon cinnamon
½ teaspoon allspice
2 tablespoons cocoa
1 teaspoon vanilla
1 cup applesauce, heated

Cream butter. Add sugar slowly. Cream until fluffy. Add egg and beat well. Add a little of the flour to the nuts. Sift remaining flour with other dry ingredients. Add flour mixture alternately with applesauce to creamed mixture. Stir in vanilla and nuts. Pour into a greased and floured bundt pan. Bake at 350 degrees for 40 minutes.
Mrs. James W. Parker
Santa Ana, California

BUTTERMILK POUND CAKE

3 cups sugar
3 cups all-purpose flour, sifted
1 cup buttermilk
2 teaspoons vanilla

1 cup shortening
½ teaspoon soda
1 teaspoon salt
5 eggs, separated

Cream sugar, shortening and egg yolks. Mix together dry ingredients. Add buttermilk alternately with dry ingredients to the creamed mixture. Beat together. Add vanilla. Fold in stiffly beaten egg whites. Grease and flour bundt or angel food cake pan. Bake 1 hour and 25 minutes at 325 degrees.
Mrs. E. M. Adams (Marjorie)
Fredonia, New York

Mrs. Carl Duck (Bonnie)
Dallas, Texas

Mrs. Ronald D. Rhodus (Virginia)
Mt. Zion, Illinois

BROWN SUGAR POUND CAKE

1 cup butter or margarine	3 cups flour, sifted
½ cup shortening	½ teaspoon salt
1 pound light brown sugar	1 teaspoon baking powder
1 cup sugar	1 cup milk
5 eggs	1 teaspoon vanilla

Cream butter, shortening and sugar. Add eggs, one at a time, beating well after each. Add dry ingredients, milk and vanilla. Beat well. Bake in tube pan at 325 degrees for 1 hour and 50 minutes. Remove from pan and cover with the following glaze while cake is hot.

GLAZE

2 cups confectioners' sugar, sifted	6 tablespoons cream or milk
3 tablespoons butter	½ teaspoon vanilla

Blend well. Spread over hot cake.
Mrs. R. William Dodson (Janelle)
Martin, Tennessee

COCONUT POUND CAKE

1 cup shortening	1 teaspoon vanilla
6 eggs, separated	1 cup milk
½ cup margarine	3 cups cake flour, sifted
3 cups sugar	2 cups coconut

Separate eggs. Let whites warm to room temperature. Beat egg yolks with shortening and margarine until well blended. Gradually add sugar, beating until light and fluffy. Add vanilla. At low speed, beat in flour alternately with milk, beginning and ending with flour. Add coconut and fold in well. Beat egg whites until stiff and fold in with spatula. Bake 1 hour and 15 minutes at 200 for 250 degrees.

Mrs. Ruben Clark	*Mrs. Jaroy Weber (Tippy)*
Louisville, Mississippi	*Lubbock, Texas*
Mrs. Richard Brogan	*Mrs. Ray W. McClung (Faye)*
Clinton, Missouri	*Little Rock, Arkansas*
Mrs. Kendall Hatton	*Mrs. E. Halliburton*
Marlinton, West Virginia	*Willoughby, Ohio*

LOUISIANA CHOCOLATE POUND CAKE

2 sticks margarine	½ teaspoon baking powder
½ cup Crisco	2 teaspoons vanilla
3 cups sugar	3 cups all-purpose flour
½ cup cocoa	½ teaspoon salt
1 cup milk	5 eggs

Cream margarine, shortening and sugar. Add eggs, one at a time, and beat well after each. Sift dry ingredients, including cocoa, together and add alternately with milk and vanilla, beginning and ending with dry ingredients. Grease and flour angel food cake pan. Pour batter into pan and bake at 325 degrees for 1 hour or until cake tests done. Do not overbake. NOTE: These directions are great, but if you are like me, you don't have time to mess with all that sifting and alternating! I usually put the margarine in the mixer bowl to soften, then come back about an hour later, dump everything else in, beat well and pop in the oven. All done in about 10 minutes. At 325 degrees it usually takes about 1 hour and 15 minutes or slightly more to get done. This cake is great with peppermint ice cream . . . especially on Sunday night after church when you want to have a few friends in for fellowship. Also good for picnics or to take to the family where "Mom" is sick.

Mrs. James R. Maples (Mary Jo)
El Paso, Texas

Mrs. Fred V. Brown (Norma)
Spartanburg, South Carolina

Mrs. Wallace Mitchell (Faye)
Gonzalez, Florida

Mrs. Carl Bailey (Louise)
Port Richey, Florida

Mrs. Ted Sisk (Ginny)
Lexington, Kentucky

Mrs. C. W. Rich
Memphis, Tennessee

WHIPPED CREAM POUND CAKE

½ pint whipping cream	6 eggs
2 sticks butter	1 teaspoon vanilla
3 cups sugar	1 teaspoon almond extract
3 cups all-purpose flour	

Beat whipping cream and set aside. Cream butter and sugar. Add flour alternately with eggs, vanilla and almond extract. Fold in whipping cream last. Bake at 325 degrees for 1 hour and 15 minutes or until done.
Mrs. Franklin Owen (Sue)
Middletown, Kentucky

PHILADELPHIA CREAM CHEESE POUND CAKE
(An Old Family Recipe From A Friend)

1 8-ounce package Philadelphia
   cream cheese
3 sticks butter
3 cups sugar
3 cups Swansdown cake flour,
   sifted

½ teaspoon salt
6 large eggs
1 tablespoon vanilla (or other
   extract of your choice)

Beat the cream cheese and butter until smooth. Add sugar gradually. Add eggs alternately with flour in which salt has been mixed (I beat eggs all together in bowl). Add extract. Bake in 300 degree oven for 1 hour and 15 minutes, or until done. Start in cold oven. Cool about 20 minutes in pan before turning out. Cake will keep indefinitely if kept tightly wrapped.

Mrs. William K. Weaver, Jr. ("B")
Mobile, Alabama

Mrs. A. O. Jenkins (Lucile)
Homer, Louisiana

Mrs. Glen G. Waldrop (Anne)
Atlanta, Georgia

Mrs. Darrell Roden (Grace)
Pensacola, Florida

Mrs. Ted Callahan
Jackson, South Carolina

Mrs. Wallace Mitchell (Faye)
Gonzalez, Florida

SOUR CREAM POUND CAKE

2 sticks butter or margarine
3 scant cups sugar
6 eggs
3 cups flour, sifted

1 8-ounce carton sour cream
½ teaspoon salt
¼ teaspoon soda
1 teaspoon vanilla

Grease and flour a 10-inch tube pan. Set oven at 315 degrees. Sift flour and soda 3 times. Add salt to egg whites. Cream butter and sugar well; add vanilla and 1 egg yolk at a time. Add flour and soda alternating with sour cream. Fold in beaten egg whites. Turn into pan and bake 1 hour and 15 minutes or until done. Makes a large, moist, velvety cake.

Mrs. Page Kelley (Vernice)
Louisville, Kentucky

Mrs. William T. Penick (Ginger)
Hyattsville, Maryland

PLUM CAKE

2 small jars Plum baby food	1 cup Wesson oil
2 cups self-rising flour	1 teaspoon cinnamon
2 cups sugar	1 teaspoon cloves
3 eggs, beaten	2 cups nuts, chopped

Mix in order given. Grease and flour tube pan. Bake 1 hour at 350 degrees.

GLAZE

½ stick butter or margarine	1 tablespoon lemon juice
1 cup powdered sugar	

Melt butter; add sugar and lemon juice. Mix till smooth. Pour over hot cake.

Mrs. John Wood (Pat)　　　　　*Mrs. Marlon Stephens (Virginia)*
Paducah, Kentucky　　　　　*Rutherford, Tennessee*

PUMPKIN CAKE

4 eggs	2 teaspoons soda
2 cups sugar	½ teaspoon salt
1 cup salad oil	2 teaspoons cinnamon
2 cups all-purpose flour	2 cups canned pumpkin

Beat eggs, sugar and oil until fluffy. Sift together flour, soda, salt and cinnamon. Add to first mixture and beat well with electric mixer. Add pumpkin and beat again. Bake at 350 degrees for approximately 35 minutes in 2 or 3 layers or oblong pan. Completely cool cake before frosting.

CREAM CHEESE FROSTING

1 8-ounce package cream cheese	1 box confectioners' sugar
1 stick margarine	Chopped nuts
1 teaspoon vanilla	

Beat first 4 ingredients with electric beater. Add chopped nuts as desired. Keep cake refrigerated.

Mrs. Billy J. Dickerson (Vesta)　　　　*Mrs. John Woodall (Carole)*
Mango, Florida　　　　　　　　　*Columbia, Maryland*

Mrs. Bill Bailey (Faye)　　　　　　*Mrs. Elwood G. Kelley (Betty)*
Elizabethtown, Kentucky　　　　　*Jefferson City, Missouri*

PRUNE CAKE

1 cup Wesson oil
1½ cups sugar
2 cups all-purpose flour
3 eggs
1 cup buttermilk
1 cup pecans, chopped
1 teaspoon soda

1 teaspoon cinnamon
1 teaspoon allspice
¼ teaspoon salt
1 teaspoon vanilla
1 cup prunes, cooked and chopped
fine

Beat together sugar and Wesson oil. Add eggs, one at a time, beating thoroughly. Sift dry ingredients together; add alternately to first mixture with flour and buttermilk. Add vanilla, pecans and prunes. Bake in large shallow pan at 350 degrees about 30 to 40 minutes or until done.

ICING

¼ cup buttermilk
1 cup sugar
1 stick margarine

1 tablespoon Karo syrup
1 teaspoon vanilla flavoring
½ teaspoon soda

Boil all together for one minute, except flavoring. Remove from heat and stir in vanilla and pour over hot cake. Cool in pan.

Mrs. Wallace Mitchell (Faye)
Gonzalez, Florida

Mrs. R. G. Van Royen
Presidio, Texas

Mrs. John W. Murphey (Alta Mae)
Heavener, Oklahoma

Mrs. Bill Bailey (Faye)
Elizabethtown, Kentucky

7-UP CAKE

1 box Duncan Hines Butter
Cake mix
1 small box instant vanilla
pudding

4 eggs
½ cup Wesson Oil
1 10-ounce bottle 7-up

Mix well and bake in 3 layers at 350 degrees for 25 to 30 minutes.

ICING

1½ cups sugar
1 large can pineapple, drained
3 egg yolks

1 stick margarine
1 can coconut

Mix together and cook until clear and thick, cooking slowly and stirring often; will look rather thin. Delicious!

Mrs. Ed Westmark (Claire)
Pensacola, Florida

WEST TEXAS RAISIN-PECAN-SPICE CAKE

*(A prize winning cake in the Trans Pecos Pecan Show
in Texas. Very Special!!)*

½ cup shortening
1¾ cups sugar
4 eggs, well beaten
¼ cup water
2 teaspoons soda
2½ cups flour
1 teaspoon cinnamon
1 teaspoon allspice

1 teaspoon nutmeg
½ teaspoon ginger
½ teaspoon cloves
1 cup buttermilk
1 cup broken pecans
1 cup raisins (dredged in 2 tablespoons flour taken from original 2½ cups)

Cream together shortening and sugar. Add well beaten eggs and soda dissolved in ¼ cup water. Sift together flour and spices. Add dry ingredients alternately with 1 cup buttermilk. Beat about 2 minutes. Dredge raisins in 2 tablespoons flour. Fold raisins and pecans in batter mixture. Bake in tube pan which has been lightly coated with shortening and dusted with flour. May be baked in bundt pan. Glaze, if desired. Bake 1 hour at 350 degrees.

Mrs. Leonard B. Lee (Elizabeth)
McCamey, Texas

QUEEN ELIZABETH CAKE

1 cup water, boiling
1 cup chopped dates
1 teaspoon soda
1 cup sugar
¼ cup butter
1 egg, beaten

1½ cups all-purpose flour
1 teaspoon baking powder
⅓ teaspoon salt
½ cup nuts, chopped
1 teaspoon vanilla

Pour 1 cup boiling water over chopped dates and soda. Let stand until cool. Mix together sugar and butter. Add beaten egg. Sift together flour, baking powder and salt. Add dry mixture to creamed mixture, then add the cooled dates. Stir in chopped nuts and vanilla. Bake in greased and floured 8x12-inch sheet pan for 35 minutes in 350 degree oven.

GLAZE

8 tablespoons brown sugar
2 tablespoons butter

4 tablespoons cream
Chopped nuts or coconut

Mix together brown sugar, butter and cream. Boil 3 minutes and spread on cooled cake. Sprinkle with chopped nuts or coconut.

Mrs. Milton Gardner (Nancy)
Thomasville, Georgia

RED VELVET CAKE

1½ cups sugar
2 eggs
½ cup butter flavored
cooking oil
1 cup butter or margarine
1 1-ounce bottle red
food coloring plus 1 bottle
buttermilk or water

1 teaspoon vanilla
2½ cups all-purpose flour
2 teaspoons cocoa
1 teaspoon salt
1 teaspoon soda
1 cup buttermilk

Cream sugar and eggs together. Add cooking oil and margarine. Mix. Add red food coloring and fill bottle with buttermilk or water and add to above mixture with vanilla. Mix well. Sift flour, cocoa, salt and soda together. Add alternately with 1 cup buttermilk to above mixture. Pour into 3 square cake pans which have been greased and dusted with flour. Bake at 350 degrees for 25 to 30 minutes.

ICING

1 box confectioners' sugar
1 8-ounce package cream cheese
1 stick butter or margarine

½ cup walnuts or pecans,
chopped
1 teaspoon vanilla

Cream together and ice cake after it has cooled. Refrigerate after first day.
Mrs. K. S. Brunson
Venice, Florida

Mrs. Dewayne Francis (Glenda)
Malden, Missouri

STACK CAKE

¾ cup shortening
1 cup sugar
1 cup molasses
3 eggs
1 cup milk
4 cups all-purpose flour

½ teaspoon soda
2 teaspoons baking powder
1 teaspoon salt
3 cups applesauce or cooked, dried
apples (best)

Mix thoroughly flour, salt, soda and baking powder. Cream shortening. Add sugar and blend well. Add molasses. Mix well. Add eggs, one at a time. Add flour and milk alternately. Beat until smooth. Pour into greased and floured cake pans. Make 6 layers. Bake at 350 degrees for approximately 15 to 20 minutes. Cool. Stack layers with dried apple filling. Cake is better after it sets for a day.
Mrs. Kendall Hatton
Marlinton, West Virginia

SNOW BALL CAKE

3 small boxes Dream Whip
1 large Angel Food Cake
1 number 2 can crushed
   pineapple, drained
Juice of 1 lemon

1 cup white sugar
1 box coconut
2 envelopes gelatin
4 tablespoons cold water

Mix 4 tablespoons cold water with gelatin. Add 1 cup boiling water. Add cup of pineapple juice and crushed pineapple. Stir in 1 cup sugar and juice of 1 lemon. Mix and chill. Whip 2 boxes Dream Whip and add to gelatin mixture. Line a 4-quart bowl with waxed paper then pinch angel food cake into small pieces. Layer cake pieces and gelatin mixture in bowl, until all is used. Chill overnight. Next day turn out on flat plate. Whip other box of Dream Whip and spread on like icing. Sprinkle with coconut.

Mrs. W. E. Pettit
Winston Salem, North Carolina

Mrs. Wallace Mitchell (Faye)
Gonzalez, Florida

Mrs. John Dunaway (Jayne)
Corbin, Kentucky

Mrs. C. E. Colton (Lois)
Dallas, Texas

STRAWBERRY CAKE

1 cup Wesson oil
1 package Duncan Hines white
   cake mix plus 3 tablespoons
   flour
4 eggs

1 cup strawberries, drained
1 cup pecans
1 cup coconut
½ cup milk or water or strawberry
   juice

Mix and bake according to directions on box.

FROSTING
1 box powdered sugar
1 stick margarine
½ cup strawberries

½ cup pecans
½ cup coconut

Mix together and spread between layers and on top of cake. Cake can be baked in 13x9-inch pan, iced and frozen for use later.

Mrs. Everett Lemay
Mt. Vernon, Illinois

Mrs. John Woodall (Carole)
Columbia, Maryland

Mrs. Bobby W. Barnett (Mary)
Bradford, Rhode Island

Mrs. Ronald D. Rhodus (Virginia)
Mt. Zion, Illinois

STRAWBERRY SHORTCAKE

1 package Duncan Hines yellow
cake mix
1 large package frozen
strawberries
1 pint whipped cream

1 package or more powdered sugar
1 teaspoon vanilla

Prepare cake according to package directions. Bake in 2 layers. Cool. Mix
whipped cream with powdered sugar until of spreading consistency. Add
vanilla. Place cooled cake on plate. Cover with strawberries and juice.
Spread cream mixture on strawberries. Add second layer. Cover top and
sides of cake with cream mixture. Garnish with strawberries or dribble a
little juice on top.
Mrs. C. E. Colton (Lois)
Dallas, Texas

SUNSHINE CAKE FOR CHRISTMAS
(Made Festive With Gumdrops – A Very Delicious Cake!)

2 sticks margarine
2 cups sugar
2 teaspoons baking powder
5 eggs
1 can Angel Flake coconut

1 cup pecans, chopped
1 pound package (4 cups) graham
cracker crumbs
2 teaspoons vanilla

Cream margarine and sugar until well blended. Add eggs, one at a time,
beating thoroughly after each. Combine crumbs and baking powder. Add
to first mixture. Mix well. Add coconut, nuts and vanilla. Pour into 3 well
greased 9-inch pans lined with waxed paper. Bake at 350 degrees for 35
minutes.

PINEAPPLE ICING
1 stick margarine
1 small can crushed pineapple

1 package confectioners' sugar
Gumdrops

Cream sugar and margarine; add pineapple. Mix well. Spread between
layers and on top and sides of cake. Garnish cake by spreading chopped
red and green gumdrops on top.
Mrs. Jerry Vines
Mobile, Alabama

SUPREME TORTE

½ cup butter, soft
1½ cups powdered sugar
2 eggs
1 small can crushed pineapple

½ pint whipped cream
1 cup chopped nuts
½ pound vanilla wafers

Crush vanilla wafers and use ½ to line a 10-inch square pan. Cream butter and powdered sugar. Add eggs and beat until smooth. Spread the creamed mixture over crumbs. Layer with crushed pineapple, whipped cream and chopped nuts. Top with remaining crumbs and chill.
Mrs. Bob Woods (Ann)
Muskogee, Oklahoma

TEXAS BRAG CAKE

1 number 2 can cherry pie filling
1 number 2 can crushed pineapple
1 box Duncan Hines yellow cake mix

2 sticks margarine, melted
⅔ cup coconut
½ cup chopped nuts

Spread pie filling in bottom of pan. Spoon pineapple over pie filling. Sprinkle cake mix over pineapple and lightly pat down. Spread coconut and nuts evenly over cake mix. Spoon margarine over top. Bake at 350 degrees for 35 to 40 minutes.
Mrs. C. E. Colton (Lois)
Dallas, Texas

VANILLA WAFER CAKE

1 pound vanilla wafers, crushed
1½ cups pecans
1 cup coconut
1½ sticks butter or margarine

5 eggs
2 cups sugar
½ cup buttermilk

Cream butter and sugar. Add eggs, buttermilk and remaining ingredients. Pour into a greased and floured 10-inch tube pan. Bake 1 hour and 15 minutes at 350 degrees.
Mrs. Bill Bailey (Faye)
Elizabethtown, Kentucky

Mrs. Damon Vaughn (Carolyn)
Bossier City, Louisiana

WATERGATE CAKE

1 package Duncan Hines White Deluxe II cake mix	1 cup Canada Dry Club Soda
1 package pistachio pudding mix	3 whole eggs
1 cup Wesson oil	½ cup walnuts or pecans, chopped

Mix cake mix and pudding mix. Add eggs, oil, nuts and club soda. Blend 4 minutes on medium speed. Pour into greased and floured bundt cake pan and bake at 350 degrees for 55 minutes. Cool for 20 minutes in pan.

FROSTING

1 large Dream Whip (2 packages) 1 package pistachio pudding mix
1 cup plus 1 tablespoon milk

Mix at high speed until of spreading consistency. Spread on cool cake.

Mrs. Glen Waldrop (Anne)
Atlanta, Georgia

Mrs. Clyde Hendricks
Fairfax, Missouri

Mrs. R. F. Smith, Jr. (Faye)
Hickory, North Carolina

Mrs. John Dunaway (Jayne)
Corbin, Kentucky

DUMP CAKE

1 can cherry pie filling	½ cup nuts, chopped
1 large can crushed pineapple	½ to 1 cup butter or margarine
1 19-ounce package yellow cake mix	

Grease a 9x13x2-inch pan or far a deeper filling use a 9-inch square pan. Dump in undrained pineapple; swirl around to fill corners. Then dump in cherry pie filling and push around until layer of fruit is even. Dump in the cake mix, sprinkling it around so that pineapple and cherries are covered. Sprinkle with nuts. Cut butter or margarine in patties and place over top. Do not mix, the dumping does it. Bake in moderate oven at 350 degrees about an hour or until nicely browned. Cake doesn't rise. It looks rather gooey and is excellent served with ice cream or whipped cream. NOTE: Coconut may be sprinkled with nuts on top if desired. Two cans sliced pie apples may be substituted for cherry pie filling for a delightful change in flavor, or use only 1 type fruit for filling.

Mrs. Samuel Burnett (Donna)
Detroit, Michigan

Mrs. Harry Girtman
Taylors, South Carolina

Mrs. Kendall Hatton
Marlinton, West Virginia

Mrs. Howard Golden
Phenix City, Alabama

Mrs. Billy J. Turner (Lucille)
Stearns, Kentucky

WALDORF ASTORIA CAKE

¼ cup shortening	1 cup buttermilk
1½ cups sugar	1 teaspoon vanilla
2 eggs	¼ cup red cake coloring
2¼ cups all-purpose flour plus	2 heaping tablespoons cocoa
2 tablespoons	1 teaspoon soda
1 teaspoon salt	1 tablespoon vinegar

Make a paste of food coloring and cocoa and set aside. Cream shortening, sugar and eggs. Add cocoa paste. Add buttermilk alternately with flour, salt and vanilla. Add soda to vinegar. Blend instead of beating. Bake in 9-inch layer pans at 350 degrees for 25 to 30 minutes. Split layers.

FROSTING

1 cup milk	1 cup butter
3 tablespoons flour	1 teaspoon vanilla
1 cup white sugar	

Mix flour with small amount of milk and make paste. Gradually add remaining milk. Cook until very thick, stirring constantly, and cool. Cream sugar, butter and vanilla until very fluffy. Add cooked and cooled mixture. Should be like whipped cream.

Mrs. Keith Hamm　　　　　　*Mrs. Jess Baker (Nita)*
El Dorado, Kansas　　　　　*Yuma, Arizona*

Mrs. J. W. Alverson (Dot)
Calhoun, Georgia

CARAMEL ICING

2 cups light brown sugar	1 teaspoon vanilla
6 tablespoons cream	Few drops almond flavoring
4 tablespoons butter	1 cup powdered sugar

Stir sugar, cream and butter together. Place over low heat. As soon as mixture begins to boil, remove from heat and add powdered sugar and flavoring. Beat until smooth enough to spread.

Mrs. Jerry DeBell (Lurline)
Columbus, Ohio

SUPER CHOCOLATE ICING

1 stick margarine
1 egg
2 cups powdered sugar
½ teaspoon salt

1 teaspoon lemon juice
1 teaspoon vanilla
2 squares chocolate, melted
½ cup pecans or walnuts, chopped

Beat together margarine, egg, powdered sugar, salt, lemon juice and vanilla in mixer until fluffy. Add melted chocolate and beat again. Remove beaters and mix in ½ cup chopped pecans or walnuts. (Mm — good on any white or chocolate cake.)
Mrs. Ted Cotten (Dorothy)
Longview, Washington

ICING FOR DEVIL'S FOOD CAKE
(Chocolate-Peanut Butter Icing)

2 cups powdered sugar
½ cup Hershey's Instant Chocolate Mix (If you use plain cocoa, use 2 tablespoons less)

¼ cup milk
¾ cup chunky peanut butter

Combine ingredients in a mixing bowl. Mix until creamy with electric mixer. Spread on cooled cake. My original recipe and a family favorite.
Mrs. Glen Paden (Alene)
Sacramento, California

LEMON CHEESE ICING

3 egg yolks
2 cups sugar
1 cup sweet milk

Juice of 3 lemons
2 tablespoons flour
½ stick margarine

Mix eggs, sugar, butter and flour. Add milk; stir while cooking. Add lemon juice. Cook until thick.
Mrs. Charles Powell (Betty)
Jasper, Alabama

Pies

ANGEL PIE

3 egg whites
1 cup sugar
½ teaspoon baking powder
¾ cup nuts, chopped

14 Ritz crackers, rolled fine
Whipped Cream

Grease a pie pan with margarine. Beat egg whites. Add sugar and baking powder. Beat mixture well. Fold in nuts and cracker crumbs. Pour in pie pan. Bake at 325 degrees for 30 minutes. Let cool and top with cream.
Mrs. L. M. Huff, Jr. (Peggy)
Carmi, Illinois

APPLE PIE

5 cups pie apples
1¼ cups sugar (save ¼ cup for crust)
2 teaspoons cinnamon
½ teaspoon nutmeg
¼ teaspoon cloves

Dash of salt
½ cup flour
2 tablespoons Real Lemon juice
2 teaspoons imitation butter flavoring
¾ cup milk

Mix dry ingredients and stir in the thinly sliced apples. Mix milk, real lemon and butter flavoring. Add to apples (If apples are frozen, mix into a pot and place on simmer on stove until crust is prepared, this will cut down on baking time.) Pour apples in unbaked pie crust and top with pie crust. Brush generously with milk and sprinkle ¼ cup sugar over crust. Cut decorative slits into pie crust for air vents. Bake 20 minutes at 425 degrees, then 30 minutes at 350 degrees or until done. Makes a large pie. Use a 10½x1¾-inch pan.
Mrs. Roland Miljevich (Cecelia)
Wakefield, Michigan

PAPER BAG APPLE PIE

1 unbaked 9-inch pastry shell	2 tablespoons lemon juice
7 cups apple chunks	½ cup sugar (for topping)
½ cup sugar	½ cup flour (for topping)
2 tablespoons flour	1 stick butter or margarine
½ teaspoon cinnamon or nutmeg	

Make a 9-inch pastry shell, or use frozen variety. Pare, core and quarter apples, then halve each quarter crosswise to make chunks, you should have about 7 cups. Place in large bowl. Make filling: Combine ½ cup sugar, 2 tablespoons flour and spice in cup. Sprinkle over apples; toss to coat well. Spoon into unbaked pastry shell. Drizzle with lemon juice. Combine ½ cup sugar and ½ cup flour for topping in small bowl. Cut in butter or margarine; sprinkle over apples to cover top. Slide pie into a heavy brown grocery paper bag, large enough to cover pie loosely; fold open end over twice and fasten with paper clips; place on large cookie sheet for easy handling. Bake in hot oven (425 degrees 1 hour. Apples will be tender and top bubbly and golden. Split bag open, remove pie, cool on wire rack. Serve plain or with cheese or ice cream.
Mrs. Andy Anderson (Eleanor)
Nashville, Tennessee

REDWOOD ROOM APPLE PIE

TOPPING

1 8-ounce package	1 egg
cream cheese	½ cup grated coconut
⅓ cup sugar	½ cup nuts, chopped

Beat cream cheese and sugar until fluffy. Beat in egg and spoon over apple filling. Sprinkle nuts and coconut over top. Bake at 325 degrees for 15 to 20 minutes or until golden brown.

FILLING

1 tablespoon cornstarch	1 tablespoon lemon juice
½ cup sugar	1 pound 4-ounce can pie-sliced
¼ cup heavy cream	apples
3 tablespoons butter	

Combine first 3 ingredients in pan. Mix well. Cook over medium heat until boiling. Stir in butter and lemon. Add drained apples. Simmer 10 minutes. Stir occasionally. Cool, then spoon in baked pie shell.
Mrs. Rodrick Turner (Mary)
Toccoa, Georgia

TRANSPARENT APPLE PIE

1 stick butter	1 tablespoon cinnamon
1¼ cups sugar	Pinch nutmeg
2 eggs, well beaten	Pinch of salt
2 tablespoons cream	
1¼ cups precooked apples (just cooked through, not mushy)	

Melt butter and mix with well beaten eggs. Add remaining ingredients. Pour into a 9-inch pie crust (single) and bake at 425 degrees for the first 10 minutes, lower heat bake until firm.

Mrs. Findley B. Edge (Louvenia)   *Mrs. John Lawrence (Laura)*
Louisville, Kentucky   *Raleigh, North Carolina*

BANANA SPLIT PIE

2 cups graham cracker crumbs	1 stick margarine, melted

Mix together and put into 9x13-inch pan.

2 sticks soft margarine	2 eggs
2 cups powdered sugar	1 teaspoon vanilla

Mix together and beat 15 minutes with mixer. Spread over graham cracker crust.

3 or 4 bananas, sliced	1 large container Cool Whip
1 large can crushed pineapple, drained	Cherries
	Nuts

Spread sliced bananas over filling. Spread crushed pineapple over bananas, then spread Cool Whip over pineapple. Decorate with cherries and nuts. Chill until firm. Serves 12.

Mrs. Wayne Ward (Mary Ann)   *Mrs. Dan Page (Elizabeth)*
Louisville, Kentucky   *Greenville, South Carolina*

Mrs. Sam Adkins (Betty)   *Mrs. Joe D. Drum (Linda)*
Somerset, Kentucky   *Denver, North Carolina*

Mrs. Kenneth Bailey (Faye)
Wake Forest, North Carolina

BLUEBERRY PIE

2 9-inch graham cracker crusts
2 3-ounce packages Philadelphia
   cream cheese
1 cup powdered sugar
1 large box Dream Whip (Use
   both packets)

1 cup chopped pecans
1 can blueberry pie filling
Juice of one lemon

Prepare Dream Whip according to directions on package. Beat cream cheese with electric mixer until smooth. Add powdered sugar. Add Dream Whip mixture. Stir in pecans and pour into pie shells. Add the lemon juice and a dash of salt to can of blueberry pie filling and drizzle over the top of the pies. Refrigerate at least 3 hours before serving.

Mrs. James B. Riley (Vera)
Gonzales, Louisiana

Mrs. Clyde Hampton (Alicia)
Hartwell, Georgia

Mrs. Melba Gardner
Newcastle, California

QUICK CHOCOLATE BROWNIE PIE

1 stick margarine
1 square chocolate
1 cup sugar

2 eggs
½ cup flour

Melt margarine and chocolate. Cool slightly and beat in remaining ingredients. Bake in greased pie pan at 325 degrees for 35 to 40 minutes. Top with ice cream.

Mrs. Elaine Horton
Pensacola, Florida

BUTTERMILK PIE

3 eggs, beaten well
1 cup sugar
½ cup buttermilk
½ or 1 stick butter, melted

3 or 4 drops lemon extract
2 tablespoons flour
1 teaspoon vanilla

Mix all ingredients and pour in an unbaked pie shell. Bake 35 to 40 minutes in 350 degree oven.

Mrs. D. A. Gresham (Dora)
Pensacola, Florida

Mrs. J. T. George (Nina)
Union Grove, Alabama

Mrs. James R. Pinkley, Jr. (Elizabeth)
Toledo, Ohio

CHERRY CREAM PIE

CRUST

17 graham crackers

4 tablespoons butter

4 tablespoons evaporated milk

Roll graham crackers. Mix together butter and evaporated milk. Stir into cracker crumbs. Press mixture over bottom and sides of a 9-inch pie pan, pressing down firmly with the back of a spoon. Bake in hot 450 degree oven about 7 minutes or until firm. Cool.

FILLING

2 tablespoons butter

1 cup sugar

3 tablespooons cornstarch

½ teaspoon salt

1 egg, beaten

1½ cups evaporated milk

2 tablespoons vanilla

2 cups cooked or canned pitted pie cherries

Cracker crumbs for top

Melt butter in double boiler. Blend in mixture of sugar, cornstarch and salt. Stir in beaten egg mixed with evaporated milk diluted with ½ cup water. Cook 20 minutes. Stir frequently. Cool. Add vanilla. Drain 2 cups cherries well. Put cherries in bottom of crust. Cover with cooked filling. Sprinkle top with cracker crumbs. Cool thoroughly before serving.

Mrs. V. A. Chron (June)

Anchorage, Alaska

LOW CAL CREAM CHEESE CHERRY PIE

1 baked 9-inch pie shell

1 package Dream Whip

1 3-ounce package Neufchatel cream cheese

1 can cherry pie filling

⅔ cup powdered sugar

Almond and vanilla flavoring

Prepare Dream Whip as usual. Beat in softened cream cheese, powdered sugar and extract. Pour into baked pie shell. Top with can of cherry pie filling. Refrigerate over night. Serves 6 to 8.

Mrs. John C. Frantz (Ruth)

Independence, Missouri

Mrs. Harry Foley

Mesa, Arizona

CHESS PIE

¼ pound butter
1½ cups sugar
1½ tablespoons cornmeal
3 eggs

1 tablespoon vinegar
1 teaspoon vanilla
1 unbaked pie shell

Beat eggs. Add remaining ingredients and mix well. Pour into unbaked pie shell. Bake at 425 degrees for 10 minutes. Reduce heat to 275 degrees and bake 30 minutes.

Mrs. Doyle Bledsoe (Mildred)
Pine Bluff, Arkansas

Mrs. Baxter Walker
Fayetteville, North Carolina

Mrs. John E. Ingram (Marjorie)
Palatka, Florida

CHOCOLATE CHESS PIE

1 cup sugar
2 eggs
1 teaspoon vanilla
1 stick margarine

1 block unsweetened Baker's chocolate
½ cup black walnuts
1 unbaked pie shell

Melt margarine and unsweetened chocolate together. Beat sugar, eggs and vanilla. Add margarine and chocolate. Blend together. Add nuts. Pour in pie shell and bake at 400 degrees for 4 to 5 minutes. Reduce heat to 325 degrees and bake for 30 minutes.

Mrs. Jewel Robertson
Sunbury, North Carolina

CHOCOLATE PIE

6 7½-ounce Hershey Almond bars
½ cup milk
18 marshmallows

1 cup whipped cream
Crumb crust
Whipped cream for topping

Heat until marshmallows are melted. Do not boil. Blend in 1 cup whipped cream when cool. Pour in crumb crust. Chill before serving. Top with whipped cream.

Mrs. Bobby W. Barnett (Mary)
Bradford, Rhode Island

CHOCOLATE ICE BOX PIE

1 can sweetened condensed milk ½ pint whipping cream
2 squares unsweetened chocolate Graham cracker crust
¼ cup water

Melt chocolate in top of double boiler. Add condensed milk and cook until very thick. Take from fire and slowly stir in water. Pour into shell and cover with whipped cream. Shill several hours before serving.

Mrs. Wallace Mitchell (Faye)
Gonzalez, Florida

SOUTHERN CHOCOLATE CREAM PIE

1½ cups sugar
4 tablespoons flour
2 cups milk
3 tablespoons butter

3 tablespoons cocoa
4 egg yolks, well beaten
¼ teaspoon salt
1 teaspoon vanilla

Mix sugar, flour, cocoa and salt. Add egg yolks, milk and butter. Cook slowly, stirring constantly until thickened. Add vanilla and pour into 2 8-inch or 1 10-inch baked pie shell. Add meringue and brown lightly.
COCONUT CREAM PIE: Omit cocoa and add approximately 1 cup coconut and vanilla. Add meringue. Sprinkle with coconut before browning.

MERINGUE
4 egg whites   Pinch of salt
½ cup sugar

Beat egg whites with salt until frothy. Add sugar gradually, beating constantly, until stiff. Spoon meringue around outer edge of filling to seal it in; spread rest over top. Bake at 350 degrees until brown, approximately 15 or 20 minutes.

Mrs. Bobby L. Eklund (Janis)   *Mrs. Bill Moore (Sue)*
Hurst, Texas   *Houston, Texas*

Mrs. William K. Weaver, Jr. ("B")
Mobile, Alabama

KENTUCKY PIE

1 stick margarine, melted	1 cup sugar
1 cup white corn syrup	½ cup chocolate chips
4 eggs, slightly beaten	1 cup broken pecans

Mix all ingredients and blend well. Pour into unbaked pie shell. Bake about 50 minutes at 350 degrees.

Mrs. George W. Smith (Carolyn)
Leitchfield, Kentucky

CHOCOLATE ICE CREAM PIE

CRUST

18 Nabisco chocolate wafers (1½ cups crushed)	⅓ cup butter, melted

Mix well and press into sheet pan or Pyrex dish about 2½-inch deep. Chill until firm.

FILLING

½ gallon coffee ice cream	1 cup whipped cream or Cool Whip
Chocolate sauce	Nuts for topping

Soften ice cream until it will spread in shell. Allow to freeze or harden. When firm, spread chilled chocolate sauce over ice cream. Put back in freezer to harden. Top with 1 cup whipped cream and sprinkle top with nuts. Cover and keep in freezer until ready to serve in squares.

CHOCOLATE SAUCE

2 squares Hershey's unsweetened chocolate	½ cup sugar
	1 small can evaporated milk
1 tablespoon butter or margarine	

Melt chocolate over hot water. Stir in sugar, and butter. Add evaporated milk. Cook over hot water until it thickens. Allow to chill.

Mrs. John Lawrence (Laura)
Raleigh, North Carolina

Use hospitality one to another without grudging. 1 Peter 4:9

CANDY BAR PIE

1⅓ cups grated coconut
2 tablespoons butter or
   margarine, melted
1 teaspoon instant coffee powder
2 tablespoons water

1 7½-ounce milk chocolate candy
   bar with almonds, broken
4 cups Cool Whip
Chocolate curls or slivered almonds

Combine coconut and butter. Press into 8-inch pie plate sprayed with Pam. Bake in 325 degree oven for 10 minutes or till coconut is golden. Cool thoroughly. In small saucepan, dissolve coffee powder in water; add chocolate bar. Stir chocolate mixture over low heat till melted; cool. Fold in Cool Whip. Pile into coconut crust. Chill in freezer several hours or overnight. (Will not freeze solid). Garnish with chocolate curls or slivered almonds.
Mrs. W. O. Crews, Jr. (Jo Ann)
Tualatin, Oregon

COCONUT CREAM PIE

1 pint milk
3 eggs
½ cup sugar
3 tablespoons flour

½ cup coconut
1 tablespoon margarine
Pinch of salt
1 teaspoon vanilla

Heat milk; add sugar, flour and butter. Add beaten egg yolks and pinch of salt. Cook until thick. Add coconut and vanilla. Cool. Have ready baked pie shell. Beat 3 egg whites with 6 tablespoons sugar and spread on top. Sprinkle coconut over meringue. Bake at 350 degrees or until light brown.
Mrs. C. E. Colton (Lois)
Dallas, Texas

CRANBERRY PIE

2 cups fresh cranberries
½ cup sugar
½ cup nuts
2 eggs

1 cup sugar
1 cup flour
¾ cup shortening, melted

Grease a 9 or 10-inch pie pan. Mix first three ingredients and spread on bottom. Beat eggs well and add 1 cup sugar. Beat until frothy. Melt butter and add flour. Add to egg mixture and beat good. Spread this mixture evenly over the top of cranberry mixture. Bake at 325 degrees for 60 minutes.
Mrs. Robert N. Hammons (Ella)
Clinton, Oklahoma

DREAM PIE

2 eggs
1 cup white Karo
1½ cups sugar
¼ cup flour
1 cup coffee cream or evaporated milk
1 cup pecans

1 cup coconut
1 teaspoon vanilla
¼ teaspoon salt
2 tablespoons melted butter or margarine
2 unbaked pie shells

Beat sugar, eggs and flour. Add Karo, cream and remaining ingredients. Pour into two unbaked pie shells. Bake at 350 degrees for 45 to 50 minutes or until tooth pick comes out clean.
Mrs. Ruby Weathers
Plainview, Texas

HEAVENLY HASH PIE

1 20-ounce can crushed pineapple
2 cups sugar
1 large bottle maraschino cherries
1 egg, slightly beaten

¼ teaspoon salt
4 tablespoons flour
6 bananas
1 cup pecans

Mix pineapple and sugar and let stand 12 to 24 hours. Drain off all the juice in a pan. Add cherry juice and bring to a boil. Beat egg; add a little water, salt, flour and add to the juice mixture. Stir until it thickens. Cool. Add chopped fruit and nuts. Put in a baked crust and serve with whipped cream. Makes two 9-inch pies.
Mrs. Bob Woods (Ann)
Muskogee, Oklahoma
Mrs. Bobby W. Barnett (Mary)
Bradford, Rhode Island

Mrs. Wesley Crenshaw (Valeria)
Jacksonville, Florida

ICE BOX ANGEL PIE

1 can Eagle Brank milk
1 lemon (juice only) or
2 tablespoons Real lemon juice

1 large carton Cool Whip
1 large can crushed pineapple
1 cup pecans, finely chopped

Prepare graham cracker crust in 9x13-inch pan. Mix all ingredients and pour into graham cracker crust. Chill several hours.
Mrs. Gary Payne (Doda)
Syracuse, Missouri

JAPANESE FRUIT PIE

1 stick margarine
1 cup sugar
2 eggs
1 tablespoons vinegar

½ cup coconut
½ cup raisins
½ cup pecans, chopped

Melt margarine; beat sugar and eggs together. Then add other ingredients. Mix and put into pie shell. Bake 40 minutes at 325 degrees.
Mrs. Mabel Ferrell   *Mrs. Gene Hobbs (Dora)*
Belvedere, South Carolina   *Sumter, South Carolina*

IMPOSSIBLE PIE

4 eggs, beaten
1¾ cups sugar
½ cup flour
2 cups milk

1 teaspoon vanilla
½ stick margarine, melted
1 7-ounce can Angel Flake coconut

Mix in order given. Butter 2 9-inch pie pans. Cook at 350 degrees for 30 minutes. Makes its own crust.
Mrs. B. W. Dougharty   *Mrs. Willard M. Milleson (Catherine)*
Santa Fe, New Mexico   *Hibbing, Minnesota*

Mrs. Roland Miljevich (Cecelia)   *Mrs. Bobby Moore (Joyce)*
Wakefield, Michigan   *Memphis, Tennessee*

Mrs. Roger Shelton
Nashville, Tennessee

LEMON PIE

1 9-ounce package Cool Whip	1 14-ounce can Eagle Brand milk
1 6-ounce can frozen lemonade	1 9 or 10-inch graham cracker crust

Mix ingredients well and pour into graham cracker crust. Chill. Very easy and delicious!

Mrs. Curtis Holland
Waco, Texas

LEMON CLOUD PIE

CRUST

1 cup all-purpose flour	⅓ cup shortening
½ teaspoon salt	1 egg

Measure flour, salt and shortening into small mixing bowl. Using lowest speed of mixer, cut shortening into flour until particles are fine. Add 1 egg; mix until a dough forms. Roll out between 2 sheets of waxed paper to circle 1½-inches larger than inverted 8 or 9-inch pie pan. Fit loosely into pan. Trim pastry from edge of shell; place extra pieces in small pan. Fold edge of pastry to form rim. Flute. Prick generously with fork. Bake at 400 degrees for 12 to 15 minutes. Cool.

FILLING

1 small package lemon pudding and pie filling mix	2 eggs
1 3-ounce package cream cheese, softened	¼ cup sugar

Prepare pudding mix according to package directions, using 2 egg yolks. Add cream cheese; beat well. Combine 2 egg whites and sugar; beat until stiff peaks form. Fold into lemon mixture. Spoon into pie shell. Chill at least 2 hours before serving. Sprinkle crumbled pastry around edge of pie.

Mrs. C. H. Sutherland (Aileen)
Travelers Rest, South Carolina

KEY LIME PIE

CRUST

1⅓ cups graham cracker crumbs ⅔ cup margarine, melted
¼ cup sugar

Mix ingredients. Press into 10-inch pie plate. Chill.

FILLING

¾ can sweetened condensed milk ¾ small Cool Whip
1 lime (juice and grated rind) 4 or 5 drops green food coloring
¾ 6-ounce can frozen limeade mix

Squeeze and grate rind of 1 lime. Mix with condensed milk and frozen limeade mix. Fold in Cool Whip. Add food coloring. Pour into graham cracker crust. Place in refrigerator and chill. Serves 6 to 7.
Mrs. Larry Mayo (Lucile)
Pensacola, Florida

MILLIONAIRE PIE

2 cups powdered sugar, unsifted 2 baked pie shells
1 stick margarine, well softened 1 cup whipping cream
1 egg 1 cup crushed pineapple, well
¼ teaspoon salt   drained
¼ teaspoon vanilla ½ cup pecans, chopped

Cream together the powdered sugar and margarine. Add vanilla, salt and egg. Mix well until light and fluffy. Spread this on the two crusts. Chill. Whip cream until stiff. Blend in the well drained pineapple and the nuts. Spoon on top of the sugar-margarine mixture and chill again.

Mrs. J. D. Grey (Lillian)   *Mrs. Robert E. Galloway (Essie)*
New Orleans, Louisiana   *Pineville, Louisiana*

Mrs. Gilbert Burks   *Mrs. Sam Adkins (Betty)*
Albertville, Alabama   *Somerset, Kentucky*

Mrs. W. E. Pettit   *Mrs. Oscar Long (Pearl)*
Winston-Salem, North Carolina   *Ashoskie, North Carolina*

MILE HIGH ICE CREAM PIE
(A beautiful dessert when you want something very special)

1 baked 9-inch pastry shell, cooled
1 pint chocolate ice cream, softened
1 pint strawberry ice cream, softened

Spread the chocolate ice cream in pie shell; top with layer of strawberry ice cream; place in freezer. (I usually freeze 1 layer at a time, it spreads easier and is really no trouble)

MERINGUE
4 egg whites
½ teaspoon vanilla
¼ teaspoon cream of tartar
½ cup sugar

Beat egg whites with vanilla and cream of tartar till soft peaks form. Gradually add sugar, beating till stiff and glossy. Spread meringue over ice cream, which should be well frozen, carefully sealing to edge of pastry. Bake in very hot oven at 475 degrees for 2 or 3 minutes or till meringue is lightly browned. Freeze pie several hours or overnight. To serve, cut in wedges with knife dipped in hot water, and drizzle with chocolate sauce.

CHOCOLATE SAUCE
4 squares unsweetened chocolate
¾ cup water
1 cup sugar
Dash of salt
6 tablespoons butter
1 teaspoon vanilla

In saucepan, heat chocolate squares and ¾ cup water together over low heat, stirring constantly, till chocolate is smooth and melted. Stir in sugar and dash of salt. Simmer till slightly thickened, about 5 minutes. Remove chocolate mixture from heat; blend in 6 tablespoons butter and 1 teaspoon vanilla. Serve warm over wedges of pie. This can be prepared ahead of time, refrigerated, then heated while you are cutting the pie.
Mrs. James R. Maplis (Mary Jo)
El Paso, Texas

MINCEMEAT PIE

½ cup sugar
½ cup syrup
½ teaspoon salt
¼ cup shortening
2 eggs
½ cup raisins

½ cup mincemeat
½ cup walnuts
½ cup pecans
1 teaspoon vanilla
2 tablespoons orange juice
1 tablespoon lemon juice

Combine sugar, syrup, salt and shortening. Bring to a boil. Beat eggs and add other ingredients. Over this slowly pour the hot syrup mixture. Cool. Pour in pie shell. Use top crust or crisscrossed strips. Bake at 425 degrees for 30 to 35 minutes.

Mrs. Barnwell Gibson (Lita)
Bamberg, South Carolina

QUICK MOCHA PIE

1½ tablespoons instant
 caffein-free coffee
2¼ cups cold milk
1 envelope Dream Whip

1 6¾-ounce package instant
 chocolate pudding mix
1 baked 9-inch pie shell or crumb
 crust, cooled

Dissolve instant coffee in milk in a deep narrow-bottom bowl. Add whipped topping mix and pie filling mix. Beat slowly until well blended. Gradually increase beating speed and beat until mixture will form soft peaks, about 3 to 6 minutes. Spoon into pie shell. Chill about 3 hours; or freeze until firm. Garnish with additional prepared whipped topping and pecan halves, if desired.

Mrs. Wallace E. Jones (Laura Jo)
St. Ann, Missouri

NO CRUST MYSTERY PIE

3 egg whites
1 cup sugar
20 Ritz crackers, crushed
1 teaspoon baking powder

1 teaspoon vanilla
1 cup nuts
½ pint whipped cream

Beat egg whites until stiff. Add baking powder, sugar and vanilla. Fold in cracker crumbs and nuts. Bake in greased pie pan at 350 degrees for 25 minutes. Let cool then add whipped cream. Let set in refrigerator over night.

Mrs. Gloria Singleton
Rankin, Texas

Mrs. Carol McCurley
Bellevue, Texas

Mrs. Lester Weekley (Aileen)
Pensacola, Florida

Mrs. James Monroe (Laura)
Ft. Walton Beach, Florida

OATMEAL PIE

1 cup milk	1½ cups quick oatmeal
4 eggs	1 tablespoon vanilla
2 cups sugar	1 cup nutmeats, finely chopped
¼ pound butter, softened	½ teaspoon salt
1½ cups dark corn syrup	2 unbaked pie shells
1 small package flaked coconut	

Place milk, eggs, sugar, butter and syrup in bowl; beat well. Add coconut, oatmeal, vanilla, nuts and salt. Divide filling evenly between pie shells. Bake at 350 degrees for 45 minutes or until filling is set. Yield: 14 servings or two pies.

Mrs. Robert E. Hall　　　　　　*Mrs. Bob Myers (Hope)*
Huron, Ohio　　　　　　　　　*Suffolk, Virginia*

PARFAIT PIE

CRUST
Line a pie plate with chocolate ice-box wafers. Place the wafers around the sides of the pie plate making a scalloped edge at top (Vanilla wafers may be used, if preferred).

FILLING

1 large can Pet milk	1 cup sugar
1 small can crushed pineapple, drained	1 package lime gelatin
	1 tablespoon lemon juice
2 eggs, beaten	Few drops green cake coloring

Place one large can of Pet milk in a shallow pan in the freezing compartment of the refrigerator and chill until it is frozen around the edges. Boil together for about 3 minutes the drained pineapple, eggs and sugar. Stir constantly as this mixture scorches easily. Dissolve one package of lime gelatin in this mixture while it is hot. Allow to cool. Add lemon juice to chilled milk and whip until soft peaks form. Fold cooled gelatin mixture into whipped milk. Add green cake coloring to tint. Pour into prepared crust and refrigerate for several hours. Pies may be frozen and will keep for several weeks. Remove from deep freeze 10 minutes before serving. Filling makes 2 8-inch pies. Strawberry gelatin may be used instead of lime.

Mrs. F. M. Dowell (Edith)
Nashville, Tennessee

RASPBERRY BAKED ALASKA PIE

1 9-inch baked pie shell, cooled
1 10-ounce package frozen
   raspberries

1 quart vanilla ice cream
Meringue

Spread half of raspberries in the bottom of the pie shell. Add ice cream and top with other half of raspberries.

MERINGUE
2 egg whites
⅓ cup sugar

16 marshmallows

Beat egg whites stiff. Add sugar and marshmallows melted in 2 table-spoons water. Beat until smooth. Spread on top of pie and place under broiler. Do not close oven door but rotate under broiler until brown. May be kept in freezer several days.
Mrs. Herman W. Cobb (Mary)
Cullman, Alabama

SPEEDY PEACH PIE

½ cup sugar
½ cup sweet milk
Dash of salt

½ cup self-rising flour
2 cups sliced peaches

Sift dry ingredients together. Add milk to make batter and beat until smooth. Grease a 1½ quart baking dish generously with margarine. Pour batter into baking dish and place sliced peaches or any fruit over the top of batter. Dot generously with margarine. Bake in oven at 350 degrees for 35 minutes. The batter comes to the top as it cooks and it is very easy to prepare and very delicious. NOTE: ½ cup plain flour may be used and 1 teaspoon baking powder added as a substitute for ½ cup self-rising flour. Cherry pie filling may be used for a cherry pie.
Mrs. Bennie Oliver (Dot)
Hamilton, Alabama

Mrs. Bill Moore (Sue)
Houston, Texas

Mrs. Robert Hughes (Ruth)
Clovis, California

Mrs. R. P. Liesmann (Eunice)
Bloomington, Indiana

Mrs. John R. Riddle (Tommye)
Birmingham, Alabama

FROZEN PEANUT BUTTER PIE

4-ounces cream cheese
½ cup confectioners' sugar
⅓ cup crunchy peanut butter
½ cup milk

9-ounces non-dairy topping
¼ cup salted peanuts, finely
  chopped
1 9-inch graham cracker crust or
  regular crust

Whip cheese until soft. Beat in confectioner's sugar and peanut butter. Slowly add milk, blending thoroughly into mixture. Fold in topping and pour into pie shell. Sprinkle with chopped peanuts and freeze until firm. Take directly from freezer to cut and serve. Makes 1 large pie. Double recipe to make 3 good-size pies.
Mrs. William C. Lamb (Miriam)
Raleigh, North Carolina

PEAR PIE SUPREME

1 16-ounce can pears
¾ cup sugar
¼ cup cornstarch
¼ teaspoon salt
¼ cup lime juice

1 teaspoon grated lime peel
Green food coloring
3 egg whites, beaten
1 baked 9-inch pie shell
1 cup whipped cream

Drain pears and slice, reserving ¾ cup syrup. Combine sugar, cornstarch, salt, ¾ cup pear syrup, lime juice and peel. Cook, stirring constantly, until thickened and clear. Cool slightly and tint with a few drops green food coloring. Fold into beaten egg whites. When cool, pour into baked shell. Spread top with whipped cream and garnish with pear slices. Serve chilled.
Mrs. George L. Karr
Fairview Heights, Illinois

PISTACHIO PIE

2 cups Ritz crackers, crushed   1 stick butter, melted

Mix butter and cracker crumbs and press in baking dish.

FILLING
2 small boxes pistachio pudding   1 quart vanilla ice cream
2 cups milk   1 package Dream Whip

Blend together the milk and pudding. Add vanilla ice cream and beat. Pour into pie shell. Beat Dream Whip and spread over top. Refrigerate.
Mrs. Jerry DeBell (Lurline)
Columbus, Ohio

SOUR CREAM PECAN PIE

3 eggs, separated   ¼ teaspoon salt
1 cup white sugar   1 cup dark brown sugar
¼ cup flour or cornstarch   1 cup broken pecans
½ pint sour cream   1 baked 9-inch pie shell
¼ teaspoon vanilla

Mix egg yolks, white sugar, sour cream, vanilla, salt and flour. Cook over low heat until very thick. (Will change color). Beat egg whites until they are holding their shape, but not stiff or dry. Add brown sugar slowly. Fold in pecans. Pour filling into pie shell and top with pecan-egg white topping. Bake at 325 degrees for 15 to 20 minutes.
Mrs. Bobbie Booker
Robbins, North Carolina

"OLD-FASHIONED" PUMPKIN PIE

3 cups pumpkin   1½ teaspoons ginger
1½ cups brown sugar   ¼ teaspoon salt
2 teaspoons cinnamon   3 eggs

In a large bowl, beat eggs until slightly frothy. Add pumpkin, sugar, spices and salt. Mix thoroughly and pour into unbaked pie shells. Bake at 350 degrees for 35 to 40 minutes or until done. Serve with whipped cream if desired.
Mrs. W. E. Pettit
Winston-Salem, North Carolina

PECAN PUMPKIN PIE

CRUST
Roll ¼ cup finely chopped pecans into crust.

FILLING

1 can pumpkin pie mix	1 can sweetened condensed milk
1 egg	

Blend and pour into unbaked pie shell.

TOPPING

½ cup brown sugar	¼ cup firm butter or margarine
¼ cup flour	
¼ cup pecans, chopped	

Spread topping over pie filling. Bake at 325 degrees for 45 minutes or until set.
Mrs. Margaret Randall
Pensacola, Florida

PRALINE PIE

⅓ cup butter or margarine	1 package vanilla instant pudding
⅓ cup brown sugar, firmly packed	and pie filling
½ cup pecans, chopped	2½ cups milk
1 lightly baked 9-inch pie shell	1 envelope instant whipped topping mix

Combine butter, brown sugar and nuts in a saucepan; heat until butter and sugar are melted. Spread in bottom of pie shell. Bake at 450 degrees for 5 minutes, or until bubbly; cool. Prepare whipped topping mix as directed on package; blend 1⅓ cups into the measured pie filling. Spoon into pie shell; chill about 3 hours. Garnish with remaining whipped topping and pecan halves, if desired.
Mrs. Wallace E. Jones (Laura Jo)
St. Ann, Missouri

SOUR CREAM RAISIN PIE

2 cups sour cream	1 teaspoon nutmeg
1 cup sugar	1 teaspoon cinnamon
2 eggs plus the yolks of 3 other eggs	1½ cups raisins
	3 egg whites
1 tablespoon flour	Unbaked pie shell

Soak raisins for 30 minutes in warm water. Mix ingredients in order listed, reserving egg whites for meringue. Pour in unbaked pie shell. Top pie with meringue. Bake in 350 degree oven for 50 minutes.

Mrs. Dale Maddux   *Mrs. C. Phelan Boone (La Verne)*
Flora, Indiana   *Batesville, Arkansas*

RASPBERRY-PINEAPPLE PIE

1 3-ounce package raspberry gelatin	⅔ cup sugar
1 16-ounce can crushed pineapple	1 small can evaporated milk

Put can of milk into freezer to chill. Place small mixing bowl and beaters in refrigerator to chill until needed. Place dry gelatin, crushed pineapple and sugar into heavy saucepan. Heat over medium heat until gelatin and sugar dissolve, stirring often. Remove from heat and let cool until needed. Whip the chilled milk in the cold bowl until thick. Fold into the gelatin mixture. Spoon into 2 graham cracker pie crusts. Chill for several hours before serving and store any leftover pie in refrigerator until ready to serve.

Mrs. Jennings Baggett (Carolyn)
Dothan, Alabama

STRAWBERRY CREAM PIE

2   cups milk
¼ pound butter
1   cup sugar
4   tablespoons flour

Dash of salt
1   teaspoon vanilla
1   pint strawberries
Whipped cream

Scald milk over low heat. Add butter to milk. Sift together sugar, flour and salt. Add to milk. Heat, stirring constantly until thick custard. Add vanilla and set aside to cool. Place 1 pint washed and hulled strawberries in cooked pie crust. Pour cool custard over berries. Top with whipped cream. Refrigerate.

Mrs. T. R. Jones (Mary)
Macon, Georgia

DELICIOUS STRAWBERRY CREAM PIE

1   small package cream cheese
½ cup confectioners' sugar
½ teaspoon vanilla

1   cup whipping cream
1   pint strawberries

Cream together sugar, cream cheese and vanilla. Beat whipping cream till stiff and fold in. Pour in crust and refrigerate. Before serving put strawberries on top.

NO-ROLL CRUST

1   stick butter or margarine
1   tablespoon powdered sugar

1   cup flour

Melt butter, mix in other ingredients. Press into pie pan with hand. Bake at 425 degrees for 8 to 10 minutes. NOTE: A fruit pie may be baked in this crust. Double crust recipe and crumble extra crust over the top. Beautiful, easy and delicious crust.

Mrs. Roger Roberto
Parma, Ohio

. . . In the third year sow ye, and reap, and plant vineyards, and eat the fruit thereof.
Isa. 37:30

STRAWBERRY COCONUT PIE

1 pint fresh strawberries	1 3½-ounce can flaked coconut,
1 cup whipping cream	toasted
3 tablespoons sugar	1 9-inch baked pie shell, cooled

Wash and slice fresh strawberries and set aside. Beat 1 cup whipping cream with 3 tablespoons sugar until soft peaks form. Fold in toasted flaked coconut and sliced berries. Spoon into baked pie shell. Refrigerate 3 to 4 hours before serving. Garnish with whole strawberries.
Mrs. Frank Campbell (Janet)
Statesville, North Carolina

MERINGUE TOPPED STRAWBERRY PIE

4 egg yolks	1 cup fresh strawberries
1 can condensed milk	1 10-inch baked pie shell
¼ cup lemon juice (3 lemons)	Meringue
1 4-ounce package cream cheese	

Beat egg yolks well; mix about ¾ can condensed milk with egg yolks. Add cream cheese to remainder of milk in can and mix well. Mix lemon juice and cheese mixture with egg yolks; add berries and pour into baked pie shell. Top with meringue. Place into oven to brown the meringue.
Mrs. Bobby Moore (Joyce)
Memphis, Tennessee

SWEET POTATO PIE

2 cups sweet potatoes, cooked and mashed	2 cups sugar
1 tall can evaporated milk	4 eggs
1 stick margarine, melted	1 teaspoon nutmeg (optional)
	1 teaspoon vanilla

Mix these ingredients together well and put into 4 unbaked pie shells. Bake at 350 degrees until done.

TOPPING

2 eggs, well beaten	2 tablespoons margarine, melted
2 cups brown sugar	2 teaspoons vanilla

Mix together and spread over the pies. Brown at 350 degrees. Recipe can be cut in half to make 2 pies.
Mrs. Jimmie E. Harley (Gayle)
Greenville, South Carolina

TEXAS CREAM PIE

¾ cup sugar
½ teaspoon salt
⅓ cup flour
1¾ cups milk

2 egg yolks, beaten
1 tablespoon margarine
1 teaspoon vanilla
2 egg whites, beaten

Mix sugar, salt and flour together. Add milk, beaten egg yolks, and margarine. Cook over medium heat stirring constantly until thickened. Add vanilla. Stir in beaten egg whites. Pour into baked pie crust. Let cool. Top with whipped cream and grate some chocolate on top of pie. NOTE: To make a chocolate pie add 3 tablespoons cocoa to above mixture.

Mrs. Roy Ladd (Hazel)
Houston, Texas

Mrs. Kenneth D. Emerson (Cleta)
Wichita, Kansas

QUEEN LEE PIE

3 eggs
½ cup sugar
½ teaspoon salt
½ cup butter, melted
½ cup honey
½ cup Karo (light or dark)

½ teaspoon cinnamon
½ teaspoon nutmeg
½ teaspoon cloves
¾ cup seedless white raisins
¾ cup walnuts, chopped
1 9-inch unbaked pie shell

Beat together first 6 ingredients. Add remaining ingredients and mix well. Pour in unbaked crust. Bake 40 to 50 minutes in 375 degree oven until set and pastry is nicely browned. Serve slightly warm or cold with whipped topping or ice cream.

Mrs. Randall Thetford (Priscilla)
Coeur D'Alene, Idaho

CALIFORNIA WALNUT PIE

½ cup butter
½ cup brown sugar
¾ cup granulated sugar
3 eggs
¼ teaspoon salt
¼ cup white Karo

½ cup light cream
1 cup California walnut meats
½ teaspoon vanilla
7 walnut halves
1 unbaked pie shell

In top of double boiler, cream together butter and brown sugar; stir in other sugar, eggs, salt, syrup and cream. Cook over hot water 5 minutes, stirring constantly. Remove from heat. Add nuts and vanilla. Pour into unbaked pie shell. Bake 50 minutes at 325 degrees. Arrange walnut halves around top and bake 15 minutes longer.

Mrs. James W. Parker
Santa Ana, California

MOTHER'S ZWIEBACK LAYER PIE OR PUDDING

CUSTARD **Make this first.**

2 cups milk
3 egg yolks
1 teaspoon vanilla

½ cup sugar
1 heaping tablespoon cornstarch

Mix in boiler and stir constantly till thick and creamy. Set aside.

CRUST

1 package zwieback, rolled
½ cup butter, melted
1 tablespoon cinnamon

½ cup sugar
½ teaspoon nutmeg

MERINGUE

3 egg whites

⅓ cup sugar

Beat egg whites until stiff peaks. Add sugar. Mix sugar, spices and rolled zwieback together well before adding melted butter. Press half of mixture in rectangular casserole firmly and smoothly. Pour on custard, then meringue, then remainder of zwieback. Bake about 20 minutes or until brown at 350 degrees. NOTE: Add a little almond extract to pudding for special flavor.
Mrs. William L. Self (Carolyn)
Atlanta, Georgia

Pastries & Cobblers

APPLE CRISP

5 to 6 apples, sliced thin
¾ cup quick rolled oats
¾ cup brown sugar

½ cup all-purpose flour
½ teaspoon ground cinnamon
1 stick margarine

Arrange apples in pan. Combine all other ingredients. Sprinkle over apples. Bake 35 to 40 minutes at 350 degrees.
Mrs. Ronald D. Rhodus (Virginia)
Mt. Zion, Illinois

APPLE RINGS

PASTRY

1½ cups flour
½ teaspoon salt

½ cup shortening
4 to 5 tablespoons cold water

Mix and chill 1 hour (if desired). Roll dough into oblong shape. Grate 4 to 6 raw apples and spread over dough. Roll like jelly roll and cut in 1½-inch pieces. Place rings in hot syrup.

SYRUP

1 cup white sugar
½ cup brown sugar

1 stick margarine
2 cups cold water

Place syrup in oven at 400 degrees. Heat until bubbly hot. Then place rings in syrup. Bake 45 minutes. Serve plain, with cream or ice cream.
Mrs. Kendall Hatton
Marlinton, West Virginia

APPLE TART

1 cup sugar
4 tablespoons butter
1 egg
1 teaspoon soda
1 cup flour

1 teaspoon cinnamon
¼ teaspoon nutmeg
2 cups apples, finely chopped
½ cup nuts, chopped

Cream sugar, butter. Add egg. Sift dry ingredients and add apples and nuts. Bake 35 minutes at 350 degrees. Serve with ice cream or whipped cream. Serves 6.
Mrs. Margaret Cooper
Baltimore, Maryland

BLUEBERRY CRISP

4 cups fresh or frozen
   blueberries
⅓ cup granulated sugar
2 teaspoons lemon juice

4 tablespoons butter
⅓ cup brown sugar
⅓ cup all-purpose flour
¾ cup quick oatmeal

Place blueberries in a 1½-quart baking dish. Sprinkle with granulated sugar and lemon juice. Cream butter, gradually adding brown sugar. Blend in oatmeal and flour with fork. Spread topping over blueberries. Bake in 375 degree oven 35 to 40 minutes. Serve plain or with whipped cream or ice cream.
Mrs. Henry B. Stokes (Etta)
Buies Creek, North Carolina

CHERRY CRISP

1 pound can crushed pineapple
1 pound can cherry pie filling
1 box yellow cake mix
1 cup pecans or walnuts, coarsely chopped
1 stick butter or margarine, melted

Place pineapple and pie filling in a 13x9-inch baking dish. Spread cake mix over the cherry-pineapple mixture. Sprinkle nuts over the cake mix. Pour butter over the top. Bake at 350 degrees for 35 to 40 minutes. Serve warm or cold with whipped topping.
Mrs. J. S. Bennett (Geneva)
Sarasota, Florida

FRUIT CRISP

4 cups fresh fruit
1 cup sugar
1 cup self-rising flour
½ cup margarine (1 stick)
¼ teaspoon salt

Preheat oven to 325 degrees. Place fruit in 1½-quart baking dish. Mix sugar, flour, margarine and salt together with fork and fnife or pastry blender until well mixed. Sprinkle mixture over fruit. Bake 1 hour. Yield: 6 servings.
Mrs. Bobby W. Barnett (Mary)
Bradford, Rhode Island

PINEAPPLE CRUNCH

1 number 2 can crushed pineapple
1 box yellow cake mix
1½ sticks margarine
¾ cup nuts, chopped

Spread pineapple in large, ungreased 8x12-inch pan. Sprinkle cake mix over pineapple. Dot cake mix with margarine. Sprinkle nuts over mix. Bake 45 minutes at 350 degrees.
Mrs. R. L. Johnson (Nelle)
Portland, Oregon

QUICK DESSERT

1 can fruit cocktail
1 box butter pecan cake mix
1½ sticks margarine

Place can of fruit cocktail in the bottom of a casserole. Add cake mix. Pat butter on top. Bake 45 minutes at 350 degrees.
Mrs. Joe Forbes (Mary Ann)
Mooresboro, North Carolina

QUICK APPLE COBBLER

1 cup flour, sifted
⅓ cup sugar
1 teaspoon baking powder
¾ teaspoon salt

Cinnamon to taste
1 egg, unbeaten
⅓ cup soft shortening
4 to 5 cups apples, peeled and sliced

Heat apples with some water added then pour into an 8x8-inch pan. Sprinkle with sugar and cinnamon as for pie. Sift flour, sugar, salt and baking powder into a small mixing bowl. Add unbeaten egg and shortening. Mix together with fork until crumbly and sprinkle over fruit. Dot generously with butter. Bake at 350 degrees for 35 to 40 minutes.
Mrs. Bernes K. Selph (Tommie)
Benton, Arkansas

Mrs. Glen Waldrop (Anne)
Atlanta, Georgia

BUSY DAY COBBLER

1 stick margarine
1 large can fruit cocktail, sweetened to taste
1 cup flour

1 cup sugar
1 teaspoon baking powder
½ teaspoon salt
⅔ cup milk

Melt margarine in deep baking pan. Pour fruit in pan. In small bowl mix flour, sugar, baking powder and salt. Pour milk in and stir well. Pour batter over top of fruit and bake for 45 minutes at 350 degrees or until golden brown.
Mrs. Joyce Moad
Jefferson City, Missouri

EASY PEACH COBBLER

1 large can sliced peaches
1 box Jiffy yellow cake mix

1 stick margarine

Pour can of peaches, juice included, into large baking dish. Pour about ¼ cup water into the peaches. Mix well. If you desire cut peaches into smaller slices. Sprinkle over them about ⅓ cup sugar. Cover entire top of peaches with the dry cake mix. Slice the stick of margarine into small slices and cover the cake mix. Bake at 350 degrees until golden brown. May be served with whipped topping or ice cream.
Mrs. Nat McKinney
Carthage, Tennessee

PEACH COBBLER

1 can Freestone peaches	Butter, softened
¼ cup sugar	1 cup Bisquick
4 tablespoons Tapioca	3 tablespoons sugar
Cinnamon to taste	2 tablespoons Wesson oil

Mix peaches, sugar and Tapioca together. Sprinkle cinnamon on top and dot with butter. Mix 1 cup Bisquick with 3 tablespoons sugar and 2 tablespoons Wesson oil and cream (melt butter). Mix thoroughly, then drop by spoonfuls on top of peaches. Bake at 350 degrees about 1 hour. This is a delicious dessert topped with ice cream.

Mrs. B. A. Carlin (Virginia)
Buna, Texas

TART SHELLS

1 roll Refrigerator Sugar Cookies

Cut roll of cookies into 36 slices and press each slice into bottom and ½-inch up the sides of a foil-lined muffin tin. Bake at 375 degrees for 10 minutes.

Mrs. Bobby Perry (Sue)
Moss Point, Mississippi

"NO ROLL" PASTRY SHELL

1½ cups all purpose flour, sifted	1½ teaspoons sugar
1 teaspoon salt	½ cup corn oil
2 tablespoons cold milk	

Sift dry ingredients into pie pan. Combine oil and milk in measuring cup. Whip with fork and pour all at once over flour mixture. Mix with fork until flour is completely dampened. Press evenly and firmly with fingers to line bottom of pan; then press dough up to line sides and partly cover rim. Be sure dough is pressed to uniform thickness. Flute edges. Bake shell at 425 degrees for 12 minutes. Unbaked shell-(custard, pumpkin and pecan) bake in hot oven at 400 degrees for 15 minutes; then reduce to moderate 350 degrees and bake until crust is lightly browned and filling tests done. Makes 1 8 or 9-inch shell.

Mrs. Bill Hickem (Billie)
Jacksonville, Florida

MERINGUE RECIPE

1 tablespoon cornstarch
2 tablespoons sugar
½ cup water

Pinch of salt
3 egg whites
6 tablespoons sugar

Mix 1 tablespoon cornstarch and 2 tablespoons sugar with ½ cup water and cook together until clear; then set aside. Add a pinch of salt to three egg whites and whip until foamy or standing in peaks, at which time you add the mixture you set aside. Continue beating until creamy. Then add 6 tablespoons sugar gradually, beating again until creamy. Pile on pie and bake 30 minutes at 325 degrees or until a golden brown.
Mrs. John Dunaway (Jayne)
Corbin, Kentucky

EASY PERFECT PIE CRUST

1 teaspoon salt
2 cups all-purpose flour, sifted
before measuring

¾ cup Crisco
¼ cup cold water

Sift flour and salt together. Cut shortening into flour the size of small peas. Gradually add cold water. Mix only until mixture can be formed into a ball. Divide mixture in half. Slightly dampen clean cabinet enough to anchor waxed paper or plastic wrap. Sprinkle top of paper with a small amount of flour. Place ½ of dough on waxed paper. Cover with waxed paper or plastic wrap and roll about ⅛-inch thick. (I use plastic wrap, it may be a little awkward at first but you will learn to work with it smoothly). Remove waxed paper. Invert pie plate on rolled dough. Remove other sheet of waxed paper. Cover dough in pie plate with plastic wrap and crimp edges to desired shape. Make sure fingers don't come in contact with dough as this will make dough tough. Remove plastic wrap or leave on and freeze. The colder the dough, the more flakier it will become so it is best made ahead and frozen. Pie crust comes out beautiful every time. Bake at 375-400 degrees.
Mrs. Joseph P. DuBose, Jr. (Sybil)
Graceville, Florida

Mrs. Bernes K. Selph (Tommie)
Benton, Arkansas

Index

Let no man despise thy youth;
but be thou an example of the believers,
in word, in conversation, in charity,
in spirit, in faith, in purity. 1 Tim. 4:12

The Pastors Wives Cookbook

c/o Wimmer Cookbook Distribution
4650 Shelby Air Drive
Memphis, TN 38118

Please send ___ copies of **The Pastors Wives Cookbook**

@ $17.95 each _____

Tennessee residents add sales tax   @ $ 1.48 each _____

Postage and handling   @ $ 3.50 each _____

TOTAL _____

Charge to Visa (   ) or MasterCard (   ) # _____

Exp. Date _____

Signature _____

Name _____

Address _____

City _____ State _____ Zip _____

Make checks payable to Wimmer Cookbook Distribution
OR CALL: 1 (800) 727-1034 OR FAX: (901) 795-9806

- -

The Pastors Wives Cookbook

c/o Wimmer Cookbook Distribution
4650 Shelby Air Drive
Memphis, TN 38118

Please send ___ copies of **The Pastors Wives Cookbook**

@ $17.95 each _____

Tennessee residents add sales tax   @ $ 1.48 each _____

Postage and handling   @ $ 3.50 each _____

TOTAL _____

Charge to Visa (   ) or MasterCard (   ) # _____

Exp. Date _____

Signature _____

Name _____

Address _____

City _____ State _____ Zip _____

Make checks payable to Wimmer Cookbook Distribution
OR CALL: 1 (800) 727-1034 OR FAX: (901) 795-9806